CHALLENGING EXTREMIST VIEWS ON SOCIAL MEDIA

This book is a timely and significant examination of the role of counter-messaging via social media as a potential means of preventing or countering radicalization to violent extremism.

In recent years, extremist groups have developed increasingly sophisticated online communication strategies to spread their propaganda and promote their cause, enabling messages to be spread more rapidly and effectively. Counter-messaging has been promoted as one of the most important measures to neutralize online radicalizing influences and is intended to undermine the appeal of messages disseminated by violent extremist groups. While many such initiatives have been launched by Western governments, civil society actors, and private companies, there are many questions regarding their efficacy.

Focusing predominantly on efforts countering Salafi-Jihadi extremism, this book examines how feasible it is to prevent or counter radicalization and violent extremism with counter-messaging efforts. It investigates important principles to consider when devising such a program. The authors provide both a comprehensive theoretical overview and a review of the available literature, as well as policy recommendations for governments and the role they can play in counter-narrative efforts.

As this is the first book to critically examine the possibilities and pitfalls of using counter-messaging to prevent radicalization or stimulate de-radicalization, it is essential reading for policymakers and professionals dealing with this issue, as well as researchers in the field.

Jan-Jaap van Eerten is a Researcher at Labyrinth Research and Consultancy in Utrecht, the Netherlands. He received his Master's degrees in Islam in the Modern World and Conflict Studies and Human Rights from the University of Utrecht in 2012 and 2013, respectively. From 2015 to 2017 he conducted research into the utility of social media counter-messaging for radicalization prevention and de-radicalization as part of the research team of Bertjan Doosje at the University of Amsterdam.

Bertjan Doosje was Professor of Radicalization Studies in the Department of Social Psychology at the University of Amsterdam, the Netherlands from 2013 till January 1, 2019. He is currently Associate Professor there. He received his PhD on stereotyping in intergroup contexts in 1995 (cum laude). Since then he has examined intergroup relations in general and, after 9/11/2001, he has developed a special focus on radicalization and terrorism.

CHALLENGING EXTREMIST VIEWS ON SOCIAL MEDIA

Developing a Counter-Messaging Response

Jan-Jaap van Eerten &
Bertjan Doosje

With the cooperation of
Elly Konijn, Beatrice de Graaf & Mariëlle de Goede

Routledge
Taylor & Francis Group

LONDON AND NEW YORK

First published 2020
by Routledge
2 Park Square, Milton Park, Abingdon, Oxon OX14 4RN

and by Routledge
52 Vanderbilt Avenue, New York, NY 10017

Routledge is an imprint of the Taylor & Francis Group, an informa business

British Library Cataloguing-in-Publication Data
A catalogue record for this book is available from the British Library

Library of Congress Cataloging-in-Publication Data
A catalog record has been requested for this book

ISBN: 978-0-367-25311-0 (hbk)
ISBN: 978-0-367-25315-8 (pbk)
ISBN: 978-0-429-28714-5 (ebk)

Typeset in Sabon
by Wearset Ltd, Boldon, Tyne and Wear

CONTENTS

ACKNOWLEDGMENTS

Narratives are powerful tools in the hands of extremist groups. To what extent is it possible to produce convincing and effective counter-narratives? In this book, we aim to answer this question. This book is based on a report that was commissioned by the Research and Documentation Centre (WODC-2607), Ministry of Security and Justice, The Netherlands. That report was authored by Jan-Jaap van Eerten, Bertjan Doosje, Elly Konijn, Beatrice de Graaf, and Mariëlle de Goede. Subsequently, we have updated the report and placed it in an international context. We thank Elly Konijn, Beatrice de Graaf and Mariëlle de Goede for their contributions.

In addition, we like to thank the following people for providing valuable and constructive comments on an earlier draft: Daniël Wigboldus (Radboud University, Nijmegen), Michael Kowalski, Frederike Zwenk, and Casper van Nassau (all from Ministry of Security and Justice, The Hague), Stijn Sieckelinck (Free University, Amsterdam), and Reint-Jan Renes (University of Applied Sciences, Utrecht).

Finally, we thank the people involved in the production of the book: Alex Howard, Ashleigh Phillips, Eleanor Reedy, Emma Critchley, and Pete Waterhouse (great editing!). Thank you very much for your friendly help and significant input.

Jan-Jaap van Eerten and Bertjan Doosje
Utrecht/Amsterdam, June, 10, 2019

1

INTRODUCTION

Violent extremist and terrorist groups across the ideological spectrum have become increasingly adept in exploiting social media to advance their goals (Bartlett & Reynolds, 2015). Among other things, they use these channels to target youngsters by using smartly crafted messages and slick videos promoting their ideas, with the aim of shaping the perceptions of these youngsters and recruiting them to the cause (van Ginkel, 2015). Islamist and far-right extremist and terrorist groups in particular have made ample use of social media for this purpose (Rieger, Frischlich, & Bente, 2017). For example, since its inception in 2014, ISIS[1] unleashed an unprecedented social media effort to spread its propaganda to thousands of online sympathizers across the world (Speckhard, Shajkovci & Bodo, 2018).

The extent and availability of violent extremist propaganda online has caused considerable public and governmental anxiety in the West. In part, because it is feared that it may radicalize individuals into violent extremism (Conway, 2016). 'Radicalization' may be understood as the process by which people increasingly adopt more extreme attitudes and behavior, which might involve approval of the use of violence by others or displaying this violence to stimulate fear in the general population in an attempt to instigate changes in society (Doosje et al., 2016). This process may lead individuals to become involved in already violent extremist or terrorist groups. For instance, online propaganda of ISIS and other extremist groups is said to have had a radicalizing effect on many youngsters, leading them to travel and become 'foreign fighters' in conflict zones such as Iraq and Iran. Yet it may perhaps also influence individuals (i.e., lone wolves; McCauley & Moskalenko, 2014) or small groups to engage in violent actions on their own.

Unsurprisingly, Western governments and other concerned actors have sought to tackle the threat of violent extremist communications online. Among the measures undertaken are 'counter-messaging' activities (also known as 'counter-narrative' messaging). These are essentially online communication activities intended to undermine the appeal of messages disseminated by violent extremist and terrorist groups (Briggs & Feve, 2013). In recent years, it has gained widespread acceptance that such efforts can help prevent and counter radicalization into violent extremism. The European Union appears also to have embraced the counter-messaging approach (Glazzard, 2017). In its Revised Strategy for Combating Radicalisation and Recruitment to Terrorism, the European Council (2014, pp. 8–9) emphasized responding "... promptly to online rhetoric supporting terrorism and to reach those most vulnerable to radicalising messages" and it explicitly encouraged efforts "... on the internet and social media to promote counter narrative messages."

Many such initiatives have been launched by Western governments, civil society actors, and private companies since then. Often, these have involved the production of multimedia content, containing messages that directly challenge violent extremist communications, which is subsequently promoted through social media (Koehler, 2016). Yet, many questions remain regarding the efficacy of these efforts. Important questions are, then, how feasible is it to prevent or counter radicalization and violent extremism with counter-messing efforts? Is it possible to produce an effective online or social media counter-messaging program? What are the important principles to consider when devising such a program? And how can the effectiveness of such initiatives be measured.

In this book, we explore the use of counter-messaging via social media as a potential means to prevent or to counter radicalization. The book is based on research we conducted for the Research and Documentation Centre (WODC) and National Coordinator for Security and Counter Terrorism (NCTV) of the Dutch Ministry of Security and Justice between 2015 and 2017. We focus on counter-messaging intended to undermine 'Salafi-Jihadi' propaganda and recruitment efforts. At the time this project was initiated, the online efforts of groups such as ISIS were at their height. Therefore, the WODC and NCTV were particularly interested in these initiatives.

Specifically, this book addresses the following research questions:

1 Why and in what manner have Salafi-Jihadi groups exploited social media to spread their propaganda?
2 What is the relation between consumption of violent extremist propagandistic content and radicalization into violent extremism?
3 How can we conceptualize counter-messaging and how has it been used via social media?
4 How feasible is it to prevent or to counter violent radicalization with counter-messaging?
   (a) And for whom may it be effective?
5 What principles can inform the development of a counter-messaging campaign?
6 How can the potential effectiveness of such an effort be determined?
7 What can the role of the government be in relation to counter-messaging efforts?

As part of the original project we have examined all these research questions using two methods:[2] (1) a literature study, and (2) (group) interviews with academics, practitioners, and youth. In this book we will rely on the findings from our literature study, coupled with the insights of academics and experts. Where relevant, the original study has been updated.

A brief outline of the book is as follows. In Chapter 2 (addressing research questions 1, 2, and 3 above), we present theoretical conceptualizations of radicalization in the existing literature, and describe what we mean when we speak about the Salaf-Jihadi movement or groups. We describe why and how Salafi-Jihadi groups have exploited social media for propaganda and recruitment purposes, and how these attempts at influencing are related to online radicalization. Subsequently, we explain what counter-messaging is and how it is used on social media. In Chapter 3 (dealing with research question 4), we address what is known about the efficacy of counter-messaging efforts and we will examine how the potential effectiveness of counter-messaging programs via social media to prevent or to counter radicalization may depend on the phase of the radicalization process of a person. Chapter 4 addresses research question 5, namely whether and how counter-messaging initiatives via social media can play a role in preventing radicalization, by examining current examples as well as by investigating the possibilities through focusing on communication campaigns in other domains. We outline potentially strong elements of counter-messaging programs as well as the potential limitations of such an approach. In Chapter 5, we describe how the potential effectiveness of such a program can be determined, including the question of whether it is possible to test such a counter-messaging program in experimental research designs (research question 6). In Chapter 6, we discuss the potential role of the government in producing or stimulating counter-messaging efforts (research question 7). Finally, in Chapter 7, we summarize and discuss the main results, outline the limitations of the current study and present potential avenues for further research.

Notes

1 Islamic State of Iraq and Al-Sham (ISIS). Also known as Dawla al-Islamiya fi al-Iraq wa al-Sham (DAISH), Islamic State of Iraq and the Levant (ISIL), Islamic State (IS).
2 In the Appendix, we describe this method in more detail and explain our choices for the people we have selected for the interviews and the focus groups.

2

COUNTERING SALAFI-JIHADISM IN CYBERSPACE

2.1 Introduction

In this chapter, we aim to provide answers to the first three research questions: (1) Why and in what manner have Salafi-Jihadi groups exploited social media to spread their propaganda? (2) What's the relation between consumption of violent extremist propagandistic content and radicalization into violent extremism? (3) What is counter-messaging and how has it been used via social media? Before we do so, it is important first to provide a general introduction to the field of radicalization (Section 2.2) and the Salafi-Jihadi movement (Section 2.3). Then, we will describe what propaganda is and why and how Salafi-Jihadi groups have exploited social media for propaganda purposes (Section 2.4.), providing some examples of their use of mainstream social media platforms (Section 2.5). Only when we have outlined how online radicalization might work (Section 2.6) are we in a position to present our conceptualization of counter-messaging (Section 2.7). We will provide some concrete examples of how it is currently used in social media (Boxes 2.1 to 2.4). We end with a summary of this chapter (Section 2.8).

2.2 What is radicalization?

What exactly is radicalization? There is no consensus definition of radicalization, and the concept remains highly contested in the literature. Although the literature offers a wide variety of definitions, many share the aspect that it is a "process that involves the adoption of beliefs and attitudes that are in opposition to the mainstream status quo and dominant sociopolitical discourses" (Macnair & Frank, 2017, p. 148).

In and of itself, adopting radical beliefs or attitudes is not necessarily problematic or negative (Davies, Neudecker, Ouellet, Bouchard, & Ducol, 2016; Macnair & Frank, 2017). It is not altogether uncommon that people hold radical views and, in most cases, this does not result in any violent or otherwise unlawful acts (Macnair & Frank, 2017). In fact, radicalization may actually be a driver of positive social change. As pointed out by Pauwels et al. (2014, p. 16) "In the course of history, 'radicals' have fought for and changed a lot of things that are now considered as normal and necessary." Think, for example of Nelson Mandela or Martin Luther King, who were at one time considered radical by many as they opposed prevailing views in society (Pauwels et al., 2014, p. 16).

However, radicalization becomes a concern when it leads to beliefs and attitudes that sanction, legitimize and compel violence as a means to achieve social change (Davies et al., 2016). As such, this chapter is concerned with 'violent radicalization' or radicalization into violent extremism, a process whereby radical views develop into "a willingness to directly support or engage in violent acts" (Dalgaard-Nielsen, 2010, p. 798). An important distinction that follows from this is the distinction between radicalism and extremism. The most important difference is that the latter accepts exercising violence as a legitimate means to achieve particular goal (Feddes, Nickolson, & Doosje, 2015).

Violent radicalization may ultimately, but not necessarily, lead to people committing acts of terrorism and other violent extremist actions. It is important to note, however, that this transfer is not inevitable (Hafez & Mullins, 2015; Pauwels et al., 2014). In fact, most individuals who support the use of violence never engage in violent acts (Khalil, 2014). In this regard, various authors highlight the critical distinction between cognitive and behavioral dimensions of radicalization (e.g., Borum, 2011; Hafez & Mullins, 2015; Khalil, 2014). Furthermore, the literature emphasizes that radicalization, in terms of developing extremist attitudes and beliefs, is one of many 'pathways' into violent extremist action (Borum, 2011; Neumann, 2013a; Pauwels et al., 2014). As stated by Borum (2011, p. 8): "Different pathways and mechanisms operate in different ways for different people at different points in time and perhaps in different contexts."

Violent radicalization can be related to a number of movements and ideologies (e.g., right-wing, left-wing, nationalist/separatist, single issue, and so on). As proposed in the introduction, we predominantly focus on violent radicalization connected to Salafi-Jihadism. Given the political and societal context when this project was initiated, this implies a specific focus and it is important to note that this means that we are not in a position to generalize many of the findings to other violent extremist contexts or groups.

2.3 The Salafi-Jihadi movement

Salafi-jihadism refers to a distinct ideological movement in Sunni Islam, which seeks to use violence and terrorism in order to establish a restoration of the *al-khilafah* (i.e., the Caliphate) and a reinstitution of perfect Divine law or sharia (which is, in fact, conflated with *fiqh*, which may be understood as the imperfect effort to interpret Divine law; Beutel et al., 2016; Rane, 2016). Salafi-Jihadism is an outgrowth of the Salafi movement, a global Sunni Islamic renewal movement that originated in Saudi Arabia (Al Raffie, 2012). The meaning of Salafism is derived from the Arabic word, *al-salaf al-salih* – meaning 'pious forefathers' – which refers to the first three generations of Muslims who, in the view of Salafists, exemplify the way that all Muslims should live today (De Koning, 2013). The Salafi movement aims to

> revitalize Islam by promoting an idealized vision of the lives of the first Muslims of the seventh century AD, and by persuading Muslims to live according to that vision; an entreaty that its followers find more just and satisfying than the life and circumstances of the present.
>
> (De Koning, 2013, p. 19)

In line with this, Salafists typically adhere to "literalist, conservative and often puritanical approaches to Islam based on an interpretation of what they perceive to be the religion's original beliefs and practices ..." (Rane, 2016, chapter 9, section 'Islamist Extremism,' para. 2). As Salafists wish to purify Islam, they are keen to distinguish themselves from what they perceive as less-strict adherents, and those groups that they consider deviant in general (Wagemakers, 2009). They also reject Muslim religious traditions and schools of jurisprudence that have developed over many centuries, and, hence, what can be described as Islamic orthodoxy.

Importantly, Salafism should not be reduced to Jihadi-Salafism. In fact, some Salafi groups respect democracy and challenge violent fractions (Roex, 2014). Scholars typically distinguish three branches: apolitical Salafism (quietist/purist), political Salafism, and Salafi-Jihadism (or Jihadi-Salafism) (e.g., Schmid, 2014, May; Wagemakers, 2009; Wiktorowicz, 2006). Our focus here is on the latter. Salafi-Jihadism is described as falling outside of the mainstream, and is only adhered to by a small minority (Rabasa & Benard, 2015; Rane, 2016). The main distinction between Jihadi-Salafism and the non-violent apolitical and political strands, is the former's willingness to support and use violence (including violence against other Muslims and non-combatants).[1]

Jihadi-Salafists legitimize violence through a selective literal interpretation of Islamic scripture. This involves a reinterpretation of the concept of jihad[2] that elevates offensive armed struggle, typically argued to be defensive, over a broader repertoire of methods of struggle that have been established in Islamic theology and jurisprudence (Lentini, 2013). Here, Salafi-Jihadi groups such as al-Qaeda and affiliates interpret the term 'defensive' as follows, "the meaning of 'defensive' extends to striking at the enemies of God wherever they are. They see themselves as vanguards who are willing to fulfill the religious obligations of jihad, even if other Muslims do not" (Rabasa & Bernard, 2015, p. 31). By exception, ISIS's self-proclaimed 'caliph' Abu 'Umar al-Baghdadi has also emphasized the offensive form of jihad, premised on the uprooting of *shirk* (idolatry) wherever it is found (see Bunzel, 2016).

In recent years, the Jihadi-Salafist movement has made increasing use of social media to help spread their propaganda and actively reach out to young people who may be susceptible to radicalization and recruitment. ISIS, in particular, has gained a solid reputation with regard to its ongoing and technologically sophisticated strategic communications campaign, in which mainstream social media platforms have played a pivotal role. In the next two sections, we outline what we understand by propaganda.

2.4 Salafi-Jihadi propaganda

The term 'propaganda' lacks a common definition. However, it is often described as a form of directed communication intended to manipulate a target audience into adopting beliefs and attitudes or engage in behaviors that serve the goals of the propagandist. This is also captured in the definition provided by Jowett and O'Donnell (2012, p. 7), which we will use throughout this book. They describe *propaganda* as "the deliberate and systematic attempt to shape perceptions, manipulate cognition, and direct behaviour to achieve a response that furthers the desired intent of the propagandist."

In democratic states, propaganda has historically come to be viewed as the preserve of undemocratic opponents. After World War I, the term became associated with dishonesty (Lee, 2018). Similar activities by democratic states have therefore been described in terms such as "public affairs," "public diplomacy," "psychological operations," and "strategic communications" (Schmid, 2014, January). Yet, as many authors have noted, whether and to what extent the different terminology marks reals differences remains a matter of debate (Lee, 2018; Schmid, 2014, January). That aside, the focus here is on how propaganda is employed by Salafi-Jihadi groups.

The propaganda of Salafi-Jihadi groups can be directed towards different target audiences and can have different purposes. It may be directed at active members (the in-group), to give instructions or legitimize their support. It may also be directed at the enemy or opponents (the out-group) in order to intimidate them, or to neutrals and potential sympathizers and recruits (potential in-group) in order to sway them to see the world on the Salafi-Jihadi groups' terms (Rieger et al., 2013). With regard to the latter, Ingram (2017) argues that the main purpose of Salafi-Jihadi and other violent extremist groups' propaganda is to convince the audience to adopt a 'competitive system of meaning' or worldview. This 'competitive system of meaning' provides: "an alternative perspective of the world compared to that presented by its opponents, that acts as a 'lens' through which to shape their supporters' perceptions, polarise their support and, ultimately, convince them to mobilise" (Ingram, 2017, p. 172).

Doosje, Loseman and Van Den Bos (2013), who use the term 'radical belief system' argue this worldview involves (a) a clear us versus them distinction, accompanied by a perceived superiority of their own group (the in-group identity) and a clearly inferior and dehumanized perception of the enemy (the out-group identity); (b) a strong perception of injustice or grievances: the in-group is threatened by the out-group; (c) a lack of trust in current institutions (politics, justice system) to address their grievances; (d) a perceived need to use violence to achieve societal and/or political changes (including the belief that such violence will be effective).

This worldview may be nurtured, supported and reinforced by (and is in fact inherent in) Salafi-Jihadi propaganda, which generally follows a similar pattern of diagnosis (what is wrong), prognosis (what needs to be done) and rationale (who should do it and why) (Ritzmann, 2017). Ingram (2016, November) speaks in this regard of a core 'pitch' or central message that can be summarized as follows:

> we are the champions and protectors of (appropriately-aligned) Muslims (the in-group identity), everyone outside of this narrow in-group identity are enemies (i.e., out-group identities or Others) who are responsible for the ummah's (Muslim community's) crises, so support us and our solutions (i.e., the militant Islamist politico-military agenda).
>
> (Ingram, 2016, November, p. 4)

Salafi-Jihadi groups utilize a diverse array of messages that play on several common themes to support and reinforce different aspects of worldview they want audiences to adopt (Ingram, 2016, November). Gartenstein-Ross, Bar and Moreng (2016) list nine of them (see also Winter, 2015; 2018). For instance, one common theme in ISIS messaging has been 'utopia,' which presents the caliphate as a pious, harmonious, and thriving Islamic state. The 'winner's message' is another one, depicting the group as "an unstoppable military force capable of defeating all enemies" (Gartenstein-Ross, Bar, & Moreng, 2016, p. 4). Yet another depicts Islam being under siege by the West, pitting the "camp of Islam" against the "camp of unbelievers."

To make their propaganda and portrayal of the world resonate with different audiences, Salafi-Jihadi groups also adapt their messaging to local conditions. For instance, they frequently draw on grievances already present among the target audience, placing the grievances in their "bigger extremist picture" (Bindner, 2018; Pauwels et al., 2014). In addition, they employ a range of appeals to seduce a diverse audience character-ized by different motivations. From emotional and social benefits (e.g., a sense of belonging, brotherhood, and a chance to become a hero; see Ritzmann, 2017; Neumann, 2015), to material needs and wants (e.g., promises of food, luxury goods, cars, and having debts paid off) (Neumann, 2015).

Salafi-Jihadi groups have utilized a range of means to sway people, from face-to-face methods, to texts, magazines, photos, film, video, and even video games. For the distribution of their messages, the internet has been of crucial importance. In recent years, social media platforms have played a particularly important role, offering various benefits. We will discuss the use of social media in the next section.

2.5 The exploitation of social media by Salafi-Jihadi groups

Salafi-Jihadi groups have long used the internet for a variety of purposes, with propaganda and recruitment being among the most important (Weimann, 2015). They have followed suit with technological advance-ments. Initially, they mainly relied on traditional websites, then they turned to interactive forums – either on the Surface or Dark Web,[3] and in recent years they have fully embraced social media.

In the 1990s many groups first established an online presence in the form of static, text-heavy websites. The aim was "to make available altern-ative platforms, circumventing the mainstream media's censorship, convey-ing unfiltered news, and disseminating ideological texts and materials that, previously, had been difficult and (sometimes) expensive to obtain" (Neumann, 2012, p. 16). By the mid-2000s, most of the groups had com-pleted the transition from static websites to interactive forums (Bartlett & Reynolds, 2015). Initially, such forums existed as part of mainstream plat-forms. However, they gradually established their own independent pres-ence, making them no longer reliant on the hosting of large internet companies (Neumann, 2012). These forums became "virtual town squares, where people met, bonded, and talked to each other – and where even the most controversial issues could be debated without fear of retribution" (Neumann, 2012, p. 16).

By the late 2000s, the use of interactive forums by many groups had started to stagnate or decline, and mainstream social media platforms such as Facebook, Twitter, YouTube, and Instagram became increasingly important channels for propaganda and recruitment, in part, due to increased online policing of forums (Bartlett & Reynolds, 2015). Yet, these platforms also offered multiple advantages. According to Weimann (2014; 2015), Salafi-Jihadi groups have three major reasons to use social media. First, they are highly popular among mainstream audiences. As propaganda and recruitment are the main purposes of Salafi-Jihadi internet usage, to follow the mainstream makes sense. Furthermore, they are particular popular among younger generations, a primary target audience. Second, they provide a user-friendly and reliable service for free, and facilitate quick dissemination of their messages. In addition, as does the internet, it allows them to circumvent to filtering of news agencies and governments (Aly, Macdonald, Jarvis, & Chen, 2016). Third, rather than waiting for individuals to stumble upon their websites and forums, social media have permitted Salafi-Jihadi groups to virtually "knock on their doors" and directly target and market their ideas to potential sympathizers and subsequently engage them in conversation: "Just as marketing companies can view members' information to find potential customers and select products to promote to them, terrorist groups can view people's profiles to decide whom to target and how to approach each individual" (Weimann, 2014, p. 3). At the same time, social media provide sympathizers with opportunities to reach out to them under conditions of relative anonymity (Weimann, 2014, 2015). A fourth reason that has been proposed by other authors, is that it provides a powerful tool for community formation (Aly et al., 2016; Rieger et al., 2013; Schils & Verhage, 2017).

Related to this, another benefit was that the advent of social media and the emergence of cheap production and editing tools also allowed individuals from around the world to take part in the production and distribution of Salafi-Jihadi propaganda (Bartlett & Reynolds, 2015; Rieger et al., 2013). In fact, much of the material that has been ascribed to Salafi-Jihadi groups isn't actually produced by them. In relation to ISIS, Neumann (2016, "Online," para. 3) notes that:

> the most influential elements of its online presence are only partly under its control, if at all. That includes fighters who post pictures on their private Facebook, Twitter and Telegram accounts and communicate in supporters in Europe via Twitter or WhatsApp; radical preachers who distribute lectures on YouTube and present themselves as religious cheerleaders; and simple 'fans' who spend their days and nights on the internet, tweeting the newest information and rumors and so exerting influence on the network of supporters.

The activities of these 'fans,' also referred to as 'Jihobbyists,' have been argued to be of particular importance for Salafi-Jihadi groups. These individuals are not directly affiliated with a particular Salafi-Jihadi group, but do consider themselves part of the movement and actively advance the agendas of these groups online (Neumann, 2012). For instance, Brachman (2009, p. 19), who has coined the term 'Jihobbyists,' suggests that:

> By hosting Jihadist websites, designing propaganda posters, editing al-Qaida videos, recording soundtracks [...] compiling speeches from famous Jihadist shaikhs and packaging them into easily downloadable files or writing training manuals, these individuals help to form the base that keeps the movement afloat.

ISIS is the group that has been especially successful in 'crowdsourcing' its messaging through a global network of supporters. Besides contributing to the volume of propagandistic material online, they have helped to enhance the visibility, accessibility and appeal of the group's content, by translating their propaganda material into various languages and repackaging it for specific audiences. For instance, in regard to the latter, Neumann (2016, "Fans," para 2.) suggests that their efforts to combine ISIS messages "with rap stars, Western brands and advertising slogans" have helped the group to appear 'cool' among a European audience. The fact that Salafi-Jihadi groups such as ISIS could rely on a dispersed network of prosumers' disseminating content and creating links to releases has also contributed to the difficulty in combatting the circulation of extremist content online (Bartlett & Reynolds, 2015).

To illustrate the ways Salafi-Jihadi groups have utilized social media for propaganda and recruitment purposes, we will describe how they have leveraged three of the most popular social media platforms: Twitter, YouTube and Facebook. It should be noted that these are by no means the only platforms they have used. Other examples include Ask.fm, Instagram, WhatsApp, PalTalk, Viper, JustPaste.it, and Tumblr, to name but a few (Ferguson, 2016). Importantly, Salafi-Jihadi groups' usage of social media has evolved in response to new technological opportunities, the emergence of new platforms, and efforts to counteract their social media presence (Bartlett & Reynolds, 2015). Related to this, since 2014, Twitter, YouTube and Facebook have all instituted more aggressive take-down policies, thereby making it more difficult to openly propagate and recruit on these popular platforms. In order to circumvent counter-measures by these companies Salafi-Jihadi groups have increasingly come to rely on more privacy-enhanced and encrypted platforms, such as Telegram (an encrypted messaging application) (Speckhard, Shajkovci, Wooster, & Izadi, 2018a), in addition to the Dark Web (Weimann, 2016).

Notwithstanding, Salafi-Jihadi groups continue to be active on Twitter, YouTube and Facebook. For example, Speckhard and colleagues have suggested that ISIS cadres create fleeting fake accounts to attract followers and redirect them to private and encrypted platforms. It often takes time before such accounts are detected and taken down. ISIS cadres have also figured out various workarounds to counteract such measures:

> On YouTube, ISIS cadres embed terrorist videos into photos, making it more difficult to detect. On Twitter, ISIS recruiters

reopen closed accounts within days, if not hours, having figured
out ways to migrate their followers to their newly reopened sites.
(Speckhard, Shajkovci, Bodo, & Fazliu, 2018; see section
"The Isis Digital Caliphate ...," para. 9)

Having said that, the following provides an overview of some of the ways
these platforms have been leveraged in recent years.

2.5.1 Twitter

Twitter is a 'micro-blogging service' with 328 million active users worldwide as at the second quarter of 2017 (Statista, 2017a). People can use
Twitter in their browser or through their app. Users can posts messages up
to 140 characters in length – so called "tweets." In these messages, media
and links to (content on) other websites and platforms may be embedded.
Users can use the hashtag symbol (#) before a relevant keyword or phrase
in their tweet to categorize those tweets. This helps them show up more
easily in Twitter searches. By clicking or tapping on a hashtagged word in
a message it shows users other tweets that include that hashtag. Accounts
can be made visible to the public at large, or to a select private audience.
Twitter allows users to 'follow' other users, so they receive the tweets they
post (Pearson, 2018). Tweets can subsequently easily be forwarded or
'retweeted' (Klausen, 2015).

Twitter has been a preferred social media platform for violent extremist
groups across the ideological spectrum (Weimann, 2015). The ability to
instantaneously and rapidly send small pieces of information to a potentially unlimited number of people free of charge (including links to content
and pages) has made Twitter an extremely valuable platform for violent
extremist groups (Dean, 2016). ISIS is particularly notorious for the way it
has leveraged Twitter. It was a key outlet for the group between 2013 and
2015. As noted earlier, in recent years, Twitter, like the other two platforms discussed here, has pursued more aggressive take-down policies, sus-
pending large numbers of ISIS-supporting accounts (Pearson, 2018).
Furthermore, since 2015, ISIS has been forced onto the back foot, both
offline and online. This appears to have had a significant impact on its
propaganda activities on the popular social media platforms we describe
here (Winter, 2018). However, Berger and Morgan (2015) estimated that,
in the autumn of 2014, no fewer than 46,000 Twitter accounts were used
by 'ISIS-supporting accounts,' with the average account having 1000 followers. However, most of the activity could be ascribed to small number
of hyperactive online supporters, numbering 500 to 2000 accounts, who
have tweeted and re-tweeted content in concentrated, high volume bursts.

ISIS has utilized Twitter for various purposes, including intimidation –
directed at both distant foes as well as local enemies – and to promote its

ideas and lure in new recruits (Klausen, 2015; Veilleux-Lepage, 2014; Vitale & Keagle, 2014). ISIS has been highly successful in leveraging the platform's crowdsourcing function for massive outreach, allowing others to positively contribute to its campaign by adding their own content, retweeting official tweets, and using popular hashtags. This has allowed the group to significantly magnify its message (Vitale & Keagle, 2014). To further the group's strategy of crowd-sourced dissemination, ISIS affiliates have also developed an Android application named, 'The Dawn of Glad Tiding.' It was temporarily available in the Android 'Play Store,' before Google removed the app for violating their terms of service. This app was advertised as a way to keep up with the latest news about the group's activities. The application allowed ISIS affiliates to automatically posts tweets including links, hashtags, and images, to the Twitter accounts of application users without upsetting Twitter's spam-detection algorithms. As such, it allowed them to flood Twitter with ISIS propaganda (Berger, 2014; Farwell, 2014; Veilleux-Lepage, 2014). At its height, app posting activity was around 40,000 tweets in a single day (Aly, 2016; Berger, 2014; Vitale & Keagle, 2014).

When this app was shut down, ISIS followed up with a large hashtag campaign, asking supporters around the world to take photos of themselves in public spaces holding ISIS flags, and then post these photos on Twitter using the Arabic hashtag 'The Friday of Supporting ISIS' or the English hashtag 'All eyes on ISIS' (Saltman, 2014). Another way in which ISIS cadres and sympathizers have used hashtags to spread their messages is so-called 'hashtag hijacking': the practice of utilizing an established, popular (and innocuous) hashtag for the purpose of disseminating one's own content or message. For instance, in 2014, ISIS supporters co-opted World Cup hashtags, such as #Brazil2014 or #WC2014. Using this strategy, any Twitter user browsing these hashtags could find ISIS tweets among regular World Cup tweets (Greene, 2015; Farwell, 2014; Veilleux-Lepage, 2014; Vitale & Keagle, 2014).

The content of ISIS-related messages on Twitter has varied. Twitter has been used to circulate links to official videos (for instance on YouTube) and publish 'video stills' of horrific acts of violence as well as to provide 'Go-Pro footage' from foreign fighters on the frontline. However, it is not merely violence that is depicted. Messages have also portrayed 'the good life' inside the Caliphate. For instance, Western foreign fighters have tweeted about touristy snapshots of the local cuisine, hanging out with friends and their new houses (General Intelligence and Security Service, GISS, 2014; Briggs & Silverman, 2014; Klausen, 2015). Some of the ways the group has used videos on YouTube will be discussed in the next section.

2.5.2 *YouTube*

YouTube is probably the most well-known video-streaming platform. According to YouTube (2017), it has over one billion users worldwide. Registered users can easily upload video content to YouTube using the website or app. The videos can then subsequently be watched by other users. Uploaded videos can be shared with either a select group of users or the general public. Users can comment on public videos and links to content can be posted on other websites and social media platforms (e.g., Twitter and Facebook) in order direct one to content on YouTube (Conway & McInerney, 2008). YouTube provides the basic features of a social networking platform. Users can create a user channel with a basic personal profile, which displays things such as friends, comments, and recently watched, posted and favorite videos (Kaplan & Haenlein, 2010; Smith, Fischer, & Yongjian, 2012; Weimann, 2015).

YouTube is one of the video-sharing platforms that has been heavily utilized by extremist groups to share propaganda and to recruit (Conway & McInerney, 2008; Weimann, 2015; Klausen, Barbieri, Reichlin-Melnick, & Zelin, 2012). Salafi-Jihadi groups recognized the potential of the platform early on. One of the groups that did so was al-Qaeda. As stated by Weimann (2014, p. 11): "In 2008, a jihadist website suggested a 'YouTube Invasion' to support jihadist media and the administrators of al-Fajr-affiliated forums, which are associated with al-Qaeda." Not long after, the success of this invasion was noted by Salafi-Jihadist on one of al-Qaeda's propaganda forums:

> After the great success accomplished by the YouTube Invasion and the media uproar it caused that terrorists are getting trained to use YouTube, we have to clarify some matters about the YouTube Invasion. It is a continuous and successive invasion of YouTube. It does not have a time frame or that it will be over after a while. No, it is ongoing and flowing. Brothers, you have to study YouTube in a detailed manner, because it will be one of the pillars of jihadist media.
>
> (Weimann, 2014, p. 11)

A well-known al-Qaeda 'cheerleader' on YouTube was American-born preacher Anwar Al-Malaki, who was killed in Yemen in 2011. In 2009, an analysis of YouTube by the British government found 1910 videos of Al-Awlaki, of which one had been viewed over 164,000 times. In addition to his YouTube videos he also ran a blog, a Facebook page and was the editor of 'Inspire,' al-Qaeda's online magazine (Weimann, 2014; Neumann, 2016). Al-Malaki was once described as the "most likeable terrorist among Western supporters" (Brachman & Levine, 2011, p. 26). Part of his popularity was because of his ability to "combine religious doctrine with colloquial Western references" (Brachman & Levine, 2011, p. 11). Al-Awlaki repackaged al-Qaeda's message into something that his English-speaking audience could not only easily understand, but could also replicate. In the late 2000s he called on his followers to perpetrate attacks on the West, and has inspired some to do so, even after his death. In fact, almost every al-Qaeda-inspired attack on the West before the Syrian conflict has been ascribed to his influence (Neumann, 2016). Among the attackers that were said to be influenced by Al-Awlaki's videos and other internet publications are Roshonara Choudhry, who nearly killed British member of parliament Stephen Timms, the couple that committed the San Bernardino attack and killed 14 people, and the brothers behind the Boston Marathon bombings, which killed three people and left many more wounded (e.g., Klausen et al., 2012; Weimann, 2014, 2015). Al-Awlaki has also been linked to the Kouachi brothers who committed the Charlie Hebdo attacks in Paris (Neumann, 2016).

The group that is probably the most notorious for the way it has leveraged YouTube is once again ISIS. Within ISIS's official media apparatus there are various media wings that have made use of the YouTube platform. They include its 'original' one, al-Furqan Media, as well as al-Hayat Media, which produces video content that is deliberately designed to speak to non-Arab-speaking youthful target audiences. ISIS has taken online videos to a new level, with carefully scripted and high quality productions, using a variety of cinematographic techniques. Some of these videos have a 'video game'-like quality (e.g., the video 'No respite'; Vitale & Keagle, 2014). Perhaps the most (in)famous example of YouTube use by ISIS, is their series of videos of violent executions. These videos mainly represent efforts to intimidate its foes and Western audiences (Veilleux-Lepage, 2014).

However, the full spectrum of the material that has been posted on YouTube by ISIS is much broader, and, among other things, includes videos that highlight battlefield successes, portray the bloodshed and violence of the enemy, romanticize the daily lives of the group's fighters, and depicts the idyllic life in and the virtues of the so-called "caliphate." Examples include the videos 'The End of Sykes–Picot,' 'The Flames of War,' 'The Clanging of the Swords I–IV,' and 'Upon the Prophetic Methodology,' which aim to legitimize the existence of the 'Islamic State' and serve as an attempt to lure in new recruits (Vitale & Keagle, 2014; Veilleux-Lepage, 2014).

Furthermore, to supplement these videos, the Hayat Media team created a series of short High Definition propaganda videos – so called 'mujat-weets' – which specifically aim to portray the movement's softer side and the prosperous day-to-day life in their Caliphate. Examples include fighters handing out candy to children, Jihadi's visiting the wounded in the hospital, and townsfolk talking about the improvements that ISIS has brought to their local village, town or city. These videos depict life in the Caliphate as stable and normal while at the same time portraying the popularity, attractiveness and strength of ISIS leadership (Vitale & Keagle, 2014).

In addition to being used for its video hosting capabilities, YouTube has also fulfilled an important function as a social networking tool (Conway & McInerney, 2008; Weimann, 2015). Specifically, YouTube comment sections as well it the site's capacity to send private messages, enable those producing and engaging with violent extremist content to quickly identify each other and establish contact (Weimann, 2015). Facebook is another platform that has been heavily used for these purposes.

2.5.3 Facebook

Facebook is the biggest social media platform, with over two billion monthly active users worldwide in the second quarter of 2017 (Statista, 2017b). This social networking service enables users to connect and maintain relationships with other members (family, friends, and strangers if desired). Users can create public or semi-public personal profiles using their personal details, and can then post 'status updates' on their profile pages or write messages to other users (Dean, 2016; Kaplan & Haenlein, 2010; Smith et al., 2012; Weimann, 2015). People can also subscribe to groups covering similar interests, for instance, on the basis of support for a particular organization (Dean, 2016).

Like the earlier-mentioned platforms, Facebook is also used for multiple purposes by a range of Salafi-Jihadi groups (Weimann, 2015). Besides being an important media outlet, Facebook – Weimann (2014) argues – has been especially important for letting violent extremists identify mainstream Islamic youth "who may be occasional viewers of jihadist content" and, in turn, link them to the more insular and private outlets. One of the strategies utilized is creating Facebook interest groups based on seemingly innocent ideals:

> As member numbers for the groups increase, jihadist material can be slowly introduced by members of the organisation to the Facebook group in a way which does not directly condone or encourage jihadist actions, and thus does not constitute a violation of Facebook policy.
>
> (Dean, 2016, p. 235)

Salafi-Jihadi extremists have also utilized Facebook groups to identify and make lists of potential devotees. By examining people's profiles and tracing their activities online, Jihadi-Salafist groups can decide whom to target and how to approach each individual or group and tailor their content in a way that resonates or 'sticks.' As such Facebook groups provide a particularly effective tool for 'narrowcasting.' Narrowcasting involves aiming messages at highly-defined segments of the public to better influence recipients. Drawing on available information on audience members, such as their subscription to particular interest groups, demographic attributes and preferences, the Jihadi-Salafist groups cleverly adapt their profiles, images, videos, appeals and so forth to match the profile of a particular group and increase the persuasive impact (Weimann, 2014).

At the same time, platforms such as Facebook have made it far easier for sympathizers to reach out to violent extremist milieus themselves, in part because those seeking to contact Jihadi-Salafists do not face the previous restrictions that often apply in more insular forums (Torok, 2016). The GISS (2014) indeed asserts that young people that are in a radicalization process actively search for like-minded individuals on Facebook. Moreover, they subsequently post Salafi-Jihadi content on their own pages, thereby potentially influencing their own circle of friends.

In sum, social media have presented extremists with powerful new avenues for both propaganda and recruitment. But how is online propaganda implicated in the process of radicalization into violent extremism? In the next section, we outline the current knowledge on this topic.

2.6 Online radicalization through propaganda?

The internet and social media have been found to be "almost always at least present in the compiled backgrounds of both individuals who have come to hold violent radical beliefs and those who have perpetrated terrorist acts" (Miller & Chauhan, 2017, p. 30). Yet, the exact nature and extent of the influence of Salafi-Jihadi propaganda on the internet and social media remain a matter of "conjecture and hypothesizing" (Aly, 2016, "Introduction," para. 2). To date, most studies have focused on studying violent extremist social media practices and analyzing the content of their online propaganda material, rather than exploring how people actually engage with online content on social media during a radicalization process (Aly, 2016, "Introduction," para. 2). Little is known about how individuals actually experience extremist content they find on social media as well as what impact it has on them, either in the short or long term (Davies et al., 2016; Edwards & Gribbon, 2013). What is, however, emphasized is that mere exposure to extremist content does not explain radicalization. Propaganda doesn't function as a 'magic bullet' or 'hypodermic needle' by which peoples thoughts and behaviors can easily or directly be controlled. Furthermore, the process of radicalization into violence is complex, dynamic and multifaceted, and may involve a variety of influences, including, but not limited to, grievances, beliefs, and social dynamics (Neumann, 2015).

Box 2.1 Two examples of online radicalization

While it always difficult to establish with great precision the role of offline versus online influences, in a number of cases we argue that online influences have played a significant role in a process of radicalization.

For instance, the two 'Boston bombers,' the brothers Dzhokhar and Tamerlan Tsarnaev, killed three people and injured more than 250 during the annual Boston Marathon on April 15, 2013. The surviving brother, Dzhokhar, has indicated that they were self-radicalized via the internet and learned how to make a bomb via a website.

Similarly, Colleen Larose, aka Jihad Jane, was convicted for terrorism-related activities in January 2014. She lived for 10 years in Michigan, USA. In 2005, after a tumultuous life, including several marriages and a suicide attempt, she converted to Islam. She had many contacts via the then-popular MySpace-tool on the internet. She was a heavy consumer of YouTube videos of Muslims being attacked by America and Israel. As a response, she posted messages that she was desperate to do something about the suffering of Muslims in the world.

Several ideas on how the exposure to extremist materials on the internet and on social media may be implicated in the processes of violent radicalization have been proposed. First, it is argued that extremist material found online may produce some sort of 'awakening' for individuals who are becoming aware of issues around the world for the first time. For instance, Muslims in Western countries may be introduced to events and circumstances on the ground in areas such as Syria, Iraq, and Palestine, which are framed by extremist groups as situations that demand revenge. For those that are already sympathizing with or supporting extremist groups, such content may serve to further harden their opinions, beliefs and attitudes (Davies et al., 2016). Related to this, exposure to extremist content, such as emotionally arousing videos that show atrocities and moral violations in conflict zones, can elicit a strong sense of moral outrage, which has been described as an important trigger to engage in extremist actions (Sageman, 2008).

Furthermore, it is suggested, when individuals are immersed in violent or graphic imagery for extended periods of time, that the amplified effects may catalyze emotional desensitization (Bartlett & Reynolds, 2015; Davies et al., 2016; Pyszczynski et al., 2006; Neumann, 2013b). For instance, Pyszczynski et al. (2006) argue that continuous exposure to death-related discourse and imagery can result in 'mortality salience' (i.e., existential threat as a result of reminders of one's own mortality), which can encourage allegiance to good versus evil worldviews and may lead individuals to become more accepting of violent actions or even willing to engage in violent actions themselves.

In a recent study into the relation between exposure to (online) violent extremist settings and (self-reported) political violence, Pauwels and Schils (2016) argue that active engagement with extremist content on social media – as opposed to passive and accidental consumption – is of vital importance. They also posit that there is a correlation between offline differential associations with like-minded peers and self-activated online engagement with political violence. In a study by the Rand Corporation (Von Behr, Reding, Edwards, & Gribbon, 2013), several assumptions about online radicalization in the literature were tested on the basis of primary data of 15 radicalized individuals, nine of whom were convicted under the terrorism legislation of the UK. They found empirical evidence to support the assumption that the internet creates more opportunities to become radicalized, arguing that for all 15 cases, the Internet was a "key source of information, communication and of propaganda for their extremist beliefs" (Von Behr et al. 2013, p. xii). However, assumptions that the internet accelerates the process of radicalization or that it promotes self-radicalization without any form of physical contact were not supported.

The online milieu in which individuals are exposed to propaganda appears to play an important role. Social media can facilitate the development of so-called 'echo-chambers': settings in which the same opinions and arguments are continuously repeated and reinforced (e.g., von Behr et al., 2013; Davies et al., 2016; Geeraerts, 2012; Neo et al., 2016; Neumann, 2013b; Pauwels et al., 2014). As a consequence, extreme voices become amplified while moderate voices die out (Davies et al., 2016; Geeraerts, 2012; Neumann, 2012, 2013b; Pauwels et al., 2014). This may result in individuals becoming more extreme in their views. Or, as put by Neumann (2013b, p. 436), it leads individuals to "acquire a skewed sense of reality so that extremist attitudes and violence are no longer taboos but – rather – are seen as positive and desirable."

Beyond exposure to propaganda, the interactive properties of these environments allow for the formation of interpersonal bonds and reinforce a sense of community, thereby enabling further socialization into extremist ideologies. This may, in turn, lead individuals to deepen their involvement with the extremist cause (Davies et al., 2016; Neo et al., 2016). As described by Neo et al. (2016, p. 8):

> The interactive features of the online platforms create the required social environment, which aim to cultivate partisanships and facilitate the assimilation of new social conduct, routines and behaviours. Furthermore, these interactions may create a sphere of influence where violent extremist groups socialize their online members to radical worldview thereby creating a ready-made antecedent for more radical ideology.

In sum, while online messages on social media, or via direct tools such as Telegram apps, are in and by themselves unlikely to lead to violent radicalization, immersion in such material and online extremist settings can potentially contribute to the process. However, more research in this area is needed.

Unsurprisingly, governments, private companies, and non-governmental actors have sought to tackle online radicalizing influences. They have done so, in part, through negative measures, suppressing extremist activities by, for example, account suspensions, take-downs, filtering, censorship, and so on (Davies et al., 2016). While some authors argue that such measures may be an effective means to limit Salafi-Jihadi online influence (see for example Berger & Perez, 2016 in relation to account suspensions), other authors argue that the effectiveness of such measures is at best limited (e.g., Davies et al., 2016). Hence, alternative measures has been sought. One measure that has been promoted to tackle the influence of violent extremist communications online is counter-messaging.

2.7 Online counter-messaging

Existing literature on counter-messaging shows a broad range of understandings of the term (Lee, 2018). Nevertheless, counter-messaging is often used to refer to communication activities intended to undermine, disrupt or counter the appeal of (propagandistic) messages disseminated by extremist groups and their supporters (Briggs & Feve, 2013; Lee, 2018). Such activities may be undertaken online and offline or in combination; we focus here on online counter-messaging activities (henceforth: counter-messaging). It should be noted that there are other descriptions for the activities described here. Narrative and counter-narrative are concepts used particularly often. However, the term narrative is, among other things, often used to describe a particular type of form of communication. As such, a narrative can, loosely speaking, be understood as "a story that contains information about setting, characters, and their motivations" (Braddock & Dillard, 2016, p. 1). Counter-messaging may, however, take a range of forms, not necessarily fitting the description of narrative. It may for instance, be a communication consisting of an isolated claim (Lee, 2018). We have opted for the term counter-messaging to enable a broad analysis.

In recent years, online counter-messaging activities have been undertaken by a range of actors, including governments, private companies, NGOs, and civil society and grassroots actors. Such activities have manifested themselves in many different forms, from 'formally' organized communication campaigns and more tailored person-to-person interventions, to citizen actors 'informally' producing digital content that is critical of extremist messages (Lee, 2018). An example of the former is #StopDhjihadisme, a campaign launched by the French government after the 2015 terrorist assault on French publication *Charlie Hebdo*, which we will discuss more thoroughly later on. 'Je suis Charlie' may be considered an example of the latter.[4] This slogan was adopted by many on social media to express solidarity with the victims of the Charlie Hebdo attack and denounce violent extremism, and it trended on Twitter. Another example relating to the same attack is 'Je suis Ahmed.'[5] Here, however, we are predominantly concerned with the more 'formal' efforts.

These counter-messaging activities can speak to a number audiences. They may be directed at the public at large to act as a bulwark against radicalization. Borrowing from public health models, one can describe these activities as a form of primary intervention. Counter-messaging may also aim to intervene with particular individuals or groups that have been identified to be vulnerable to radicalization or show an affinity towards Salafi-Jihadi and other violent extremist groups (secondary prevention/intervention). Those that are already radicalized and have aligned themselves with Salafi-Jihadi groups may also be targeted. This can be referred to as tertiary prevention or intervention (Gielen, 2017; Harris-Hogan, 2016; Lee, 2018; Rieger et al., 2018). The ultimate aim of the activities in the area of tertiary intervention is to convince those who have turned to violent extremist groups to abandon the path they are on (Gielen, 2017).

Counter-messages come in an array of formats, such as text, pictures, videos. Oftentimes, senders have focused on video material, which is subsequently disseminated and promoted through social media (Koehler, 2016; Rieger et al. 2018). Depending on the target audience, different types of counter-messages have been used. As put forward by Neumann (2012, p. 34), messages may:

> involve challenges to the violent extremists' ideology and to their political and/or religious claims; messages that aim to 'mock, ridicule or somehow undermine their credibility'; contrasts between violent extremists' grandiose claims and the reality and/or consequences of their actions; or positive alternatives that cancel out or negate the violent extremists' ideology or lifestyle.

Many counter-messaging campaigns have, however, focused on directly challenging extremist messages (Koehler, 2016).

To provide more clarity in regard to the wide range of activities that have come to be referred to as counter-messaging, Briggs and Feve (2013) of the Institute for Strategic Dialogue (ISD) have developed useful a 'counter-messaging spectrum.' They distinguish between three categories of counter-messaging, involving different actors, target audiences, and messages: (1) counter-messaging; (2) alternative-messaging, and (3) government strategic communication. Within this spectrum, one of the approaches strictly fits the term counter-messaging. Yet, as these authors note, in practice distinctions are not always that clear. Often there is overlap between them. In our current analyses we include all three as forms of counter-messaging. In subsequent sections we will describe all three approaches, offering some examples of initiatives that have been undertaken.

2.7.1 Counter-messaging

Strictly speaking, 'counter-messaging' involves messaging activities that aim to "... deconstruct, discredit and demystify violent extremist messaging" through means such as ideology, logic, fact or humor (Briggs & Feve, 2013, p. 14). Such efforts may, for instance, aim to pick apart extremist ideologies or undermine the legitimacy and credibility of extremist groups through ridicule. Counter-messaging efforts are often targeted towards audiences that are already further along the path of radicalization, ranging from sympathizers, passive supporters to those more or less active within extremist groups (Briggs & Feve, 2013, p. 14). They may aim to achieve a number of goals, including de-radicalization of those already radicalized. They also aim to spread the seeds of doubt among 'at risk' audiences (i.e., among those people who potentially are exposed to or seek out extremist content). Such efforts may take the form of, and include, an online communications campaign, but they may also involve more targeted and tailored efforts such as person-to-person interventions. Counter-messages may be disseminated by many different actors. It is suggested that some may be better positioned to act as a 'sender' than others. For instance, religious scholars could potentially be well-positioned – if they have religious authority and credibility to project a 'religious' or 'ideological' counter-message, whereas this may be difficult for the government (we will explore this difficult position further in Chapter 4). One example of a counter-messaging effort offered in the literature is the 'Say No To Terror' campaign (see Box 2.2).

2.7.2 Alternative-messaging

The second category, 'alternative-messaging,' mainly involves activities focused on "promoting moderate centre-ground alternatives that work to undercut extremist messages and messengers, and that can help to create communities of interest and movements for positive change against violent extremism" (Briggs & Feve, 2013, p. 2). Activities may, for instance, aim "to influence those who might be sympathetic towards (but not actively supportive of) extremist causes, or help to unite the silent majority against extremism by emphasising solidarity, common causes and shared values" (Briggs & Feve, 2013, p. 12). This may include messages that highlight values such as democracy, freedom, rule of law, equality and respect for human rights (Dafnos, 2014). Unlike counter-messages, alternative

---

Box 2.2 'Say No To Terror' campaign

The 'Say No To Terror' campaign provides an example of an online counter-messaging effort instigated to respond to the messaging of groups such as al-Qaeda. It comprises a dedicated website that provides links to the 'Say No To Terror' campaign on Twitter, Facebook, and YouTube (Weimann, 2015). The website, which is written entirely in Arabic, hosts information content as well as videos, posters, and forums. As outlined by Aly, Weimann-Saks and Weimann (2014), it presents a counter campaign that aims to challenge the validity of terrorism, the legitimization of violent jihad, as well as the authority of the leaders of Jihadi extremist groups. It aims to do so by communicating incentives and benefits for resisting terrorism that appeal to both the cultural and religious values of the target audience. In contrast to al-Qaeda's message that imposes on Muslims a religiously sanctioned moral duty to wage a violent Jihad, the 'Say No To Terror' campaign draws on Islamic cultural history to impose a religiously sanctioned moral obligation to protect themselves and their communities from extremism and terrorism. The salient themes in the content of the campaign comprise a narrative that emphasizes the criminal nature of (witting and unwitting support for) Jihadi terrorist and extremist groups, highlights the hypocrisy of their narrative (among other things, by highlighting Muslim victimization terrorism), and depicts the terrorist leaders as liars and manipulators, whilst simultaneously reinforcing traditional Islamic leadership models. The origins and motives of the campaign are unclear as 'astroturfing' is being utilized, a procedure in which the sponsors of a message or organization (e.g., political, advertising, religious, etc.) are masked, creating the impression that it originates from grassroots participants. However, according to Aly et al. (2014), content and distribution strategies suggest the source is either affiliated with or sympathetic to the Saudi Arabian government.

---

messages do not explicitly intend to directly challenge extremist messages, but aim to undercut and displace them (Beutel et al., 2016). Like counter-messages, they may be disseminated by many different actors. The campaign 'Dare to be Grey' provides an example of an alternative-messaging effort by Dutch students (see Box 2.3).

2.7.3 Government strategic communication

The third and final category is government strategic communication, which is, as the term implies, inherently the domain of the government. Government strategic communication involves efforts of government actors

> to ensure that government positions and policies are clearly articulated and directed to the right audiences; that government actions

---

Box 2.3 'Dare to be Grey'

A recent Dutch example of an alternative narrative campaign is 'Dare To Be Grey.' This initiative aims to amplify the voice of the grey 'middle ground,' which is "being drowned out by the extreme voices of today," and aims to "put a stop to the polarization that is dividing [Dutch] society through promoting an open debate" (Dare to be Grey, 2017). It facilitates an online platform against polarization through different social media channels, including Facebook, YouTube, and Instagram, and a dedicated website. It intends to raise awareness by disseminating videos, images, photos and online articles as well as offering a platform for people on which people can tell their 'grey' story. Their campaign also has offline components, Dare to be Grey organizes regular events. It is also developing an educational program and magazine. According to one of those involved who took part in one of our focus groups, rather than directly challenging extremist narratives, they wanted to encourage and inspire the grey mass (on all sides of the political spectrum) to put forward a strong alternative message that can compete with those on the fringes. The initiative was developed by a group of students from the University of Utrecht, who took part in the 'Peer 2 Peer: Challenging Extremism' contest, a competition that is co-sponsored by the US Department of State, and by Facebook. The program encourages college students from universities from around the world to develop an online social media campaign and digital products that contribute to countering extremism (EdVenture Partners, 2017).

---

that are especially helpful in building relationships with key constituencies are amplified; and in some cases directly challenging misinformation about government....

(Briggs & Feve, 2013, p. 8)

This may include public awareness activities (Briggs & Feve, 2013; van Ginkel, 2015). The earlier mentioned 'Stop Jihadism' campaign may be considered as one example (see Box 2.4).

2.8 Summary

In this chapter, our aim was to provide answers to a several questions, namely: what is propaganda? How has social media been leveraged by groups affiliated with the Salafi-Jihadi movement for propaganda purposes? How does online propaganda relate to radicalization? And what is counter-messaging?

Propaganda is understood here as "the deliberate and systematic attempt to shape perceptions, manipulate cognition, and direct behaviour to achieve a response that furthers the desired intent of the propagandist"

Box 2.4 'Stop Jihadism'

One example of a government strategic communication initiative is the #StopDhjihadisme campaign that was launched by the French Government shortly after the January 2015 terrorist attacks on the office of the satirical magazine, *Charlie Hebdo*, and a kosher supermarket in Paris. Part of this campaign perhaps bests fits the 'strict' description of counter-messaging. Besides sharing information on Twitter and Facebook with the aim of dissuading would-be jihadists from joining Jihadi groups, the initiative also produced and disseminated a YouTube video that depicts the heinous reality of daily life in territories conquered by ISIS. However, in addition, the French government has launched an educational and informative website for the general public, and more specifically, "those close to young people on the path of radicalization (teachers, associations) as well as young people themselves." According to the French Government, the website was established to allow citizens to "better understand the issues and the means to combat terrorism" (Gouvernement.fr, 2015, "#StopJihadism"). Among other things, the website presents information on how to "decrypt" propaganda and manipulation techniques used on the internet by Jihadist recruiters and displays an infographic that is supposed to help identify potential jihadists. It also conveys information about the government's resources and actions concerning the fight against terrorism.

(Jowett & O'Donnell, 2012, p. 7). Salafi-Jihadi propaganda can be directed at a range of audiences and may have different purposes. It may be directed at 'foes' and 'friends,' and potential sympathizers and recruits. The main aim of the recruitment propaganda is to convince audiences to adopt a 'competitive system of meaning' or worldview, with the ultimate aim to stimulate behavior that is conducive interests of the Salafi-Jihadi groups.

In terms of distribution of their propaganda messages, social media have become highly important in recent years. Social media offer various advantages to extremist groups, they are cheap, easy to use, facilitate broad dissemination of messages, and allow the extremist groups to be part of the mainstream. Furthermore, social media allow extremist groups to circumvent the interference of intermediaries such as news agencies. Social media also enable them to reach out to their audience directly and engage them in a conversation. Such media also make it easier for audiences to reach out to the extremist groups. Lastly, social media enable anyone to take part in the production and dissemination of propaganda, allowing them to reach audiences outside of their traditional orbit.

Salafi-Jihadi groups have used a range of social media to disseminate their propaganda messages. Some well-known examples include Twitter, YouTube and Facebook. More recently, they have come to rely increasingly on more private and encrypted platforms in addition to the Dark Web. The exact nature and extent of the influence of Salafi-Jihadi propaganda on radicalization processes is not yet clear and deserves further study. Nevertheless, the literature suggests propaganda in and by itself is unlikely to lead to radicalization into extremism. However, it may contribute to the process.

One of the responses suggested to counteract the influence of Salafi-Jihadi propaganda on the internet and social media is online counter-messaging. 'Online counter-messaging' is used here to refer to organized online communication activities intended to undermine, disrupt, or counter the appeal of (propagandistic) messages disseminated by extremist groups and their supporters. A fine distinction can be made between: (1) counter-messaging (e.g., activities that challenge extremist messages head on); (2) alternative messaging (e.g., activities that aim provide a positive altern-ative); and (3) strategic communication by the government (e.g., activities that, among other things, provide insight into what the government is doing).

Notes

1 Whereas only the Salafi-Jihadism is inherently violent, it should be noted that the non-jihadist variants are often regarded as extreme by the prevailing norms of West European societies, which is at odds with European secular freedoms (e.g., the separation of state and religion, popular sovereignty, and respect for minority rights), and is opposed to integration into mainstream West European societies (De Koning, 2013; Schmid, 2013). Moreover, some believe that due to a lack of 'firebreaks' between more mainstream Salafism groups and movements and extremist fringes, involvement in the former can potentially provide a gateway to the latter (Rabasa & Bernard, 2015). In this sense, it has been suggested that these groups and movements are a 'conveyer belt.' However, others argue that the more mainstream Salafi groups may actually function as a 'firewall' that pre-vents those radicalizing from strolling further along the path towards violent extremism (Schmid, 2013).

2 It needs to be noted that the concept of jihad refers in its most fundamental form to an internal spiritual struggle. This spiritual struggle is also referred to as the Jihad al-Akbar or the 'greater jihad.'

3 As Weimann (2016) explains, one can describe the internet as composed of different layers: the 'Surface Web' is the 'upper-layer,' which can easily be accessed using traditional search engines such as Google or by directing your web browser to a specific, known website address. However, the content of the 'Deep Web,' the 'deeper' layers of the internet, are not indexed by these search engines. A segment of the Deep Web is the so called 'Dark Web,' which contains intentionally concealed content that can only be accessed through specialized browsers.

4 Devichand, M. (January 3, 2016). *How the world was changed by the slogan 'Je Suis Charlie.'* Retrieved on September 7, 2017, from www.bbc.com/news/blogs-trending-35108339.

5 The policeman who died in the streets of Paris in front of the Charlie Hebdo office.

3

COUNTER-MESSAGING

An effective means to prevent or counter radicalization?

3.1 Introduction

In the previous chapter, we have dealt with research question 1: 'Why and in what manner have Salafi-Jihadi groups exploited social media to spread their propaganda?,' research question 2: 'What's the relationship between consumption of violent extremist propagandistic content and radicalization into violent extremism?,' and research question 3: 'What is counter-messaging and how has it been used via social media?.' We now turn to research question 4, namely: 'How feasible is it to counter or prevent violent radicalization with counter-messaging? And for whom may it be effective?' First, we provide an overview some recent criticisms of the counter-messaging approach, raising questions regarding their efficacy (Section 3.2.). Second, we provide a model of the radicalization process (Section 3.2) and discuss the theories that articulate how people are less likely to be influenced by counter-messages depending on the extent that they identify strongly with an extremist group and the views the group espouses (Sections 3.3 to 3.7). In Section 3.8, we summarize the main conclusions that we draw from this analysis.

3.2 Criticisms of counter-messaging

In recent years, various critiques of counter-messaging have been offered. In addition to expressing ethical concerns (e.g., Lee, 2018), authors have raised questions regarding the efficacy of the counter-messaging approach. As noted by many, there is currently a near total lack of published evaluations of counter-messaging efforts, and evidence supporting the notion that counter-messaging is an effective means to counter radicalization is absent (e.g., Beutel et al., 2016; Ferguson, 2016; Lee, 2018; Reed, Ingram, & Whittaker, 2017).

This may be because the study of counter-messaging is a new field, but it also has something to do with the nature of these initiatives. For instance, they often aim to prevent radicalization and/or dissuade an individual from engaging with an extremist organization, and it is difficult to measure a non-effect (e.g., radicalization that does not occur; see Davies et al., 2016; Kim, Lee, Marguleas, & Beyer, 2016; Lee, 2018; Lindekilde, 2012; Romaniuk, 2015; Romaniuk & Fink, 2012; Vidino, 2010). In addition, (de)radicalization processes are complex and many variables may confound outcomes. Hence, it is difficult to identify and draw a causal link between changes in attitudes and/or behaviors and counter-messaging efforts (Radicalisation Awareness Network, RAN, 2015). Put differently, if any positive changes can be observed, it may be difficult to pinpoint whether they are in fact due to the effort undertaken.

However, this does not necessarily mean that counter-messaging efforts do not work. A lack of evidence is not the same as evidence to the contrary. Put differently, at present, it is hard to draw conclusions whether these programs are (in)effective. Yet, authors have put forward a number of criticisms that point to potential problems. A recent report from Reed, Ingram, and Whittaker (2017) summarizes several of the issues.

First, as outlined in the previous chapter, it is still a matter of considerable debate how directly exposure to online violent extremist content is connected to engagement with violent extremism. As put forward by Reed et al. (2017, p. 11): "Although the vast majority of terrorist actors share and engage with extremist narratives, suggesting a correlation, there is still little evidence to support the notion that exposure to extremist content has a causal effect on future violent extremism activity." Furthermore, research has found that developing extreme ideas and beliefs is not necessarily a precursor for violent extremism, and that many violent extremist do not 'radicalize' in any traditional sense. All of this undermines the notion that extremist narratives have a direct causal effect on extremist action.

Yet, at the same time, these authors also argue we should not oversell this notion, given that there is ample evidence that suggests that messaging can have an effect on consumers. Furthermore, the fact that violent extremist groups have invested heavily in their propaganda efforts indicates that they expect it to have some benefit for their recruitment efforts, which should not be ignored. Notwithstanding, they conclude "the dearth of empirical evidence assessing the relationship between extremist propaganda and violent actions should also make us less confident in any conclusions in both this relationship and the efficacy of narratives that counter such propaganda" (Reed et al., 2017, p. 12). We agree with these authors that more research is needed to develop a thorough understanding of this relationship.

Second, in part due to the relative infancy of the field, there has been a sizable gap between the volume of counter-messages and the propaganda of groups such as IS. While the amount of counter-messaging efforts has increased in recent years, the teams working on these efforts have typically been understaffed as well as underpopulated, and their efforts have vastly been outweighed by that of groups such as ISIS (Reed et al., 2017; Berger, 2016).

Third, counter-messaging is often criticized because of the focus of many efforts. Efforts are often defensive in nature and merely respond to the messages of violent extremist groups. Such an approach may well be counter-productive. Elsewhere, Reed (2017a, para. 3) proposes that: "unless absolutely necessary, campaigns should avoid responding to the opposition's messages," because this "simply repeats and re-enforces their messaging" and allows "them to set the ground on which the communication battle will be fought." As such, this may help Salafi-Jihadi groups rather than weaken them. Moreover, counter-narrative efforts often times directly aim to counter or rebut the information provided by extremist groups. As we will explain more thoroughly in the next section, people who become more aligned with violent extremist groups, and the ideas they espouse, may well disregard such messages outright. In fact, such efforts may well backfire.

Fourth, it is argued that campaigns are often one-sidedly focused on countering ideological aspects of violent extremist messaging. As other authors (e.g., Davies et al., 2016, p. 78) have pointed out: "Individuals are drawn into violent extremism for a host of reasons, many of which are unrelated to ideology." Furthermore, for those who become sensitive to violent extremist groups, the attraction typically lies not so much in the specifics of the ideology, but in the nature of the 'radical belief system' that is offered (Doosje, Loseman, & Van Den Bos, 2013; Pauwels et al., 2014).

In addition to the above mentioned issues, an important question remains: who should be the target audience of counter-messaging efforts? Although counter-messaging initiatives are not limited to a single audience (given the porous nature of the internet and social media), campaigns might attempt to address specific audiences, for instance individuals who are already further along the path of radicalization, or the initiatives could focus on audiences further upstream. In the next section we will explain that, if one still wants to invest in a counter-messaging campaign, the latter focus is more likely to offer some return on investment. In addition, it might perhaps be possible to consider the use of counter-messaging with members who indicate having some hesitations or doubts about the group. In both these cases (prevention and de-radicalization of doubtful members), such messages may not directly be disregarded and could perhaps have some influence, if even indirectly or with some delay.

3.2 The narrow focus of a radical person

Many models of the radicalization process articulate certain phases, from moderate to extreme. For example, Moghaddam (2005) has introduced a staircase model to terrorism that describes people going from the group floor with grievances, to the fifth and final floor, in which they commit an act of terrorism. In line with this model, Doosje et al. (2016) present a process model of radicalization that involves three steps: (1) a sensitivity phase, (2) a group membership phase and (3) an action phase (see Figure 3.1).

According to this model, the majority of people have a shield of resilience against violent extremist influences and reject their message outright (left side of the figure). However, there are micro (personal level) factors, meso (group level) factors and macro (societal level) factors, that may threaten an individual's resilience shield, creating a 'cognitive opening' (see also Wiktorowicz, 2004; Pauwels et al., 2014). At a certain moment his/or her resilience shield may fall apart, which can lead the person to engage with violent extremist. At this side of the model, prevention efforts might strengthen the shield of resilience, making people more likely to be able to resist persuasive attempts by radical groups. These prevention efforts might include presenting people with counter-messages.

Equally important for the current question about the potential use of counter-messaging, according to this model, is that it is shown that members of extremist groups have another shield of resilience, namely against de-radicalization forces (right side of the figure). Generally speaking, this shield enables them to resist any influencing attempts from moderate sources. This makes it less likely that counter-messaging efforts or any other de-radicalizing forces from outside their group will have an

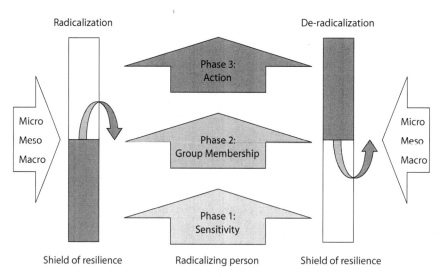

Figure 3.1 The (de)radicalization process and its determinants.

Source: Doosje et al. (2016).

effect, to the extent that the group has become really important to the individual and has prepared the individual to counter-argue the persuasion attempts. This argument is line with various literatures, as well as our interviews and focus groups.

However, it should be noted that, in some cases and under some circumstances, this shield of resilience of a radical person may fall apart, allowing a process of de-radicalization to start (i.e., rejection of attitudes and beliefs that underlie support for a violent ideology). This is usually preceded by a process of 'disengagement,' which is characterized by a change in behavior (i.e., stopping using violence and leaving the radical group). Yet, it certainly does not ensure it. There are many examples of people who are disengaged, but not de-radicalized (e.g., see Horgan, 2008). Indeed, disengagement without de-radicalization appears to be the rule rather than the exception (Schmid, 2013).

Important for the current discussion, Doosje et al. (2016) also argue that a (radical) person's focus becomes narrower with each consecutive step in the radicalization process. More specifically, it is predicted that to the extent that a person identifies strongly with the group (and the group with the individual), there are strong forces to becoming a strong and cohesive group. As such, this group will be motivated to isolate itself from outside influences that may undermine its narrative.

In the subsequent sections, we first describe five influential theories that predict that when people reach a certain level of extremism, they are less likely to be influenced by counter-messaging efforts.

3.3 Theory 1: Cognitive dissonance theory

The first theory to back up our argument that counter-messaging programs may face substantial challenges when aiming to influence those that are already committed to extremist groups and the views they espouse, is the theory of cognitive dissonance (CDT; Festinger, 1957).

In essence, CDT postulates that individuals seek consistency among their cognitions. Cognitions can be thought of as elements of knowledge about behaviors, perceptions, attitudes, beliefs, and feelings (Harmon-Jones & Mills, 1999). When two or more cognitions that are relevant to each other are inconsistent, individuals will experience an unpleasant mental tension or discomfort, called cognitive dissonance. To use a classic example of Festinger (1957), knowing that smoking is detrimental for your health is likely to cause dissonance if a person smokes. CDT asserts that people have a motivational drive to reduce dissonance, as well as a tendency to avoid situations and information that are likely to increase it.

When dissonance reaches a sufficient level, people will engage in dissonance-reduction work. The amount of dissonance is determined by the number of dissonant and consonant elements, and the importance of those elements. To reduce dissonance, individuals can change one of the dissonant cognitions, add consonant or remove dissonant cognitions to reduce the overall level of inconsistency, or decrease the importance of the elements involved in the inconsistency (Harmon-Jones & Harmon-Jones, 2007; Simon, Greenberg, & Brehm, 1995). Typically, dissonance-reduction efforts focus on the cognitions that are less resistant to change.

To illustrate using the example of the smoker, people could stop smoking, which would indicate a change in their behavior (consonant with the belief that smoking is bad for health). Yet, it may be easier to change their cognitions about the effects of smoking, for instance by seeking out information that questions the harmful effects (reducing dissonant cognitions). Alternatively, individuals could seek the positive effects of smoking (adding consonant cognitions). The smokers may also come to adopt the position that the dangers of smoking are negligible in comparison with the joy they get from it (altering the importance of cognitions; Harmon-Jones & Mills, 1999).

Individuals often experience dissonance when they do something that conflicts with their prior attitudes or beliefs. When there is no obvious external cause for that behavior, people have the tendency to adjust their attitudes and beliefs to correspond more closely with their behavior. Even when they know this behavior is wrong. This is because knowledge about behavior is usually quite resistant to change (Harmon-Jones & Mills, 1999; Harmon-Jones & Harmon-Jones, 2007). As noted by Harmon-Jones and Harmon-Jones (2007, p. 8) "… if a person behaved in a certain way, it is often very difficult to undo that behavior." In a similar vein, people often start to believe what they say (de Wolf & Doosje, 2010/2015). Applying this to radicalization, the more often people make statements that are more extreme than their actual views, the more they start to believe in those statements (Veldhuis & Staun, 2009). De Wolf and Doosje (2010/2015) explain that this process is often leveraged by radical groups when grooming new recruits. New members are encouraged to voluntarily and publicly make 'moderate' statements and promises in support of the radical group and its ideology. When these requests are honored, they align their attitudes and beliefs with their actions, which make them more amendable for future, more significant requests. This mechanism has been referred to as the 'foot-in-the-door-principle.'

Additionally, CDT proposes that people experience dissonance when they engage in an unpleasant activity to obtain some desired outcome. The dissonance will be greater, the greater the unpleasant effort required (Harmon-Jones & Mills, 1999). One way to reduce the dissonance is by evaluating the reasons for engaging in that activity more positively (i.e., add consonant cognitions) (Harmon-Jones, Harmon-Jones, & Levy, 2015). People who want to become part of an extremist group typically need make major sacrifices (e.g., in money, time, behavior, energy, socially); by demanding these investments from (potential) members such groups discourage 'free entry' and 'free exit' (Demant, Slootman, Buijs, & Tillie, 2008). For example, new recruits are often encouraged to 'break bridges' with family and friends and adopt an ideology that may conflict with their original beliefs and attitudes (De Wolf & Doosje, 2010/2015; Doosje et al., 2016). CDT suggests that the more people (have to) sacrifice, the more they will believe that these sacrifices are worth it. This will lead radicalizing people to become even more committed to their extremist group and views (De Wolf & Doosje, 2010; Veldhuis & Staun, 2009). After all, in case of a change of opinion or disengagement from the group, the costs would all have been for nothing (Demant et al., 2008).

Particularly important for our current undertaking, CDT suggests that people will generally be motivated to resist influencing attempts when they lead to incongruent or conflicting cognitions (Tormala, 2008). This is likely to hold especially for those that are highly invested in extremist groups and causes – among other things, because investments in the group increase the cognitive-dissonance costs of deviation from the group and their way of thinking. Dalgaard-Nielsen (2013) suggests that 'hardcore' members, who are part of the inner core of extremist networks or groups who have made substantial investments in the name of their commitments will be particularly reluctant to go through these cognitive revisions:

> ... having committed crimes, served time in prison, broken with friends or relatives, and/or submitted to various forms of hardship in the name of their extremist commitment, [extremists] will be highly resistant to embark on the supposedly rather fundamental cognitive revisions required, if they were to admit to themselves that they had been misguided.
>
> (Dalgaard-Nielsen, 2013, p. 107)

She therefore argues that "as a point of departure, we should expect that external attempts at influencing attitudes in order to promote exit will face substantial challenges" (Dalgaard-Nielsen, 2013, p. 107).

Importantly, arousing cognitive dissonance, for instance through counter-messaging efforts, can be a strategy to get people to reconsider their positions. However, it should be noted that it may be quite difficult to effectively expose committed extremists to such dissonance-arousing information. Dissonance research indicates that people are more inclined to examine information that confirms their positions, and to often avoid information that is contradictory (Harmon-Jones, 2012), phenomena termed respectively 'selective exposure' and 'selective avoidance' (Fransen, Smit, & Verlegh, 2015). Biases that have been found to be more pronounced when individuals hold stronger, more extreme attitudes on an issue (e.g., Brannon, Tagler, & Eagly, 2007). Also, one should be careful, as dissonance arousing efforts may well lead to results that were not intended. If the information presented in a counter-message manages to trigger sufficient cognitive dissonance, but is not persuasive or convincing enough to change a person's attitudes or beliefs (which may well be the case when they are strongly held; Howe & Krosnick, 2017), this may lead the person to intensify his original position – a phenomenon also referred to as a 'boomerang effect' (Jervis, 2017).

In sum, cognitive dissonance theory suggests that those undertaking counter-messaging efforts will have a hard time influencing those who have invested heavily in extremists groups. Not only will these individuals be reluctant to expose themselves to information that may arouse dissonance, they will be highly resistant to embark on fundamental cognitive revisions. Ultimately, according to this cognitive dissonance perspective, such efforts may even back-fire as they may serve to strengthen the original beliefs and attitudes.

3.4 Theory 2: Psychological reactance theory

The second theory, Psychological Reactance Theory (PRT; Brehm, 1966; Brehm & Brehm, 1981) is a well-known framework for understanding why people may be inclined to resist influence attempts. PRT is based on the assumption that people generally value their perceived freedom to act, think and feel as they want. In short, the theory proposes that when individuals perceive a third party is threatening or constraining their freedom, they experience 'reactance.' Reactance is an unpleasant motivational state, comprised of anger and negative cognitions (e.g., counter arguing), which motivates individuals to engage in cognitive and behavioral efforts to reassert their freedom (Steindl, Jonas, Sittenthaler, Traut-Mattausch, & Greenberg, 2015). To provide what may be a recognizable example, consider an occasion when parents tell a child not to wear particular clothes to school, but the child believes that he or she is free to decide what to wear. The child is likely to experience reactance and will be motivated to restore his or her freedom. In consequence, he or she may decide to wear the clothes to school anyway (Miron & Brehm, 2006).

With respect to persuasive communication, the theory assumes persuasive messages may be perceived as a threat to behavioral or attitudinal freedom, and, as such, may arouse reactance. For example, on the attitudinal side, people may want to feel free to hold a particular position on issues (e.g., pro or con), alter their position, or not adopt a position. Any persuasive message that attempts individuals to adopt certain positions may be construed as threats to such attitudinal freedoms (Eagly & Chaiken, 1984). Once reactance is aroused, individuals will be driven to restore their freedom, which may cause a 'boomerang effect' similar to the one described before. Namely, individuals may change their attitudes in an opposite direction of the advocated position (Burgoon, Alvaro, Grandpre, & Voulodakis, 2002; Miller, Burgoon, Grandpre, & Alvaro, 2006). Other freedom-restoring responses that have been suggested include observing others restoring the threatened freedom, subjectively increasing the attractiveness of the threatened freedom (and decreasing the attractiveness of the alternative option) (Miron & Brehm, 2006). A particularly damaging response may be source derogating, which may be accompanied by hostility or aggression towards the source. This is because it will undermine the reference power and credibility of the influencing agent. This can lead to diminished influence over the long term (Miller, Lane, Deatrick, Young, & Potts, 2007).

The magnitude of experienced reactance depends on the importance of the threatened freedom, the proportion of freedoms threatened and the perceived magnitude of the threat (Burgoon et al., 2002). Furthermore, it has been found that reactance may differ according to the traits of the target group. Arguably relevant for our current endeavor, research indicates that adolescents and young adults are likely to be particularly reactance prone, and are more strongly inclined to reject persuasive messages perceived as attempting to control them in any kind of matter (Hong, Giannakopoulos, Laing, & Williams, 1994). Grandpre, Alvaro, Burgoon, Miller, and Hall (2003) suggest that this may be attributed to characteristics related to a transitional stage of adolescence.

In addition, message characteristics have been found to affect the magnitude of reactance. Generally speaking, all aspects of a message that overtly force a certain attitude or behavior upon someone (i.e., that obviously show persuasive intent) may arouse reactance (Franssen, Smit, & Verlegh, 2015). Studies on the use of language indicate that messages using explicit, forceful, dogmatic, controlling, and threat-to-choice language are more likely to be perceived as threatening freedom, and will increase the amount of reactance, often resulting in an undesirable boomerang effect (Dillard & Shen, 2005; Miller et al., 2007; Quick & Considine, 2008; Quick & Stephenson, 2008). For example, Dillard and Shen (2005) found that phrases such as "No other conclusion makes any sense" and "There is a problem and you have to be part of the solution" will arouse reactance. Also, studies indicate that messages using imperatives such as you "ought to," "need to," "should," etc., can increase perceptions of a threat to freedom (Steindl et al., 2015).

Limited attention has been paid to the issue of reactance in the context to counter-messaging campaigns, although it has been put forward by some authors as a possible explanation for negative responses elicited by counter-messages (Ernst et al., 2017). Reactance theory has also been evoked in discussions on the potential negative effect of communicative strategies of de-radicalization programs. For instance, work by Braddock (2014) and Dalgaard-Nielsen (2013) suggests that de-radicalization programs that directly and overtly attempted to challenge beliefs and promote alternate, state-sanctioned beliefs and behaviors through discussions have the potential to backfire and strengthen extremist attitudes as a result of evoked reactance.

Taking the above into account, the main takeaway from Psychological Reactance Theory is that, arguably, counter-messages – especially those that overtly and forcefully attempt to challenge (or 'counter') extremist attitudes and behaviors and encourage others – may well lead people to engage in freedom-restoring responses. Not only may it lead people to reject the message, it may well cause a boomerang effect.

3.5 Theory 3: Social judgment theory

The third theory that predicts little effect of a counter-messaging among already radicalized people is the Social Judgment Theory (SJT; Sherif & Hovland, 1961; Sherif, Sherif, & Nebergall, 1965). The central tenet of this theory is that the effectiveness of persuasive communication efforts will depend upon the way in which the receiver evaluates a persuasive message (O'Keefe, 2016). They will not do so purely on the merits of what is advocated in the message; rather, people assess the advocated position and compare it with their own attitude. Subsequently, they will determine whether they should accept what is advocated (Perloff, 2010).

Of course, on any given issue there are likely to be a variety of positions or points of view available. Take for instance the issue of 'abortion.' One may hold that abortion should be illegal or alternatively think that women should be permitted to have an abortion whenever they request it. One may also hold a variety of intermediate positions that vary in the amount of restrictions imposed on abortion. A person is likely to assess various positions differently. One may have one preferred position, but find others more or less acceptable or tolerable. There may also be positions one finds objectionable or is ambivalent about (O'Keefe, 2016). SJT aims to specify these reactions by proposing that people have different 'latitudes' (i.e., 'judgmental categories') that exist on a continuum. The 'latitude of acceptance' consists of the range positions that a person finds acceptable, including his or her most preferred position (the 'anchor'). The 'latitude of rejection' contains those positions that the individual finds objectionable, including the most objectionable position. In between there is a 'latitude of non-commitment,' a range of positions to which the person has no commitment or is indifferent (Perloff, 2010). With respect to persuasive communication, whenever a position that a message advocates is judged to fall within one's latitude of acceptance or non-commitment, attitude change in line with that position is likely to occur. An advocated position that is perceived to fall in the latitude of rejection yields little or no effect, or may lead to attitude change away from the advocated position (i.e., the 'boomerang effect') (O'Keefe, 2016).

The SJT further proposes that somewhat ambiguous messages that advocate positions that belong to a person's latitude of rejection may be contrasted. This means that they are perceived as even further away from a person's own position (i.e., 'contrast effect'). Here, the 'anchor' serves as the main reference point. In similar fashion, when the advocated view is in the latitude of acceptance, the message may be perceived as closer to the person's own position (i.e., 'assimilation effect'). In the latitude of non-commitment, either the assimilation or contrast effect may occur. The location of the boundary point at which assimilation effects stop and contrast effects begin is not clear (O'Keefe, 2016). However, O'Keefe (2016) suggests that this may be closer to the latitude of rejection than the latitude of acceptance.

The SJT suggests that attitude change is likely to occur when there is a certain discrepancy between the position advocated in the message and the receiver's position. However, this is true up until the point that the message falls in the latitude of rejection. Importantly though, the structure of a person's latitudes on an issue is presumed to be influenced by 'ego-involvement.' Ego-involvement is often understood as the degree to which an individual is 'involved in an issue,'[1] which often goes hand in hand with holding an extreme position on an issue. When people are highly involved in an issue, their latitude of rejection increases, which results in a decrease in the size of the latitude of acceptance and non-commitment (O'Keefe, 2016). Hence, it follows that they will find fewer positions acceptable. A contrast effect will occur if communication is perceived as farther away from a person's own stand than it really is, thus causing a negative shift in attitude (Sherif et al., 1973). People who are highly involved tend to do this more frequently, even with mildly disagreeable positions. Furthermore, they will only assimilate ambiguous messages when the advocated positions are generally consistent with their attitudes. As such, people who are highly involved in an issue are generally harder to persuade (Perloff, 2010).

When involvement in an issue is very high, people's thinking on issues can take on an extreme, black-or-white quality, in which there may effectively be only two judgmental categories. There is no middle ground, things are either good or bad (O'Keefe, 2016). People who go through a process of radicalization may come to adopt a black-and-white, absolutist worldview that structures their thinking on whole range of matters. This process is stimulated by socialization in a radical group (e.g., through mechanisms of indoctrination and isolation) (de Wolf & Doosje, 2010/2015). SJT suggests that these individuals will be highly resistant to just about any message that is not adjacent to their own view on the issue. Those undertaking an influencing attempt may be able to advocate safely a position that is only moderately discrepant with the person's preconceived attitude and falls within the latitude acceptance. When a message ends up in the latitude of rejection, it will be contrasted, it will be perceived as farther away from a person's position than it really is (de Wolf & Doosje, 2010/2015).

Once more, the implication is that those undertaking counter-messaging efforts need to be careful when targeting these individuals, as they have very little wiggle room. Given that the Social Judgment Theory suggests that advocated positions cannot veer too much from a person's pre-existing positions, one ideally has a clear picture these individuals' latitudes of acceptance and rejection before one undertakes influence attempts. The theory raises substantial doubts as to whether influence efforts that aim to offer a direct rebuttal of rigidly held positions can be successful. According to the theory, in all likelihood, messages that do so are rejected outright.

3.6 Theory 4: Social identity approach

The fourth theory that can explain why it is difficult to de-radicalize radical individuals (via online counter-messaging or in any other manner) is the social identity approach. This approach refers to two related theories, namely Social Identity Theory (SIT; Tajfel & Turner, 1979; 1986) and Self-Categorization Theory (SCT; Turner, Hogg, Oakes, Reicher, & Wetherell, 1987). Before we address the relevance for this particular research question, we first provide a sketch of the basic tenets of this approach (for a broader outline see Hornsey, 2008), because it articulates the importance of group membership, which is highly relevant in the context of radicalization and de-radicalization (Doosje et al., 2016).

The social identity approach asserts that the (social) identities that we derive from our group memberships form an important part of our self-concept. Social identity refers to a definition of the self in terms of a shared social category based on intergroup comparisons. The concept of social identity can be distinguished from personal identity, which refers to definitions of self in terms idiosyncratic attributes and interpersonal relationships (Baray, Postmes, & Jetten, 2009). The social identity perspective argues that our cognitive representation of self may vary depending on whether the personal identity or social identities are made psychologically salient. When a particular social identity is salient, it becomes the basis for self-conception, in turn influencing how we think (attitudes), feel (emotions) and act (behavior; Ellemers, Spears, & Doosje, 2002).

SIT postulates that the salience of a particular group membership will induce a motivation to positively differentiate that group (i.e., the in-group) from other relevant groups (i.e., out-groups) on valued dimensions of comparison (Reicher, Spears, & Haslam, 2010). This motivation is believed to be underpinned by a variety of factors, such as the need to establish and maintain a positive identity (Tajfel & Turner, 1979), reduce subjective uncertainty (Hogg, 2000) and achieve optimal distinctiveness (Brewer, 1991). This results in a tendency to favor one's own group over other groups (i.e., in-group bias) which can be reflected in attitudes, emotions and behaviors.

The degree of identification with the in-group is assumed to moderate this tendency. One important prediction derived from this approach is that high identifiers are more inclined to selectively seek out favorable information about the in-group in order to bolster their self-concept. Similarly, they tend to avoid negative information about their group that could threaten their favorable sense of self (Appiah, Knobloch-Westerwick, & Alter, 2013; Knobloch-Westerwick & Hastall, 2010). Or as put by Knobloch-Westerwick and Hastall (2010, p. 518), "individuals seek out particular messages that enhance their social identities, essentially by providing favorable social comparisons with out-groups."

Furthermore, SCT argues that when social identity is salient, people experience a cognitive shift such that perceptions of self and others will become group-based, eliciting a tendency to conform to in-group norms. More specifically, it is argued that when a social identity becomes salient, people come to perceive themselves and others less as unique individuals, and more in terms of group memberships. When this occurs, there is an assimilation of the self to an in-group prototype (i.e., a process termed 'depersonalization'; Smith & Hogg, 2008). A prototype may simply be understood as a cognitive representation of group norms (Moran & Sussman, 2014). When a group prototype becomes an internalized part of our self-concept through assimilation, we assign the in-group norm to ourselves, and tend to think, feel, and behave accordingly. We do so even in the absence of surveillance of other group members. In addition, we will judge others in terms of their conformity to the in-group prototype (Smith & Hogg, 2008).[2]

Social identity theorists argue that such norm-based influence may have a considerable impact on attitude change attempts. The key point is that when social identity is salient, the in-group norm will come to serve as a standard for validity judgments in relation to persuasive information. As such, it is predicted that in-group messages will be perceived as more valid than out-group messages, and that people will be more influenced by in-group members than out-group members (Smith & Hogg, 2008). When individuals identify more strongly with the group, these norms exert more influence (Moran & Sussman, 2014).

Research supports the notion that persuasive messages stemming from an in-group source are generally more effective than those stemming from an out-group source (e.g., Mackie, Gastardo-Conaco, & Skelly, 1992; McGarty, Haslam, Hutchinson, & Turner, 1994). This effect is suggested to be due to people's use of source information not only as a heuristic cue to accept the in-group's position. It is also suggested that people process in-group information in a rather systematic manner (Wyer, 2010). This holds particularly when the message pertains to issues that are group-defining or group-relevant, and when the source is a prototypical group member (Smith & Hogg, 2008). To the extent that messages are considered to be derived from an out-group source, they are typically not processed deeply (Mackie, Worth, & Asuncion, 1990). This is especially the case when out-group members articulate a critical or anti-normative message (Esposo, Hornsey, & Spoor, 2013). According to Esposo et al. (2013, p. 394), "their message is likely to be rejected regardless of whether it is objectively 'right,' well-considered, well-justified, or well-argued."

Of course, anti-normative information can potentially also stem from someone who is perceived as an in-group member. Research suggests that when someone or a minority within the in-group advocate a position that differs from other in-group members, they are not likely to be influential. As argued by Marques, Abrams, Páez, and Hogg (2001, p. 401), the "perception of someone as being a deviant discredits and devalues them, and reduces their persuasive potential." In fact, the 'black sheep effect' predicts that the other group members may well derogate and reject the deviant in-group member more strongly than out-group members. Furthermore, under certain circumstance, a boomerang effect may occur, thus, they may change their attitudes in the opposite direction than that which the deviant advocates (Bazarova, Walther, & McLeod, 2012). The black sheep effect has been demonstrated in a variety of studies (Marques, Abrams, Páez, & Martinez-Taboada, 1998; Marques, Yzerbyt, & Leyens, 1988). Moreover, also been shown that the black sheep effect is stronger when identification is relatively high (Coull, Yzerbyt, Castano, Paladino, & Leemans, 2001).

Particularly important for our current endeavor, highly entitative social groups that display strong ideological premises (e.g., extremist groups) strengthen socio-psychological processes that encourage a salient group identity and enforce assimilation into prototypes and group norms (Harris, Gringart, & Drake, 2014; Harris, 2011). Harris et al. proposed that "[t]hese groups emphasise their distinctiveness and impose boundaries between themselves and the mainstream, which enhance the strong connections between members and fosters the 'us and them' mentality." The cohesive nature of these groups is argued to make members highly resistant to any form of disruptive influence (Harris et al., 2014, p. 4).

Thus, the Social Identity Approach indicates that group membership is crucial in explaining how people process information: people are generally more likely to be persuaded by someone from their own group than by a member of an out-group. This has implications when considering the source of an online counter-messaging program: when people perceive the message as stemming from an out-group, they are not easily persuaded by the content, no matter the quality of the materials and the arguments. Even when a message is considered to stem from an in-group member, to the extent that it is perceived as against the norms of the in-group, this member is usually less persuasive and in fact may fall from grace and become a black sheep.

Equally important from the current perspective, both tendencies (i.e., to discredit information stemming from an out-group source and from a deviant in-group source) are particularly strong for people who identify strongly with their group. This is due to the fact that they are more likely to perceive the world in terms of their group membership. At the same time, they are motivated to keep a 'healthy distance' from out-groups and anti-normative in-group members. This effect will be especially pronounced when these are highly entitative groups with strong ideologies, such as extremist groups. For these reasons, from a Social Identity Approach, an online counter-message to these highly identified people may fail to fall on fertile soil.

3.7 Theory 5: SIDE model of deindividuation effects

The fifth theory also argues that people are less likely to be persuaded when they feel connected to a group, is the Social Identity Model of Deindividuation Effects (SIDE) model. This is a well-established theory on computer-mediated-communication (CMC), grounded in the social identity approach (see previous section). We treat it separately because this theory predicts that the effects of a norm-based influence may be even more pronounced in online groups. It is argued that the scarcity of individuating cues in CMC further depersonalizes social perception of others and the self. This is believed to heighten group identification and perceived in-group homogeneity, in turn enhancing conformity to the in-group norm (Lee, 2006; Spears, Lea, Postmes, & Wolbert, 2011),[3] provided the social identity is initially salient and the group norm is known or can be inferred (Tanis & Postmes, 2003). Under these circumstances, it is argued that the in-group-norm will be more influential in CMC in comparison with face-to-face communication (Sassenberg, Boos, & Rabung, 2005).

The predictions of the SIDE model have received considerable support (for a review, see Spears, Lea, & Postmes, 2001). For instance, Postmes, Spears, Sakhel, and Groot (2001) conducted an experimental study pertaining to the conditions under which individuals conform to group norms in an online environment. Groups were requested to discuss a policy dilemma of a hospital concerning efficiency versus patient care priorities. It was observed that anonymous discussants, unwittingly primed with a particular norm, were more likely act consistent with (and socially transmit) that norm, than were non-anonymous discussants. This effect grew stronger over time.

Besides predicting that anonymous online interaction can enhance conformity to group norms, SIDE theorists have also suggested that it enhances the group polarization process that we referred to in Chapter 2. Group polarization refers to a consistent finding in social psychological research that, following frequent interactions with like-minded others in closed groups, people tend to endorse more extreme positions in the direction in which the group was already leaning (Lee, 2007). Some authors suggest that online settings such as those provided by social media provide ideal environments for this phenomenon to occur, as they allow individuals to pro-actively select groups to join (and which not) and to seek out like-minded (and avoid dissimilar) others. Within these groups (i.e., echo chambers), participants face both normative and informational influences that move them further towards more extreme and inflexible positions. As explained by Geeraerts (2012, p. 26), "[b]ecause participants in homogeneous groups share similar perspectives, they do not express opposing views. Furthermore, as a normative influence, participants might adjust their opinions to the expectations of other group members who are more extreme." In turn, this make people less open or even hostile to dissimilar others and counter-attitudinal viewpoints.

The SIDE model suggests that a lack of individuation information in online social interaction may further enhance this process. It assumes that group polarization is a function of identity salience and occurs as group members converge towards a polarized in-group norm (Postmes, Spears, Lee, & Novak, 2005). That is, people move toward a more extreme position in the direction of the in-group norm, even beyond the average position, in order to maximally differentiate themselves from (implicit) out-groups (Lee, 2007). The SIDE model predicts that anonymous online social interaction will foster group identification and conformity to group norms, resulting in greater group polarization (Spears et al., 2011). Several studies provide evidence in line with this prediction (e.g., Lee, 2007; Spears, Lea, & Lee, 1990). For instance, in a CMC experiment, Lee (2007) found that de-individuated group members exhibited stronger identification with their anonymous group members and were also more likely to polarize their opinions than individuated counterparts.

3.8 Summary

In this chapter, we have addressed research question (4), namely 'How feasible is it to counter or prevent violent radicalization with counter-messaging? And for whom may it be effective?.' To summarize, evidence supporting the notion that counter-messaging is an effective means to counter radicalization is currently absent. At present, it is therefore hard to draw firm conclusions about whether these programs are (in)effective. A number of problems with these initiatives have been identified. First, the underlying assumptions of these initiatives can be questioned. Second, there is a sizable gap between the volume and quality of counter-messages and violent extremist propaganda. Third, concerns have been raised regarding the nature of many counter-messaging efforts, as many have been 'defensive' and have focused on directly challenging the ideological aspects of Salafi-Jihadi messaging.

Furthermore, on the basis of five theoretical perspectives (cognitive dissonance theory, social judgment theory, psychological reactance theory, social identity approach and the SIDE-model), we argue that the greater the extent that people become committed to violent extremist groups and the views they espouse, the less likely they are to be influenced by counter-messaging efforts. This may especially be the case when the strategy utilized is one of rebuttal. The individuals may be hard to reach as well as difficult to move. In fact, they may adopt positions in the other direction than intended as a reaction to this persuasive attempt (i.e., a boomerang effect). Thus, counter-messaging campaigns may not be a very effective tool to de-radicalize those who are already far along the path of radicalization.

Having articulated the clear limitations of any online counter-messaging campaign in terms of reaching those already far along the path of radicalization, we argue that, if any success is to be expected at all from such efforts, the payoff is likely to be more significant among those who show some curiosity or sympathy for extremist groups and the views they espouse, but are not yet committed to them (i.e., when they still are in the sensitivity phase of the model described by Doosje et al., 2016). Of course, to successfully target and influence these individuals a whole range of other factors may need to be considered (see Chapter 4).

In addition, despite the fact that there are good and solid theoretical reasons to expect that counter-messages may not work for those already far along the path of radicalization, it is an interesting question whether or not such efforts may have some effect when some individuals from violent extremist groups show a glimpse of doubt about their group and its goals. In terms of the model by Doosje et al. (2016) presented earlier, for some individuals, the shield of resilience may show signs of holes or weak spots. May counter-messages therefore fall on fertile grounds for such individuals and plant the seed of a question? It is important to consider how to design such a counter-messaging campaign (mainly for preventive purposes and for the individuals who show signs of doubts about their group). Which aspects of a counter-messaging campaign need to be considered? These questions will be addressed in the next chapter.

Notes

1 According to O'Keefe (2016, p. 22), who describes the concept of ego-involvement, a person can be said to be involved with an issue

> when the issue has personal significance to the individual, when the person's stand on the issue is central to his or her sense of self (hence ego-involvement), when the issue is important to the person, when the person takes a strong stand on the issue, when the person is strongly committed to the position, and so forth.

2 Social influence can also occur under conditions when personal identity is salient. Social influence under social identity salience has been termed 'interpersonal influence' and is fostered by interpersonal bonds. When personal identity is salient, social influence may also be driven by individuals' striving for distinctiveness from their communication partners as well as fulfilment of other personal needs (Sassenberg & Jonas, 2009).

3 Under conditions of personal identity salience, deindividuation is assumed to obstruct interpersonal influence as it hinders the development of interpersonal bonds that are the basis for interpersonal influence (see also the previous note) (Sassenberg, Boos, & Rabung, 2005).

4

PRINCIPLES FOR
DEVELOPING COUNTER-
MESSAGING CAMPAIGNS

4.1 Introduction

In this chapter, we address research question 5: What principles can inform the development of a counter-messaging campaign? Thus, we examine the key principles that may guide the development and implementation of a social media counter-messaging program addressing potential radicalization, given the limitations discussed in the previous chapters. These limitations include that a counter-messaging initiative might not be effective among those who have already passed the first stage of radicalization (see Chapter 3). The current chapter will therefore address research question 5 mainly in a preventive sense. However, as argued earlier, despite the fact that members of radical groups, generally speaking, will not be inclined to read materials from outside their sphere, some individuals who show signs of disengagement with the group might be possible targets for a tailored campaign.

Overlooking the literature, it is clear that evaluations and effect studies for counter-messaging campaigns are sparse and it is currently hard to draw conclusions as to whether these efforts are effective. Unsurprisingly, it is difficult to find any evidence-based research findings from which valid prerequisites for an effective counter-messaging initiative can be drawn. However, the field of 'strategic communication' has a long history and is not the limited domain of countering violent extremism (CVE). It is inherently multidisciplinary and draws on literature from a wide variety of subfields including, but not limited to health promotion, (social) marketing, and public relations. The broader literature is rich in descriptions of practices and approaches that are *associated* with more successful communication efforts. In the following we will therefore supplement findings from the literature on counter-messaging (and counter-extremism more generally), with findings from the broader communication literature. In addition, we will present insights from the various experts we have interviewed.

General theories from mass communication have gradually evolved from one-directional sender-message-receiver models toward more dynamic and interactive models, including feedback loops and the agency of both sender and receiver. The latter do more justice to contemporary mediated communication processes including social media. Hence, we will try to outline key principles that can be derived from many such smaller theories from the perspective of a counter-messaging program. In brief, key principles are outlined in subsequent sections, and we follow the general steps in setting up a communication campaign:

1   Research and planning (using theory; assessing the context-specific drivers of radicalization, identifying, analyzing and segmenting the audience, drawing lessons from (former) violent extremists; assessing available resources; and setting goals and objectives – Section 4.3).
2   Program development and design (developing the message, and selecting credible messengers; selecting dissemination channels – Section 4.4).
3   Implementation (disseminating the message, and possible risks and challenges – Section 4.5).

In Section 4.6, we outline the risks and challenges. Finally, in Section 4.7, we summarize the findings from this chapter.

4.3 Start a campaign with research and planning

From the literature in communications science, it is clear that in the starting phase of a campaign, conducting research is essential. It is vital to develop a thorough understanding of the topic at hand, define the problem and the audience, gain insight into program strategies that may prove fruitful, and develop an outline and global plan of how the program will be designed. In the following, several important aspects in this phase are described in the following subsections: use of theory (subsection 4.3.1); assessing the context-specific drivers of radicalization (subsection 4.3.2); identifying, studying and segmenting the audience (subsection 4.3.3); learning from (former) extremists (subsection 4.3.4); assessing available resources (subsection 4.3.5); and determining goals and objectives (subsection 4.3.6).

4.3.1 Make use of theory

A first important principle that can be drawn from broader communication research is that the application of theory (or rather theories) is a *sine qua non* for the design of effective communication efforts (e.g., Rossmann, 2015; Egner, 2009; Korda & Itani, 2013; Noar, 2006; Noar, Palmgreen, Chabot, Dobransky, & Zimmerman, 2009; Perloff, 2010). What distinguishes effective from ineffective communication campaigns is that the former "reflect painstaking application of theoretical principles" whereas the latter "are based on 'seat of the pants' intuitions" (Perloff, 2010, p. 332). Indeed, one of the most comprehensive meta-analyses of online health promotion interventions demonstrated that programs based on theory generally had greater effect than those that were not (Webb, Joseph, Yardley, & Michie, 2010).

The health promotion literature suggests theory can inform programs in a variety of ways. For instance, communications programs that are generally more effective than others are grounded in thorough analyses that define the problem or situation to be addressed in the context in which it occurs. In addition to empirical evidence, theory can help to provide insight into the nature of a problem and its causes, determinants and mechanisms, and assist in identifying the range of factors that program developers might seek to modify through their effort. Furthermore, theories suggest ways to drive change in attitudes and behaviors and can guide program planners in the development and implementation of program elements (Green, 2000). Beyond drawing on or borrowing from existing theory, it is also argued that program planners do well to articulate a sound, program specific 'theory of change,' which specifies how a program hopes to cause a desired outcome (Waldman & Verga, 2016). Such a theory explicitly spells out "each hypothesized logical [and theoretical] relationship linking program design to eventual program effects," and is, among other things, valuable for evaluation and monitoring purposes (Egner, 2009, p. 331).

Sound theoretical underpinnings are important. as without a full rational appraisal of the issue or problem in a given context as well as potential solutions, one easily falls in the trap of focusing on "wrong or inappropriate variables (i.e., miss the target completely)" or tackling "only a proportion of the combination of variables required to have the desired effect (i.e., hit only a few of the total number of possible targets)" (Green, 2000, p. 126). To illustrate, a program that is designed to dissuade audiences from engaging in particular behavior, for instance smoking, is highly unlikely to succeed if it does not effectively address its known determinants. One could argue the same for a program that aims to address radicalization, whether it is focused on cognitive or behavioral radicalization.

Given the lack of solid empirical studies on both (online) radicalization and counter-radicalization processes, a sound theoretical foundation seems particularly important for communication activities addressing violent radicalization. As argued by Davies et al., (2016), those undertaking counter-messaging efforts should, at a minimum, take into account what is known about the factors that are purported to animate radicalization processes. While they recognize that there is no 'grand theory' of radicalization and that the reasons why individuals radicalize into violent extremism are not yet fully understood, they also point out that there is growing consensus that a wide range of inter-related factors may be implicated in (violent) radicalization. Indeed, a range of studies points towards a complex interaction between factors at the micro, meso and macro level (e.g., Borum, 2011; Doosje et al., 2016; Khalil & Zeuthen, 2016; Pauwels et al., 2014; Ranstorp, 2010; Schils & Verhage, 2017; Schmid, 2013; Veldhuis & Staun, 2009; Vergani et al., 2018; Vidino, 2010).

These authors found this complexity to be add odds with how counter-messaging efforts are currently set up. They reviewed eight counter-messaging initiatives, and found that all applied an understanding of particular extremist or terrorist groups and the ideology they conveyed to the construction of counter messages. Yet they had little interest in social processes and the push and pull factors that are often involved in radicalization. As such, the authors wondered whether there was any utility in these programs. According to these authors, "given their incomplete theoretical underpinnings of these campaigns, it would be difficult for these programs to meet their desired aims" (Davies et al., 2016, p. 78).

In sum, use of theory is an essential strategy for developing an understanding of the problem at hand and can help to enhance the effectiveness of communication efforts. Theory-driven approaches are more likely to produce results and return on investment.

4.3.2 Assess the context-specific drivers of radicalization

Developing an understanding of why individuals become involved in violent extremism is clearly a challenging task. Yet, at the outset of a campaign, it is recommended to consider and assess factors that may provide the breeding ground for the acceptance of the Salafi-Jihadi message and could drive and sustain engagement with associated groups in the context in which the campaign is undertaken (Davies et al., 2016; Gielen 2017; Khalil & Zeuthen, 2016; Zeiger, 2016). Besides being important for reasons mentioned in the previous section, it may help to avoid biased assumptions such as those pertaining to supposedly 'vulnerable populations,' and instead can steer counter-messaging initiatives to audiences that might be most impacted by efforts. Furthermore, an assessment of factors may inform aspects of an appropriate messaging approach (Zeiger, 2016).

The literature offers various frameworks that may assist in identifying and developing a better understanding of factors that may drive radicalization in a given context (e.g., Doosje et al., 2016; Khalil & Zeuthen, 2016; Pauwels et al., 2014; Schils & Verhage, 2017; USAID, 2009; 2011; Veldhuis & Staun, 2009; Vergani et al., 2018). An often used framework is provided by USAID (2009; 2011), and makes a distinction between factors that may 'push' individuals towards violent extremism and factors that draw them towards it, so called pull-factors. Some authors have, however, argued that this framework may be too simplistic. For instance, Khalil and Zeuthen (2016) argue that the push/pull framework is often inconsistently interpreted, which may result in factors being overlooked. They suggest it may be beneficial to distinguish more clearly between factors at different levels of analysis (i.e., the micro-, meso- and macro-level), and have provided a framework that comprises three interrelated categories: 'individual incentives' (micro-level), 'enabling factors' (meso-level) and 'structural motivators' (macro-level). To give an illustration of the types of factors that may be relevant, we will partially draw on this framework. Importantly, the specific factors involved may vary according to the context and individuals involved. Furthermore, different factors may become more or less prominent during different phases of the radicalization process (Doosje et al., 2016).

Radicalization processes are influenced by 'structural motivators' which are linked to factors at the macro-level. These may include socio-economic, cultural and political conditions such as inequality and marginalization, poor governance, and human rights violations, but also factors such as external state interventions in the affairs of other nations (Khalil & Zeuthen, 2016; in the USAID framework they are described as 'push' factors). These macro-level factors may give rise to grievances and can contribute to attitudes that are supportive of violent extremism. Yet, in and by themselves, they do not explain radicalization into violent extremism (Khalil & Zeuthen, 2016). Many people may experience such circumstances, but only few are driven towards violent extremism. As such, these factors have been described as indirect causes (i.e., 'causes of causes' or 'root causes') of violent extremism (e.g., Pauwels et al., 2014).

There is no such thing as a clear profile of violent extremists, yet certain conditions at the individual level (micro-level) have been found to make individuals more susceptible to violent extremism. The second category of 'individual incentives' is comprised of "economic, security-based and psychosocial incentives that are conditional on the individual in question" (Khalil & Zeuthen, 2018, p. 2; they are largely similar to the 'pull'-factors described in the USAID framework). Individual 'demands' may lead one to become more prone to the reach of violent extremist groups or for individuals to seek them out themselves. Among other things, such factors may include the need for a sense for purpose, belonging, identity and justice, the desire for adventure or status, and expected material rewards or rewards in the afterlife (Khalil & Zuethen, 2016; see also Feddes et al., 2015). For instance, Doosje et al. (2016) describe how in the 'sensitivity phase' (see previous chapter), feelings of insignificance may be caused by a loss of status, a strong feelings of humiliation, or poor career prospects (e.g., personal failure, substance abuse, criminal activities). In this situation, extremist groups may become attractive to individuals, as they can be well-equipped to "foster or restore feelings of significance by providing recruits with a sense of belonging, respect, heroism, status and the notion to fight for a holy cause" (Doosje et al., 2016, p. 81). Another important factor in this phase is the need to reduce personal uncertainty. When people become uncertain, they may become incentivized to identify strongly with a group that can reduce that uncertainty. Groups that offer a distinctive and clearly defined identity and associated normative beliefs and behavioral rules may be particularly attractive. Violent extremist groups may be especially well-suited to reducing personal uncertainty, as these highly distinctive groups offer a clear profile, a solid structure, and a black-and-white world view that provides clear answers to complex questions and prescribes certain actions (e.g., Doosje et al., 2016; Hogg, 2014; Hogg, Kruglanski, & van den Bos, 2013).

Finally, at the meso-level, it is possible to distinguish 'enabling factors,' such as the presence of radical mentors in an individual's social circle or significant others with social ties to violent extremist groups, access to radicalizing settings online, or a lack of family support. Khalil and Zeuthen (2016) argue that these factors enable violent extremism rather than motivate it. Exposure to violent extremist settings, through self-selection, social selection and outreach by violent extremist groups, is typically necessary for radicalization into violent extremism to occur. Individual needs or 'demands' need to be met with a relevant 'supply' (Lindekilde, 2016). In the sensitivity phase, individuals may for instance become exposed (online/offline) to violent extremist groups through friends and family members (i.e., social selection; Doosje et al., 2016; Lindekilde, 2016). Violent extremist groups also consciously create opportunities for exposure, for instance, by organizing study circles or engaging in (online) propaganda activities (Lindekilde, 2016). Through indoctrination and socialization offline and online, individuals may subsequently become more strongly invested in violent extremist groups and ideas. Some studies indicate that a lack of family support may also influence the radicalization process. For instance, a review on the role of families suggests that unstable or problematic family situations may prompt individuals to become more receptive to violent extremist groups and that parents, who could potentially act as a buffer, often do not respond adequately when they are confronted with potential signals of radicalization (Sikkens, van San, Sieckelinck, & de Winter, 2017).

From these insights we can draw several lessons for counter-messaging activities. First, online counter-messaging should always be considered as part of a broader approach to tackle radicalization into violent extremism, given that such activities alone cannot provide an answer for many of the factors that are believed to drive radicalization into violent extremism. Second, counter-messaging initiatives intended to directly prevent radicalization may want to focus on audiences who are at risk of exposure to extremist influences (to the extent they can be identified), rather than target audiences who are not likely to be exposed, given that some form of exposure is typically considered necessary for radicalization into violent extremism to occur (Berger, 2016). However, as we have argued in the previous chapter, given that those who already show strong support for violent extremist groups and ideas are unlikely to be a worthwhile target audience, perhaps it is best to focus on those individuals who show some curiosity towards violent extremist groups. However, some authors have also argued against this position. For instance, Speckhard and Shajkovci (2018) have argued that counter-messaging activities should target broader audiences who are not interested in violent extremist groups to make certain that they remain not interested. However, as we will see in the next section, there are also arguments against this position. Of course, campaigns can also have other purposes, which may make it relevant to target other, broader audiences as well.

Lastly, the framework makes clear that individuals may not only be attracted to extremist groups for ideological reasons. Rather, the groups may also be attractive as they promise fulfillment of other needs (e.g., the need for adventure, or the need for belonging to a group). If this is the situation, than counter-messaging focused on refuting erroneous ideological interpretations is unlikely to be sufficient to divert individuals from radicalization into violent extremism (Davies et al., 2016). Rather, those undertaking a campaign should give consideration to the different needs and motivations of individuals, and address them by providing a viable alternative. Importantly, as these needs may differ, various alternative paths may need to be offered.

4.3.3 Identify, analyze and segment the audience

A second step in the assessment of the specific context is identifying the target audience of a campaign. Depending on the purpose of the campaign, audiences may differ. As well as individuals that may be open or sympathetic to, or are starting to seek out, violent extremist content online, the target audience could for instance also comprise people who may be able to exert an influence over these individuals (Zeiger, 2016). In some cases, it may perhaps also be relevant to target broader populations. Importantly though, audiences are never monolithic groups. Not only may members of the audience differ in characteristics such as needs and values, they may well respond differently to certain communications. Moreover, it is unlikely that all members of the audience can be reached utilizing the same approach. Thus, different communication strategies and messages will be necessary for different people. Within the broader communication literature it is therefore generally recommended that program planners carefully define and segment their target audience(s), and customize their communication strategy accordingly (e.g., Boslaugh et al., 2005; Egner, 2009; Kreuter & Wray, 2003; Noar, 2006; Noar, 2011; Noar, Harrington, & Aldrich, 2009; Slater, 1996; Slater, Kelly, & Thackeray, 2006; Snyder, 2007; Thackeray, Neiger, Hanson, & McKenzie, 2008).

The basic idea of audience segmentation is dividing a heterogeneous audience into relatively homogeneous subgroups (i.e., segments) on the basis of meaningful attributes that are either known (or presumed) to be related to the issue under consideration and desired outcomes (Boslaugh et al., 2005). This process is considered to be a prerequisite for developing messages that are responsive to the circumstances, needs, predispositions, and other relevant characteristics of the audience (Kreuter & Wray, 2003). Likewise, segmentation will largely drive the selection of other aspects of communication strategy (e.g., channels, and credible sources; Noar, 2011; Slater, 1996). The importance of audience segmentation cannot be overemphasized. A failure to adequately segment is may render a campaign ineffective.

There is no overriding segmentation strategy for every situation. Differences in objectives, populations, contexts, and circumstances will necessitate different segmentation decisions. However, as a general rule, the more narrow and homogeneous the segment, the more targeted strategies and approaches can be and the more likely that they will be effective (Noar, 2011). Thus, ideally you want to have a perfectly tailored strategy for each person. This may be especially important when targeting those that show curiosity towards extremist groups and ideas. While the digital era offers unique opportunities for individual tailoring, in practice this may not always be feasible, for instance due to limited resources (Slater et al., 2006).

There is an almost infinite number of variables on which audiences can be segmented. Arguably, the simplest segmentation approach is to subdivide audiences on the basis of demographic variables (e.g., age, gender, race or ethnicity, social class, religion) and geographic location (e.g., city, region) (Boslaugh et al., 2005; Egner, 2009). This approach is fairly common in other fields, such as health promotion (Boslaugh et al., 2005). However, it is frequently argued that segmentation on the basis of geo-demographic homogeneity alone may only be of limited use for developing meaningful strategies and messages. This is because, among other things, it tends to lead to subgroups with great intra-segment variance (e.g., Boslaugh et al., 2005; Rimal & Adkins, 2003). Hence, rather than using geodemographic variables alone, the health promotion literature recommends using more sophisticated strategies and giving consideration to cultural psychographic, attitudinal, and behavioral variables and/or combinations of these and other variables (Boslaugh et al., 2005).

Related to this, geographic and demographic variables have been used for targeting (online) radicalization prevention efforts towards supposed vulnerable communities, typically Muslim communities (Harris-Hogan, Barrelle, & Zammit, 2016). In line with the argument above, critics have argued these initiatives inherently end up with too broadly defined audiences. As a consequence, such efforts do not reach those most in need of attention and largely draw in the wrong crowd, namely mainstream Muslims (Richardson, 2013; Harris-Hogan et al., 2016). Moreover, it is asserted that such initiatives may label entire Muslim communities 'suspect' or 'a security threat,' and may well alienate Muslims who feel they have unfairly been singled out solely due to their religion and/or Arab background (Berger, 2016; Richardson 2013). In addition, it has been pointed out that targeting too broad an audience could potentially increase curiosity in extremist groups and their ideologies (Berger, 2016). As such, rather than countering (violent) radicalization, such efforts may be counter productive. Whatever the purpose of a campaign, one is ill-advised to take the 'scatter-gun approach.' Rather, campaigns should carefully segment their audience and match their message and strategies accordingly if they want to have an impact.

In order to do so effectively, rigorous audience research is necessitated (e.g., Egner, 2009; Fink & Barclay, 2013; van Ginkel, 2015). For instance, van Ginkel (2015, p. 9) argues that it is important that those undertaking a counter-messaging campaign gain insight in:

> the profile of the target group, the question of with whom its members are in contact, the background that its members come from, the level of education or professional experience that they have, their (former) interests, and the sources used to find information.

This may only be the tip of the iceberg. The main point, however, is that one needs to learn as much as possible about the target audience, and that decisions related to the target audience should be informed (as much as possible) by data instead of presumptions (Noar, 2011). It has become increasingly possible to harness the power of social media data to gain insight into the audience. We will explore some of these and other strategies in Chapter 5.

It should be noted that it may not always be possible to conduct a very thorough audience analysis, as it requires sufficient resources (e.g., finances, time, and technical know-how). Moreover, not all information can be found with open search research (Van Ginkel, 2015). As pointed out by van Ginkel (2015), it might even be necessary to create legal powers for certain authorities to conduct a particular kind of analyses thoroughly. Furthermore, it may necessitate proper funding and cooperation to facilitate the exchange of information and knowledge. This may not always be feasible for small-scale efforts.

Thus, in the planning phase of the campaign, defining the specifics of the target audience is an important step to take into account when designing a counter-messaging campaign. In the previous chapter, we concluded that counter-messaging campaigns may be best targeted in a preventive manner. However, from this literature, it is clear that a too broad scatter-plot approach may run the risk of being ineffective and counterproductive. Thus, ideally, a campaign should aim to focus on specifically targeted individuals or a segment of a group.

4.3.4 Learn from (former) extremists

It is important to develop a thorough understanding of the themes that run through the messaging (or narratives) of Salafi-Jihadi groups when one wants to engage in counter-messaging efforts (e.g., Ashour, 2011; Braddock & Horgan, 2016; Hedayah & ICCT, 2014; van Ginkel, 2015; Zeiger, 2016). This allows one to better tailor appropriate counter- or alternative messages, for example, because it may help one to identify weaknesses in their message that can be exploited (Zeiger, 2016). A good understanding may not only help identify what is overtly expressed within terrorist messages, but also what is meant by those messages and how the messages may be potentially be interpreted (Braddock & Horgan, 2016). Hence, a third step in conducting an assessment of the specific context may be an analysis of the themes leveraged by violent extremist groups in their messaging.

Various studies offer preliminary insight into the themes leveraged by specific Salafi-Jihadi groups (e.g., Winter, 2015; Gartenstein-Ross et al., 2016; Zelin, 2015). Importantly, such studies typically assess the themes intrinsic in the messaging of a Salafi-Jihadi group at a single point in time. However, thematic shifts and changes may occur over time in response to unfolding events and developments (Winter, 2018). For instance, in Winter's (2015) study of ISIS propaganda intended to intimidate enemies and draw new recruits, 'utopianism' was the most prominent theme: ISIS messaging presented the so-called caliphate as a utopian society where recruits could live as heroes (others themes were: brutality, mercy, victimhood, war and belonging). However, in 2018, there was a significant thematic rearrangement in the group's propaganda; its story had shifted away from 'utopianism' towards 'warfare' (Winter, 2018). "As its territories hemorrhaged and its leadership disintegrated, the Islamic State was at pains to prove to supporters that it remained a potent and, broadly speaking, winning force" (Winter. 2018, pp. 113–114). This, suggests that conducting such an analysis should not be a one-time event. Furthermore, it is important to keep in mind that messaging may differ according to the context.

Importantly, as suggested earlier, beyond looking at what violent extremists are saying, it is also vital to consider why their message may resonate with an audience in the first place. The audience should be the primary consideration in any counter-messaging effort. In this regard, former extremists may be able to provide extremely useful information.

They have first-hand experience in terms of why they themselves decided to join an extremist group and may also have insights into other members' motivations and reasons. As such, they can provide information about the factors that people may have (had) to join a group and, more specifically, the role played by extremist messaging. In addition, they may also have ideas in regard to what types of counter-messages may resonate. Furthermore, former members may have insight into the structure of groups and supporting networks, for example they have ideas about who might be susceptible to counter-messaging and who is not. For these reasons, former extremists can offer unique and highly insightful information for creators of a counter-messaging campaign. In Box 4.1 below we provide one example of an effort in the realm of counter-messaging in which former extremists have played a prominent role.

Box 4.1 Drawing on the experience of former extremists: the One2One program

An example of a social media effort in which former extremists have played a prominent role is provided by a pilot project of the Institute for Strategic Dialogue (ISD), a project that was set up as a partnership with Curtin University and members of the Against Violent Extremism (AVE) network. The One2One program aimed to devise a methodology and test the viability of an approach "based on directly messaging those openly expressing extremist sentiment online and seeking to dissuade them from following that path" (Frenett & Dow, 2015, p. 18). The team made use of the Facebook tool called 'Graph Search' to identify at-risk candidates that openly endorsed and promoted right-wing or Jihadi extremist messages online. Once identified, profiles were passed on to former extremists to verify their 'at-risk status' and 'at-risk' candidates were contacted by the former extremists using the Facebook peer-to-peer messaging system in conjunction with a 'pay to message' functionality in order to elicit a conversation. According to Frenett and Dow (2015), the results of the early stage effort appeared to be quite promising. Yet, they also note that it was a short-term study and it was limited to publicly accessible social media data. They could not effectively measure any long-term shifts in cognitions or behaviors. That having been said, of those individuals that were willing to respond (43 percent of those considered at risk of falling into what they termed 'violent Islamism'), a majority were willing to engage in a 'sustained conversation,' which they defined as an exchange of more than five messages. They also found that engagement rates were affected by the variables, tone and anonymity. When former extremists revealed their true identities, shared their experiences, and used a more casual tone, engagement rates were higher. Anonymous communication and antagonistic and aggressive tones led to lower engagement rates.

4.3.5 Assess the available resources

Another recommendation is that those undertaking a counter-messaging initiative should think carefully about their available resources. In comparison with other approaches, it is argued that social media provide a relatively cost-effective means to reach both broad and specific target audiences (Freeman, Potente, Rock, & McIver, 2015; Gold et al., 2012; Hanna, Rohm, & Crittenden, 2011). While social media tools are available for free or at limited costs, running a campaign on social media evidently still requires resources. In fact, several studies in the field of health promotion indicate that the development and implementation costs are often higher than previously expected (Evers, Albury, Byron, & Crawford, 2013, Freeman et al., 2015; Gold et al., 2012). Developing and implementing a social media program can be time- and labor-intensive, especially when the chosen messaging strategy requires continuous content creation and responsive interaction and feedback (Freeman et al., 2015). Importantly, this is not to say that an engaging social media content strategy necessarily always needs to involve excessive creative development and production costs (Hanna et al., 2011).

Furthermore, familiarity with social media from personal experience is typically not enough to run an efficient program in a social media setting. In fact, it may require a multidisciplinary team with a broad range of skills and knowledge (Gold et al., 2012). Time and resources may be required to foster skills and competencies necessary to communicate effectively in social media (Evers et al., 2013; Freeman et al., 2015; Gold et al., 2012). Team members may for instance require training on the functionalities of different social media platforms, how users engage and interact in social media environments, the development of shareable content, and social media analytics (Freeman et al., 2015; Gold et al., 2012). Gold et al. (2012) also note that one should be aware that building and maintaining multidisciplinary collaborations may require time and financial investment.

In the case of insufficient resources, it may be valuable to partner up with other organizations and stakeholders in order to expand them (Weinreich, 2011). Even if this is not the case, this may be valuable. In particular, soliciting meaningful participation of actors at the grassroots level in campaign planning, design, and implementation may benefit the effectiveness of campaign efforts (e.g., Egner, 2009; Global Counter-Terrorism Forum, GCTF, 2013; Snyder, 2007; Macnair & Frank, 2017; Radicalisation Awareness Network, RAN, 2017). They can help to develop locally relevant counter-messages and may be more effective and credible in delivering the message than governments and statutory organizations (GCTF, 2013; RAN, 2017; also see Section 4.4.2.). Of course, soliciting community participation may require continued investment in building relationships and trust.

Thus, even though running an online counter-messaging campaign may be cost effective, developing and implementing a social media strategy may require a team with diverse theoretical and practical knowledge and technical expertise and skills, which are associated with relatively higher costs. Therefore, it is important to carefully consider available resources. Also, it is fruitful to build connections and enlist involvement of actors at the grass root-level.

4.3.6 Determine goals and objectives

An often mentioned and rather self-evident (yet, not always thoroughly implemented) best practice is setting clear goals and objectives (e.g., Beutel et al., 2016; Briggs & Frenett, 2014; Macnair & Frank, 2017; Snyder, 2007; Zeiger, 2016). There are many distinct target audiences for counter-messaging efforts, which may require different types of campaigns, communication strategies and messages (RAN, 2015). Determining clear goals and objectives is vital as it will guide the development of appropriate approaches and will help determine whether the program was a success. Goals tend to be formulated in more abstract terms and identify desired end-states to which an effort is directed, whereas objectives are more narrowly defined descriptions of achievements that are needed to arrive at the desired outcomes (Veldhuis, 2012).

The Institute for Strategic Dialogue (Reynolds & Tuck, 2016; Tuck, 2017) provides some general pointers in regard to objective setting. First, they should be well defined and specific about the desired effect. What kind of changes should occur? Second, they should be established around measurable (or observable) criteria, "with campaigners confident before the inception of the campaign that they will be able to discern, from available metrics and evaluation activities, whether or not they were achieved" (Reynolds & Tuck, 2016, p. 10). Lastly, they should be realistic, taking in account matters such as the time-span and the intended audience of a campaign, budget and other resources.

4.4 Designing your program

In developing a communication campaign, and thus also in developing a counter-messaging campaign, a more specified campaign strategy will be made on the basis of initial research and planning. In this phase of program development and design there are several important aspects to consider: developing messages (Section 4.4.1), selecting credible messengers (Section 4.4.2), and determining the modes of dissemination (Section 4.4.3.).

4.4.1 Developing the message

Another factor that should be considered when one undertakes a counter-messaging campaign involves the messages themselves. What are important aspects to take into account when constructing messages? The literature on effective messaging is very broad, here we choose to discuss four important factors: (1) the content of the message; (2) the form of the message (2) message sidedness; (3) emotional appeals.

4.4.1.1 The content of the message

Needless to say, what messages communicate is of primary importance. Below, we will discuss some suggestions that we think are worthwhile to consider when constructing counter-messages. First, there is no silver-bullet approach to developing effective messages. In fact, campaigns might be most successful when they combine a diverse array of messages tailored to the characteristics of the audience and the specifics of the context. However, it should also be noted that authors have argued that counter-messages should be consistent across modalities in terms of the themes they promote, and, ideally, they should support a consistent overarching message or 'pitch' (Braddock & Morrison, 2018; Ingram, 2016, June; Ingram & Reed, 2016). Otherwise they may appear ad hoc and confusing at best, or contradictory at worst (Ingram & Reed, 2016). In any case, counter-messages may want to address the range of needs that members of an audience may have. As outlined earlier, individuals may have different needs that Salafi-Jihadi groups may cater for. These needs may, for instance, be related to identity and belonging, to thrill-seeking, to serious ideological concerns and/or to existential questions (e.g., Feddes et al., 2015). Salafi-Jihadi groups such as ISIS actively try to tap into those needs in their messaging. It is important to create equally appealing messages which provide an alternatives to the benefits they offer to people.

For instance, in one of our interviews, Rieger[1] suggested that counter-messages may aim to provide a sense of belonging and a positive identity (related to the identity seekers type; see Section 4.3.3). She argues that an important motivation of those who are drawn to extremist groups is that these groups provide potential members with a

> sense of belonging, a sense of we all belong together, relatedness, which is even more important for individuals who feel out of society already, or out of their peer groups. So, counter messages would, in my opinion and in the opinion of our research group, make a good point if they also showed 'hey, there is a place for you in our society, you can belong to other groups that are not extremists'. Give this sense of social groups being together instead of being alone.

Second, reframing may work better than offering a direct rebuttal to extremist propaganda. Thus, instead of getting involved in an (ideological) confrontation, counter-messages should "acknowledge the concerns that underwrite much of the sympathy toward extremist groups without validating the violent means that extremists advocate" (Beutel et al., 2016, p. 40). After such an acknowledgment, one may be in a more legitimate position to offer alternative, legal paths to address such grievances. While doing so, it may be important to provide concrete suggestions as to what one can actually do, something that Salafi-Jihadi groups also do. As argued recently by Hamid (2018, section "Issues with Current Messaging Strategies," paragraph 2):

> even if the messages reach and resonate with the target audience, if they do not offer the viewer something they can actually do, or some offline group they can actually get involved with, then the resonance will wear off with no change in behaviour.

Hence, he argues it is important to link online messaging with potential offline actions (see also Section 4.4.3).

Third, as extremist messaging tries to promote a simple, binary black-and-white understanding of the world (us versus them, good versus bad, etc.), a response may then be to provide a more nuanced view by introducing alternative perspectives (Beutel et al., 2016). This can be achieved in various ways. For example, rather than placing an extreme importance on one group membership alone (i.e., the radical group), it is helpful to articulate the multiple identities that people possess and the various groups that they belong to (e.g., national group, gender group, family). A good example of such an effort is the program "Being Muslim, Being British." This program aims to promote a balanced view of the self by increasing the complexity of the self that may be associated with positive anti-violence outcomes (Liht & Savage, 2013). Another aim might be to discredit the black-and-white perception of group membership (i.e., being a good Muslim versus not a good Muslim) and trying to convince people of a more nuanced view of the group membership, in which grey areas can exist.

Fourth and relatedly, counter-messages could aim to provide an alternative perspective on the actors that are portrayed as enemies in the messaging of Salafi-Jihadi groups. For example, presenting concrete examples of out-group members who do not fit the standard depiction of members of the "enemy group" might represent an approach in which a seed of doubt might be planted. A potential downside of such a strategy might be that people start a process of sub-typing, in which they create an exception for a small number of members, but keep the overall negative image of the out-group intact. Generally speaking, if one aims to persuade people, trying to create some form of similarity between the audience and the out-group might work best, as people are more likely to take a message seriously when it comes from a similar rather than a dissimilar other source.

Fifth, if those that want to engage in a campaign aim to engage in a more direct rebuttal, a strategy to consider is highlighting the potential inconsistencies in narratives by the terrorist group. Alternatively, it might be possible to pay attention to the potential inconsistencies between the behavior of terrorists and the content of their messages (e.g., Braddock & Horgan, 2016; i.e., leveraging the so-called 'say-do gap,' see Chapter 6). This might be the killing of innocent Muslims by ISIS. Or it can be a focus on the harsh conditions when living in a terrorist group (such as in former ISIS-territory; Beutel et al., 2016).

Sixth and finally, we advocate the use of simple messages. More complex messages might not be perceived as intended (or not at all), in particular by people under stress. Stress makes people respond to messages in a simple and biased manner, undermining the effectiveness of complex messages (e.g., Ingram, 2016, November). Then again, too simplistic messages might not be effective either. One needs to strike the right balance, taking into account the members of the target audience.

Importantly, the nature of messages is more complex in social media campaigns in comparison with traditional media channels (Shi, Poorisat, & Salmon, 2016), and we will discuss this in Box 4.2.

4.4.1.2 Narratives and non-narrative messages

The relative effectiveness of messages that are presented in a narrative format as compared with a non-narrative format has attracted considerable attention from researchers. Non-narrative messages include expository and didactic forms of communication, providing reasoned arguments and factual evidence in support of an advocated position (Kreuter et al., 2007). Loosely speaking, a narrative message provides "a story that contains information about setting, characters, and their motivations" (Braddock & Dillard, 2016, p. 1). This may, for instance, be an anecdote or testimonial. It should be noted that both message types are not necessarily mutually exclusive alternatives and evidence for their effectiveness is mixed. A non-narrative message may well integrate a narrative example. Similarly, a narratively structured message may contain non-narrative information such as arguments (Bilandzic & Busselle, 2012). Researchers have sought to determine the relative effectiveness of narratively structured messages in comparison with other, non-narrative forms of communication. However, it appears difficult to compare the different message types and often elements are included that may provide alternative explanations. Yet, research does show that narratively structured messages can influence "recipients' beliefs, attitudes, intentions, and behaviors such that they

---

Box 4.2 A 'fixed' message?

Social media allow users to comment on and reshape messages, which could potentially interfere with or even undermine the intended effects of campaign messages (Shi, Poorisat, & Salmon, 2016). For instance, several studies found that user-generated comments that appear alongside messages impact on audience evaluations of the content (e.g., Kim, 2015; von Sikorski & Hänelt, 2016). To illustrate, Kim (2015) conducted a web-based experiment to examine the impact of comments on audiences' evaluations of online news. It was found that comments that appeared right below new stories significantly affected participants perception of news acceptance among public audiences, which, in turn, had significant effects on participants' news evaluations. Thus, this indicates that others' comments had an indirect effect on audiences' evaluations of online news. The effect of comments on audience evaluations of content may be particularly relevant in the context of counter-messaging initiatives, given that counter-messages may very well spark negative or abusive responses.

For example, Ernst et al. (2017) studied user comments beneath eight videos tagged with #whatIS, which were released on YouTube as part of the counter speech campaign 'Concepts of Islam' (i.e., Begriffswelten Islam) between October 12, 2015 and January 16, 2016. These videos were published by the German Federal Agency of Civic Education (i.e., *Bundeszentrale für politische Bildung* (BpB)) in cooperation with popular actors on YouTube in Germany. The aim of the campaign was targeting "stereotypical representations and discussions generating biased opinions towards Islam respectively Muslims in Germany" (Ernst et al., 2017, p. 3). Ernst et al. (2017) applied qualitative content analysis on a randomly selected sample of user comments that appeared beneath these videos and found that comments dealing with negative prejudices and stereotypes towards Muslims and/or Islam dominated the data. In addition, they also identified some comments which hinted at hate speech. Yet they also found positive consequences of these videos; namely, users discussed the topics and themes of the videos on a large scale. However, as these authors point out, it raises questions as to what extent these videos have achieved their original goal, and how counter-messaging campaigns can avoid this particular phenomenon and foster discussion in a more civilized manner. More research on the impact of user comments on message evaluation as well as how counter-messaging campaigns can effectively deal with potentially negative or abusive responses is needed.

---

move into closer alignment with viewpoints espoused in those narratives" (Braddock & Dillard, 2016, p. 18). Furthermore, of interest for our current endeavor, narrative messages are believed to offer several persuasive advantages when resistance is to be expected.

The power of narrative messages stems in part from their unthreatening nature (Weimann, 2015). Persuasive intent is often less obvious in narrative messages as compared with non-narrative messages. As a result, recipients may be unaware that a message is trying to persuade them (Hoeken & Fikkers, 2014). In this regard, a relevant feature is the context in which the narrative is presented. For instance, in so-called entertainment education, narratives are embedded in entertainment programming to convey a message (Slater, 2002). In practice, these are often health messages directed at reducing risk behavior (e.g., HIV prevention; Moyer-Gusé, 2008). When people do not expect or are unaware of persuasive intent, various forms of resistance to persuasion are less likely to occur (Dal Cin, Zanna, & Fong, 2004; Moyer-Gusé & Nabi, 2010). It is also an effect of the narrative format itself (Cohen, Tal-Or, & Mazor-Tregerman, 2015). In narrative messages, standpoints and arguments are often implied (i.e., ingrained in the story and portrayed through events and characters) as opposed to explicitly stated, which is believed to make it harder to argue against them (Dal Cin et al., 2004; Hoeken & Fikkers, 2014; Kreuter et al., 2007). Because narrative messages present experiences of other people, it is also suggested that they may be more difficult to refute to begin with (Dal Cin et al., 2004).

It is also proposed that the processing of narrative messages differs in important ways from the processing of non-narrative messages. In traditional dual process models, such as the Elaboration Likelihood Model (ELM; Petty & Cacioppo, 1986), ability and motivation to engage in more effortful elaboration impacts on how a message is processed. Perhaps the most frequently mentioned factor that induces motivation is personal relevance of an issue (i.e., issue involvement). When motivation and ability are high, people process a message via a central route, in which the relevant arguments in favor and against are carefully weighed. When motivation and ability are low they do so via the peripheral route, in which people pay more attention to non-message related cues, such as the identity of the source (e.g., a celebrity advertising a product). It is argued and demonstrated that more durable attitude change is happening when a persuasive message is being processed via the central rather than the peripheral route. However, when confronted with narratives, involvement with the topic or issue addressed is assumed to be less relevant, and other factors such as involvement in the narrative, identification with story characters, and emotions evoked or emotional involvement are believed to be more important. For this reason and several others (see Igartua and Vega, 2015), dual process models are assumed to be less suitable for explaining narrative persuasion processes.

Researchers have used different labels to describe narrative involvement (e.g., transportation, engagement, absorption). Despite the different terms, the shared idea is that narratives are potentially capable of inducing a state where one "primarily [engages] with the storyline while one's own real-world environment or real life becomes less prominent," which is accompanied by an "increased cognitive and emotional response to the unfolding events in the narrative" (Moyer-Gusé & Dale, 2017, p. 2). Perhaps the most commonly used term is 'transportation' which has been defined as "an integrative melding of attention, imagery, and feelings, focused on story events" (Green, 2004, p. 248). Several studies have found that transportation is associated with enhanced persuasion (e.g., Escalas, 2004; Green, 2004; Green & Brock, 2000). One explanation suggests that when individuals are thusly carried away, they are less able and motivated to contradict story points. Consequentially, when an individual is sufficiently transported, he or she is less likely to counter argue, in turn, making it more likely that narrative-consistent attitudes are accepted (Moyer-Gusé & Dale, 2017).

The degree of identification with characters has also been found to be positively associated with narrative effects (e.g., de Graaf, Hoeken, Sanders, & Beentjes, 2012; Hoeken & Fikkers, 2014; Igartua and Vega, 2015). However, identification has been conceptualized in many different ways by different researchers across various studies. For instance, it is commonly used to refer perceived similarity to and liking of the characters (Konijn & Hoorn, 2005). Another conceptualization describes identification as a process whereby an individual loses self-awareness and temporarily comes to adopt the perspective, feelings, and goals of a specific character with whom he or she identifies (Cohen, 2001). There are several explanations for the role of identification in narrative persuasion. Among other things, it is suggested that messages conveyed by characters with whom one identifies are more likely to be attended to, remembered, and learned. It has also been proposed that identification can facilitate the process whereby individuals become involved in a narrative (Cohen, Weimann-Saks, & Mazor-Tregerman, 2017), as suggested, this may reduce their ability and motivation to counter-argue.

In each of these constructs, emotions evoked, or emotional involvement, is an important underlying mechanism. In general, narrative messages are believed to be particularly powerful when they evoke strong emotions. Results of experimental studies (Konijn, van der Molen, & Van Nes, 2009) provide evidence that emotions and being emotionally involved overruled the knowledge that some narrative was fictional or 'fake' (even though this was explicitly stated beforehand). Participants in an emotional state attributed more realism to what was presented as a fictional narrative and subsequently attributed more information value than participants who were not in an emotional state. This is explained by the lower and higher pathways in processing information in our brains, in which emotions take control precedence (see Konijn et al., 2009). Thus, when a counter-narrative message connects emotionally to the recipient, particularly when connecting to relevant needs, desires, and goals related to the emotions evoked, this increases the likelihood that it will be effective (see Section 4.4.1.3).

In sum, narrative messages are believed to offer several benefits and therefore may be useful to utilize the narrative format in a counter-messaging campaign. It should be noted, however, that research on narrative persuasion has predominantly focused on narratives advocating a clear, pro-social and consensual message that does not need to overcome strong counter attitudes (but see Cohen, Tal-Or, Mazor-Tregerman, 2015). Clearly, in the case of counter-narrative messages addressing (violent) radicalization, strong counter-arguing can be expected. Nevertheless, the emotion-evoking strength of narrative formats in particular seems to be promising in reducing cognitive reflection and adding persuasiveness, through enhancing perceived realism and the information value of the message content.

4.4.1.3 Message sidedness

While some authors question the effectiveness of an approach that relies too much on logic and argumentation, others assume such an approach may still prove effective in relation to those who are in the initial phase of radicalization. For instance, Schmid (2015, p. 3) argues that

> While the fanatical extremists of ISIS might no longer be open to rational, persuasive arguments, many of those not yet fully radicalised might still have open minds. They can be confronted with facts and rational reasoning and might then be able to see ISIS for what it is....

He provides a series of argumentative elements that can be utilized to counter a dozen claims of ISIS that underpin key parts of its core message. Others have suggested such an approach may perhaps be fruitful in an earlier stage, in order to build resilience against radicalizing influences (e.g., Mann et al., 2015).

Taking this approach, one may want to consider how much attention should be directed to opposing viewpoints or perspectives. The degree to which messages consider opposing viewpoints is called 'message sidedness.' Messages that only present those arguments in favor of a particular proposition or only from the perspective of those undertaking the influence attempt are commonly referred to as one-sided messages, while a two-sided message presents the arguments in favor of a proposition but also considers the opposing arguments and acknowledge the existence of opposing views (Allen, 1991). Two-sided messages often include pro and con arguments as well as refuting the latter. The question of whether one-sided or two-sided messages are more effective has garnered much attention in the communications literature, albeit typically in relation to non-narrative messages containing solid arguments and factual information.

Allen (1998) and O'Keefe (1999) conducted meta-analyses of research regarding one- and two-sided messages, and both reached the same conclusion: two-sided messages are more likely to influence audience members than one-sided messages, but only when they refute opposing viewpoints. Two-sided messages are believed to gain their persuasive advantage by enhancing the credibility of the source (see Section 4.3.2.) as well as providing cogent arguments for why opposing views are wrong (Perloff, 2010).

Furthermore, it is suggested that the recipients' prior knowledge about and stance towards an issue may influence the effectiveness of both types of messages. One-sided messages have been argued to be more effective when the message recipients are uninformed about an issue. In contrast, two-sided messages are more likely to be effective when the audience is well-informed (e.g., Sorrentino et al., 1988). One-sided messages are also suggested to be more effective if audience members are already favorably predisposed towards message assertions, whereas two-sided messages are more effective when message recipients are predisposed against message recommendations (Keller & Lehmann, 2008). Thus, in view of a counter narrative strategy, two-sided messages seem more likely to be effective.

Mann et al. (2015) suggest that one approach to two-sided messages, referred to as 'inoculation,' can potentially be used to build and strengthen youth's 'resilience' against extremist and radical propaganda on the internet. The inoculation theory (McGuire, 1964) holds that, analogous to the process of vaccinating individuals against a virus by administering a low dose of that virus, it is possible to inoculate individuals by exposing people to messages providing a weakened argument against an attitude they hold (Banas & Rains, 2010). As explained by Banas and Miller (2013), an inoculation message contains two key components: threat and refutational preemption. The threat component provides an individual with the motivation to bolster his or her attitudes. One way to elicit threat is through forewarning of an impending persuasive attack. This calls attention to the vulnerability of an individual's existing attitudes, thereby motivating persuasion resistance. The refutational preemption component provides arguments or evidence the individual can use against the impending attack. This component serves two purposes. It provides individuals with means to counter the persuasive attack and allows them to practice defending beliefs through counter arguing.

Research indeed indicates that inoculation messaging might be an effective strategy for conferring resistance to influence attempts. A meta-analysis by Banas and Rains (2010) shows that inoculation strategies are consistently effective in enhancing people's resistance to attitude change. Moreover, they found that that inoculation messages were more effective than messages that provide mere support for individuals' initial attitudes. The efficacy of inoculation has been demonstrated in a wide variety of contexts (e.g., health, politics, marketing; see Compton (2012) for a review).

For instance, inoculation has been shown to be a helpful strategy for discouraging children from smoking cigarettes (e.g., Pfau & Van Bockern, 1994; Pfau, Van Bockern, & Kang, 1992) and drinking alcohol (e.g., Godbold & Pfau, 2000). It has also been used successfully to confer resistance among supporters of political candidates to attack messages from opposing candidates (e.g., Pfau & Burgoon, 1988; Pfau, Kenski, Nitz, & Sorenson, 1990). However, its usefulness for strengthening resilience against extremist messaging has not been studied (Mann et al., 2015). Banas and Miller (2013) did show that inoculation can be applied to confer resistance against propagandistic conspiracy theory messages. Their study provides preliminary evidence that brief, cognitively focused inoculations can reduce the effectiveness of comparatively longer and emotionally charged persuasive messages.

4.4.1.4 Messages designed to arouse emotions

An oft made recommendation in the literature on counter-messaging is that messages should concentrate on arousing emotion rather than rely on facts and logical arguments. In line with this suggestion, studies in political science have shown that people remember information better when it is presented in a manner that arouses emotions (e.g., fear, enthusiasm, anger) than when it is presented in a neutral manner (e.g., Civettini & Redlawsk, 2009). However, just as there are many emotions, there are a wide variety of emotional appeals that could be leveraged in messaging. Interestingly, the utility of different 'emotional appeals' has only received very limited attention within the specific context of counter-messaging. However, the broader literature on emotional appeals in persuasion provides insights. This literature overwhelmingly focused on fear appeals, but some attention has also been given to other emotions, such as humor and regret. In this section, we provide a short outline of this literature.

Before we do this, it is important to note, however, that a message may be designed to evoke a particular emotional state, but may not be successful in doing so. For instance, what may be considered fearful for those designing a campaign, may not be considered fearful by message recipients (O'Keefe, 2016). This seems particularly the case with adolescents who may, for example, consider the gory graphics on cigarette packages kind of humorous rather than scary (Konijn, 2008). Likewise, warning messages may create boomerang effects among this age group (Bijvank, Konijn, Bushman, & Roelofsma, 2009; Veldhuis, Konijn, & Seidell, 2014).

Furthermore, an appeal may not only arouse the intended emotion but also other emotions. To illustrate with an example from the field of health promotion, Dillard et al. (1996) reviewed 31 AIDS prevention fear appeals and found that 30 evoked change in more than one emotional state. Moreover, while most research focuses on the impact of a certain emotional appeal after messages are viewed, more recently it has also been suggested that message recipients may experience a flow, or evolution, of emotional experience over the course of a message, which could impact its persuasiveness. Although this still needs further study, it is suggested that presenting information with carefully patterned emotionally evocative sequences may enhance the effectiveness of messages (Nabi, 2015).

With this in mind, in the following, we discuss fear- and humor-based appeals, which have attracted some attention in the literature on counter-messaging. Both aim to arouse an emotional state in order to achieve persuasive effects. A related way to harness emotion for persuasion is through the anticipation of emotional states, which we discuss subsequently.

FEAR APPEALS

Fear-based appeals are commonly used to confront people with the negative consequences of not adopting message recommendations, under the assumption that this will motivate people to follow or perform the recommendations (Rogers & Mewborn, 1976). As explained by Ruiter, Kessels, Peters, and Kok (2014), in theory, effective fear-based appeals provide two types of information. First, they present a threat (e.g., lung cancer) to which a person is deemed to be susceptible (e.g., smoking cigarettes may cause lung cancer), and which is severe (e.g., lung cancer may be fatal). Both the elements of severity and susceptibility are believed to be necessary to arouse fear (however, these are often implicit assumptions, hardly tested). Second, they need to provide a prospect of averting the threat by providing recommendations for a protective response. This acceptance of the recommendation is promoted by presenting the suggested response as effective in negating the threat (i.e., response efficacy) and by boosting a person's perception that he or she can effectively execute this response (i.e., self-efficacy). When the recommended response is perceived to be effective and feasible to an individual, he or she is likely to adopt the recommendations. Importantly, though, when this is not the case, and people think they cannot avert the threat, this may prompt defensive and even counterproductive responses. Although fear appeals have been widely used in various fields and a number of studies have shown their effectiveness, their utility is not uncontested. Studies on health promotion (Peters, Ruiter, & Kok, 2013, Ruiter et al., 2014), and crime prevention (Petrosino, Turpin-Petrosino, & Buehler, 2003) indicate that fear appeals are often ineffective and may even backfire (cf. Konijn, 2008).

Limited attention has been paid to fear appeals in counter-messaging efforts. Jacobson (2010) suggests that fear appeals could potentially be an effective message strategy for certain counter-radicalization purposes, for instance in order to bring home the reality of why individuals should be afraid to engage in violent activities (in this regard he uses the example that fear may deter those that want to engage in suicide attacks). However, recently, Beutel et al. (2016) argued that, given their dubious record in various fields, fear appeals are best to be avoided in this context. Yet, they add that this does not mean that there may not be some utility in messages that have some "shock value." Given the above and the specific target group, we conclude that the approach of fear appeals might not be a very effective strategy for designing counter-messages in the context of (violent) radicalization.

HUMOR APPEALS

Humor-based messaging has been utilized in various domains, including commercial advertisements, entertainment, and health. However, findings concerning the persuasive effectiveness of humor-based appeals have been mixed and contradictory. Yet, there is evidence that humor "has the potential to enhance psychological states associated with persuasion" (Nabi, 2016, p. 3). Then again, studies also raise several concerns that warrant careful consideration.

For instance, a meta-analysis in the field of advertising (Eisend, 2009) found that humor can increase attention to the message, and positively affect attitudes toward the brand, the message, and purchase intentions.

> Contrary to the assumptions of previous reviews, there is no evidence that humor impacts positive or negative cognitions, and liking of the advertiser. The meta-analytic findings clarify some ambiguous prior conclusions: humor significantly reduces source credibility, enhances positive affect, ABR and purchase intention.
>
> (Eisend, 2009, p. 1)

In fact, it was found that humor may even detract from the credibility of the source (see Section, 4.4.2).

Another line of research has focused on the use of humor in entertainment(-education) programming. In this context, studies (Moyer-Gusé, Mahood, & Brookes, 2011; Nabi, Moyer-Gusé, & Byrne, 2007) have found that while humor-based entertainment content may lead to a reduction of counter-arguing, which could benefit persuasion, it also stimulated participants to trivialize (Moyer-Gusé, Mahood, & Brookes, 2011) and discount the message more (Nabi, Moyer-Gusé, & Byrne, 2007). Elsewhere, it has also been argued that the fun or laughter evoked by the humorous appeals of a message may overrule the content of the message, which can then not be remembered (Konijn, 2008). Thus, humor-based content could potentially fall flat.

Studies on humor and persuasion typically do not differentiate between different types of humor. Yet authors have proposed that various types of humor can be differentiated (e.g., slapstick, clownish humor, irony, satire, etc.; e.g., Buijzen & Valkenburg, 2004). Recent research provides preliminary evidence that different types of humor may impact differently on message recipients. A study by Iles and Nan (2017) considered the differential effects of ironic and sarcastic versus no humor appeals in health-related advertising messages. They found that sarcasm has a 'detrimental effect' on persuasion. Irony also reduced the persuasive effectiveness, albeit to a lesser extent. Compared with no humor, the use of sarcasm reduced overall negative affect, increased counter-arguing, and decreased perceived argument strength. Likewise, it was found that irony increases counter-arguing. Their study indicates it may be fruitful to consider different types of humor, instead of treating it as a 'generic' concept. The study by Iles and Nan (2017) suggests that certain types of humor could not only fall flat, but could potentially be counter-productive.

In relation to counter-messaging the utility of humor has received only limited attention. Bartlett, Birdwell, & King (2010) argue that the use of satire could potentially help strip extremist groups from glamour and mystique (although they emphasize that governments should refrain from utilizing it). They point out that sustained satire has historically played an important role in undermining the popularity of extremist movements such as the Ku Klux Klan. Others have pointed out the risks, and argue it should be utilized with great caution. For instance, Goodall, Cheong, Fleischer, and Corman (2012, p. 73) assert that humor is a weapon with a double edge: "Just as an off-color joke can offend your co-workers or sour a personal relationship, humor has the potential to be divisive and motivating in ways that are detrimental to larger policy goals."

Beutel et al. (2016) suggest that knowing the target and intention of a humor-based message is crucial. They speculate that if the target of humor-based messages is, for example, a terrorist leader, with the intention of undermining his or her credibility and having potential recruits no longer look up to him, this may increase the potential of such a message strategy. However, when it is intended to ridicule the potential recruits and their motivations and concerns, this may well be taken as an insult and backfire, eliciting defiance as a response. Likewise, Kruglanski[2] suggests mockery and ridiculing carries the potential to backfire "they may mock you right back." Taking all of the above into account, we conclude that humor is perhaps best utilized with great care and the potential risks should be carefully analyzed from various perspectives beforehand.

Having said that, it should also be pointed out that some studies do indicate that humor-based messages may have a particular persuasive advantage. That is, humor has been found to be a factor that may enhance interpersonal sharing of messages and interaction. For instance, Campo et al. (2013), who studied the effects of a pregnancy prevention campaign, found that campaign exposure and the use of humor (i.e., clownish-humor, surprise, absurdity) "was a significant predictor of talking with and/or showing the campaign to others" (Campo et al., 2013, p. 4). Related to our particular subject matter, a recent study by the Centre for the Analysis of Social Media (CASM) of the Demos Institute (Bartlett & Krasodomski-Jones, 2015) examined the extent to which different types of 'counter-speech' (i.e., a "common, crowd-sourced response[s] to extremism or hateful content") are produced and shared on Facebook across four countries (Bartlett & Krasodomski-Jones, 2015, p. 5). They found that the most popular tone of posts on counter-speech pages across the three countries was a funny or satirical tone.[3] The popularity of a post was measured by the amount of interactions content generated (i.e., likes, comments, and shares). Usually these posts parodied extremist language on hate-pages related to issues such as immigration, religion, and race. Of course, this does not do away with earlier mentioned concerns. In Box 4.3, we further discuss the relation between emotions and message sharing.

ANTICIPATED REGRET

Rather than arousing emotions directly and offering a recipient a way to deal with the aroused feelings, appeals may also focus on drawing people's attention to positive or negative feelings that are to be expected if a particular recommendation is (not) followed (O'Keefe, 2016). Put differently, messages may prompt people to imagine how they might feel if they (do not) follow a certain course of action, which can influence their intentions and actions. In this regard, studies have often focused on anticipated regret. Regret has been described as a negative emotion experienced when an individual realizes or imagines that the current situation could have been better had he or she previously chosen or acted differently (Sandberg & Conner, 2008). The assumption is that people do not like to experience regret as a result of their choices. Clearly, individuals may anticipate regret, which can serve as a motivation to (not) engage in certain behaviors. It is suggested this may hold in particular when the consequences of a high-risk activity are severe and irreversible (van der Pligt & Vliek, 2016). As such, it has been suggested that encouraging people to anticipate regret may impact their intention to engage in risky behaviors.

The potential of evoking anticipated regret in influence attempts has been evidenced in a variety of studies, in particular in the field of preventative health behaviors. Researchers have found anticipated regret can influence a range of health- and safety-related behaviors, such as substance use, safer sex practices, vaccinations, organ donation and road safety offences (see Koch 2014 for a review). A meta-analysis of Sandberg and Conner (2008) revealed a strong relationship between anticipated regret and behavioral intentions, and a moderate link between anticipated regret and behavior. Recently, another meta-analysis (Brewer, DeFrank, & Gilkey, 2016) provided similar findings. In addition, they concluded that anticipated action regret [i.e., anticipated regret from engaging in an behavior] had smaller associations with behavioral intentions related to less severe and more distal hazards, but these moderation findings were not present for inaction regret [i.e., anticipated regret from engaging in behavior].

(Brewer et al., 2016, p. 1264)

To the best of our knowledge, the utility of strategies that use anticipated regret has not yet been studied in the domain of prevention of radicalization. However, de Wolf and Doosje (2010/2015) suggest it may have some potential as a strategy to encourage those attracted to radical groups to consider the possible negative emotional consequences of their decisions and actions.

In sum, the counter violent extremism literature holds that counter-messages should arouse emotion in the target audience. However, limited consideration is given to which emotions should be aroused. The broader literature on emotional appeals indicates that it may be best to avoid using fear-based appeals. Certain types of humor might be useful, but humor-based messaging also carries clear risks and should be used with caution. Leveraging anticipated regret may have some potential to address (violent) radicalization, but research in the area of CVE is lacking. Dealing with younger age groups (e.g., adolescents) may further complicate suggestions as this particular developmental stage is characterized by increases in aggressiveness, sensation seeking, and risk behavior, during which emotional appeals and warnings may easily backfire. Among these warnings, gruesome or horrific messages may, for example, be considered 'humor.'

Box 4.3 Emotions and message sharing

The effective dissemination of counter-messages in a social media context may in part be dependent upon the degree to which a message is shared. Whilst the aim for counter-messages is typically not to go 'viral,' as it implies untargeted message dissemination (RAN, 2015), the literature on 'virality' and online word-of-mouth does provide some interesting insights with regard to what message features increase the likelihood that a message is retransmitted. Although research in this domain is relatively new, some studies suggest that content that is emotionally-charged and evokes high-emotional arousal is more likely to be shared. This is not only useful to 'get the word out.' As explained by Nabi (2016), this also creates the opportunity for repeated message exposure for the individual doing the sharing. Repeated exposure is associated with greater message effectiveness.

An often cited study in this domain (Berger & Milkman, 2012) is focused on how emotions affect email sharing of articles from the *New York Times*. Using a dataset of nearly 7000 *New York Times* articles, they investigated

---

how the valence of content (i.e., whether content is positive or negative) affects whether a message is highly shared. They further studied how specific emotions (e.g., awe, anxiety, anger, sadness) evoked by content, and the arousal or activation they induce, impact transmission. Their study found that positive content is more likely to be shared than negative content. However, the study points out that social transmission is more complex than valence alone. Arousal is argued to be key. The authors found that content that evoked high-arousal emotions – regardless of whether they were positive (awe) or negative (anger or anxiety) – was more likely to be shared than content that elicited low-arousal emotions (i.e., sadness).

The role of emotion has also been examined in relation to social media. Analyzing two datasets of more than 165,000 tweets, Stieglitz and Dang-Xuan (2013) found that Twitter messages that are emotionally-charged tend to be retweeted more often than messages that are neutral. In another study, Nelson-Field, Riebe, and Newstead (2013) examined the sharing of 800 videos (commercial and non-commercial) on the Facebook platform. In particular, they looked at the emotional responses these videos evoked, and the likelihood of audiences to share those videos given the evoked emotion. Their findings correspond with those of Berger and Milkman (2012). They found that the degree of arousal is the primary driver of the sharing of video content. They also found that valence plays a role in the sharing of video content. Videos that elicited positive emotions were more likely to be shared than those that evoked negative emotions (no matter the degree of arousal). However, while it was found that valence mattered, it did so to a lesser degree than arousal. While they recommend evoking a positive emotional response over a negative one, they argue that when it comes to sharing "it is less important that the emotion felt be a positive one, than that it should be strongly felt" (Nelson-Field et al., 2013, p. 210).

Similar results were found by Guadagno, Rempala, Murphy, and Okdie (2013). They conducted an experiment to explore what videos were most likely to be forwarded. They found that individuals who reported strong emotional responses to a video reported greater intent to spread the video. Furthermore, their results suggest an "arousal hierarchy." Videos that elicited positive emotions were most likely to be forwarded. Videos that evoked a diffuse arousal were more likely to be forwarded than negatively arousing or non-emotional videos. Finally, they found that videos evoking negative emotions were more likely to be shared than non-emotional videos. As well as these studies there are several others that suggest the importance of emotion in message sharing.

Thus, these studies and others suggest that messages that are emotionally-charged and arousing are likely to be shared (cf. Felten, Taouanza, & Keuzenkamp, 2016). In particular, messages are more likely to be shared when they elicit positive emotions rather than negative ones or no emotions at all. At the same time, messages eliciting some negative emotions are more likely to be shared than messages that elicit no emotion at all. These notions are worth taking into consideration when constructing messages.

4.4.2 Select credible messengers

The term 'source' is often used to refer to either the sender of a message or the model that appears in the message to deliver the information, demonstrate behavior, or provide a testimonial (Atkin, 2004; but see Box 4.4). The literature on counter-messaging generally holds that even when messages are perfectly crafted, the source (here more commonly referred to as 'the messenger') should be perceived as credible in order for the message to be convincing to a target audience (e.g., Braddock & Horgan, 2016; Briggs & Feve, 2013; Davies et al., 2016; Fink & Barclay, 2013; van Ginkel, 2015; Weimann, 2015; Zeiger, 2016). The importance of so called 'source credibility' is widely echoed in the broader research literature on persuasion.

What exactly constitutes source credibility? Source credibility is commonly understood as "the believability of a source" as interpreted by the message recipient, and is composed of two primary dimensions: trustworthiness and expertise (Metzger & Flanagin, 2013, p. 211). However, other dimensions may impact on the believability (or effectiveness) of a source as well, such as attractiveness, likability, similarity and familiarity (Atkin & Rice, 2012).

When a source is perceived as credible, then recipients are generally more likely to accept the message claims, and in turn influence attempts are more likely to have an effect. However, the level of 'fit' also matters. For example, a famous athlete will not fit an advertisement for alcoholic beverages. In this respect, the old-fashioned image of a sexy lady used to sell cars stems from a classical conditioning approach (Konijn, 2008), but clearly is a misfit in today's society. Furthermore, it is clear that the assessments of credibly in an online environment is often much complex than in previous media contexts (see Box 4.4).

In the context of counter-messaging, counter-violent extremism experts and practitioners suggest various sources that can potentially serve as credible sources (e.g., Braddock & Horgan, 2016; Briggs & Feve, 2013; Davies et al., 2016; van Ginkel, 2015; Weimann, 2015; Zeiger, 2016). However, which messenger will in fact be effective will heavily depend on the context and the audience members in question. As noted by Weimann (2015), different countries, regions, communities and groups, may require different approaches. As suggested above, it is also vital to consider the messages one wants to relay.

As will be explored further in Chapter 6, it is commonly assumed that governments may not be the most effective messengers for counter-messaging efforts, although they can engage in other forms of strategic communication (e.g., Briggs & Feve, 2013; Davies et al., 2016; Romaniuk, 2015; van Ginkel, 2015; Weimann, 2015). Among other things, this is due to "say-do" gap. This refers to a perceived gap between governmental rhetoric and actions (Romaniuk, 2015). Messages are believed to be more likely to strike a chord when they originate from the grassroots level. As argued by Bouwman in one of our interviews,

> it is very important that it occurs from within the group. And that you do not play the expert and say "we're gonna develop all the materials." If you really want to apply a positive strategy, it is very much stemming from their own community.[4]

In the subsections below, we discuss some commonly mentioned examples of potentially credible sources, including: former extremists, victims of extremist violence, youth, family members, and other community actors.

Box 4.4 Source credibility in online environments

The social media contexts present several challenges for traditional conceptualizations of 'the source' and credibility evaluation. Among other things, authors have noted that online information may lack traditional credibility indicators such as the identity of the person, group or organization who posted the message. Source information may be unavailable, masked, or entirely missing. Source information may also be difficult to interpret (Metzger & Flanagin, 2013) due to the "multiplicity of sources embedded in the numerous layers of online dissemination of content" (Sundar, 2008, p. 74).

To illustrate, Sundar and Nass (2001) explain there are three layers of sources in online and social media environments: (1) visible sources; (2) technological sources; and (3) receiver sources. Visible sources are "the sources seen by the receiver to be delivering the message or content" (Sundar & Nass, 2001, p. 58). They are frequently perceived as the originator of the information, while they may just be information gatekeepers. Technological sources are technological interfaces, which may be perceived as an original source, no matter that they are not independent. Lastly, receivers of information themselves can become a source in social media environments (Hu & Sundar, 2009). To illustrate, in the context of a counter-messaging effort, a visible source may, for example, be a civil society organization or someone involved in a campaign posting a message. A technological source might be Facebook, Twitter or Instagram. To become a receiver source, the recipient of a message may post a like, add a comment, or do a repost after having received a message (Shi, Poorisat, & Salmon, 2016).

As suggested above, communication through these platforms is often not a linear process, whereby a sender directly relays a message to a receiver. Instead, multiple layers of source may exist for a message (Shi et al., 2016). To illustrate, a video containing a counter-message may be originally posted by a particular civil society organization (the original promoter) on YouTube, but someone may pick it up from a Facebook post on a friend's page who himself picked it up through a blog. Which of these sources is most likely to resonate with the recipient as the source? Whereas one might argue that it is the civil society organization who initially distributed it, another might say it is the friend or the blog – and the latter might be more persuasive than then former (Hu & Sundar, 2009). It appears that the perceived credibility of each of these sources as well as their interaction could potentially impact how audience members evaluate message claims (Hu & Sundar, 2009; Shi et al., 2016).

Importantly, as suggested earlier, receiver-sources may potentially add to, change, and repurpose the message as they see fit (e.g., add a comment, change its content, etc.). If one further takes into account that sources and content of a message also interact to influence message recipients' credibility evaluations, one comes to understand how complex the concept of source credibility actually is within contemporary social media environments (Metzger & Flanagin, 2013, see also Shi et al., 2016).

Adding to the complexity, some scholars have suggested that traditional credibility indicators may play a less prominent role in how users locate and make judgments about information they encounter online (e.g., Metzger, Flanagin & Medders, 2010). Traditional approaches may include assessing source credentials and biases, and verifying quality or accuracy of information. However, some studies indicate that information consumers on social media and the internet often do not engage in such evaluation processes. Instead, they often rely on a diversity of heuristics to assess the credibility of both sources and information (e.g., reputation, social endorsement, consistency, self-confirmation, expectancy violation, and persuasive intent (Metzger & Flanagin, 2017).

Only recently has research started to touch upon these issues in relation to counter-messaging campaigns (see, for an example, Braddock & Morrison, 2018), and further studies are warranted.

4.4.2.1 Former extremists

It is commonly assumed that leveraging the voices of former violent extremists (i.e., 'formers') and foreign fighters (i.e., 'defectors') may prove to be effective (e.g., Ashour, 2011; Braddock & Horgan, 2016; Briggs & Feve, 2013; Gartenstein-Ross et al., 2016; Hedayah & ICCT, 2014; Macnair & Frank, 2017; Neumann, 2015; van Ginkel, 2015; Weimann, 2015; Zeiger, 2016). Just as with former criminals, formers alcoholics or former drug addicts, it is believed that 'formers' are more likely to be perceived as 'street credible,' as they have experienced the life as an extremist first-hand. Furthermore, they may be perceived as more credible because they have shared similar grievances and views (Gartenstein-Ross et al., 2016). On the other hand, it is also proposed that they can probably better relate to the experiences of those individuals attracted to violent extremist groups, as they have gone through similar processes themselves (Zeiger, 2016).

On similar grounds, Rieger[5] suggests that in comparison with other sources, they may perhaps have "greater potential to raise doubt in young adolescents or in young adults who are maybe more extremist." Talking from direct experience, they may also be able to tell a powerful story about the reality of life as an extremist or jihadi and their disillusionment with the group (Weimann, 2015). In this regard, Kruglanski[6] points out that stories of formers can show that

> that joining extremist groups does not provide glory and fame like they expect. According to our analysis a major motivation for joining is this quest for fame and glory [...]. If people who left extremism can recount their experiences about how they were humiliated, how they were mistreated, how they were given second or third rate jobs, came to serve as cannon fodder just to be killed. These kind of messages can be effective to show they are not treated in a glamorous, glorified manner.

As such, it is argued that formers may represent a powerful voice that could potentially help prevent vulnerable individuals from joining these groups.

However, one should be aware of challenges, limitations and risks when one aims to solicit the involvement of formers. First, it is quite difficult to find formers willing to speak out against their former group (Hedayah & ICCT, 2014). They may want to leave that part of their lives behind them or may not want to have public profiles (Hedayah & ICCT, 2014; RAN, 2015). In addition, some may fear repercussions or harassment by members of the former group (Briggs & Feve, 2013; Hedayah & ICCT, 2014). In addition, it may be stressful for them to speak out about their experiences. It is important to give consideration to their safety and well-being (Briggs & Feve, 2013). In relation to ISIS defectors, McDowell-Smith, Speckhard, & Yayla (2017, p. 56) proposed: "Not surprisingly many are not psychologically healthy having been seduced into the group because of needs they hoped the group would meet and as a result of post-traumatic stress after serving in conflict zones inside a horrifically brutal organization." They also mention issues of trust: "Others are not trusted enough by law enforcement to be used in that capacity as they vacillate in their opinions about the terrorist group they formerly endorsed or belonged to" (McDowell-Smith, Speckhard, & Yayla, 2017, p. 56). It is indeed possible that those that have defected still harbor the Salafi-Jihadi worldview. Hence, they should be carefully vetted beforehand. Lastly, soliciting the involvement of formers may not be appreciated by parts of the population, given the formers previous involvement in violent extremism. Initiatives that do so may well open themselves up to criticism and accusations (Gartenstein-Ross et al., 2016).

Thus, formers may potentially be in a good position to deliver persuasive counter-messages, as they can directly relate to their audience and can deliver a message from their own direct experience. However, there are some noteworthy limitations, challenges, and risks involved with working with formers. There are several examples of counter-messaging efforts that leverage formers as messengers. In Box 4.1 we described one such effort. In Box 4.5 we provide another example. Namely, a Facebook campaign that has used defector testimonies in videos. Using pre-recorded videos is one method that may help mitigate some of the risk mentioned above. For instance, because there is no danger that a former will say anything off message in a video edited by campaigners (Speckhard, Shajkovci, Bodo, & Fazliu, 2018).

Box 4.5 Former extremist as a source

The International Center for the Study of Violent Extremism (ICSVE) has recently run multiple counter-messaging campaigns in various countries using videos featuring the testimonies of ISIS-defectors (e.g., Speckhard, Shajkovci, Bodo, & Fazliu, 2018; Speckhard, Shajkovci, Wooster, & Izadi, 2018a). Among them was a Facebook ad awareness campaign that ran in the United States, UK, Canada, and Australia in December 2017. According to Speckhard, Shajkovci, Wooster and Izadi (2018b, pp. 52–53)

> The purpose of these awareness campaigns was to reach as many English-speaking individuals in the United States, UK, Canada, and Australia […] to drive engagement with the ICSVE-produced counternarrative videos and raise awareness about the dangers of joining or considering joining a violent extremist group like ISIS.

As these authors note, it is difficult to observe and report any cognitive shifts as a result of the campaign, and they only provide a short-term measurement (see Chapter 5 on evaluation methods). However, they found that the ad generated a reach of over one million and more than 600K views. The authors also performed a qualitative analysis of comments on the videos, and argued that the campaign initiated relevant discussions on the dangers emanating from violent extremist groups such as ISIS. However, not all responses were constructive. On the basis of their analysis, they argued comments could roughly be divided into three categories. The first category comprised comments that were anti-ISIS, the second comments in defense of Islam. A third category was however comprised of anti-Islam speech. Furthermore, there were many commentators that attempted to discredit the videos. Importantly, as we have argued earlier (see Box 4.2), counter-messages may trigger responses that are the very opposite of what campaigns may want to evoke, and which could have negative consequences (Ernst et al., 2017).

4.4.2.2 Victims

A second potential credible source are victims of violent extremism. With proper training, coaching and support, victims of terrorist violence may also be able to fulfill a role as messengers (e.g., Beutel et al., 2016; Briggs & Feve, 2013; Davies et al., 2016; Hedayah & ICCT, 2014; RAN, 2016; Schmid, 2012; van Ginkel, 2015; Zeiger, 2016). Victims may be particularly effective messengers because they can speak with the unique moral authority as a survivor or witness (Beutel et al., 2016). In addition, testimonies of victims can potentially serve a strong preventative function by giving a face to and humanizing those that are attacked as well as highlighting how ordinary people can be affected and how they cope with these terrible situations (see '*Handbook: Voice of Victims of Terrorism,*' RAN, 2016). Van de Donk[7] adds that the personal stories of survivors and relatives of victims can highlight the real impact of violence, which can potentially serve as a reminder that violence is not a solution. Importantly, he also suggests that leveraging the voices of victims against those that are already far along the pathway to violent extremism may actually be counter-productive. Their testimonials might serve to justify already committed extremists in their convictions. As with former violent extremists, when leveraging the voices of victims, careful consideration should be given to their personal well-being and security (Hedayah & ICCT, 2014). Survivors have been used in a variety of projects, one of them being the well-known 'Against Violent Extremism' project (see Box 4.6).

Box 4.6 Victims as a source

A commonly mentioned example of an initiative in which victims play an important role is the Against Violent Extremism Network (AVE). The AVE is overseen by the Institute for Strategic Dialogue (ISD) in London, and is the largest existing network of victims and former extremists. It was founded at the Summit Against Violent Extremism in 2011, and is the result of a partnership between the ISD, Jigsaw (formerly Google Ideas), and the Gen Next Foundation. The AVE brings together 'formers' and 'survivors' and seeks to use the lessons, experiences, and networks of those who have first-hand experience of violent extremism and amplify their voices. In addition, it aims to serve as an incubator for initiatives that contribute to tackling violent extremism, including those in the area of counter-messaging. Members are enabled to connect through the website and social media channels and exchange ideas, work together, find potential investors, partners, and volunteers, and amplify their message (Against Violent extremism, n.d.-a). According to its website, the network has helped to establish more than 2600 connections and launch more than 80 projects.

4.4.2.3 Family members

Family members could potentially also be key messengers that can challenge the messages and appeal of violent extremist groups (e.g., Saltman & Frenett, 2016; van Ginkel, 2015; Weimann, 2015; Zeiger, 2015). At an interpersonal level, they are well-positioned to detect early signs of radicalization, and engage in dialogue to present a counterweight. Mothers, in particular, have been suggested to have a great deal of emotional influence on their children, and messages stemming from them could potentially have a strong impact (Saltman & Frenett, 2016). Yet, the radical person might be someone who has drifted away from their family, often with conflicts, and is not responsive to family anymore (Sieckelinck & de Winter, 2015). Hence, it is suggested that capacity building and training may be needed before families and relatives can fulfill such a role (van Ginkel, 2015). Additionally, it has been pointed out that family members may play an important role in persuading individuals to drop out of extremist and terrorist groups (Jacobson, 2010; Weimann, 2015). For instance, Jacobson (2010) points out that renewed ties and contacts with family members have led some individuals to reconsider their membership in such groups.

Beyond the interpersonal level, it is suggested that these voices can also be leveraged in online campaigns. Some campaigns have aimed to spread the stories of family members of violent extremists (see Box 4.7). It is suggested their testimonials can potentially provide a powerful alternative or counter-message that can serve a preventative function (Zeiger, 2016).

4.4.2.4 Youth

Young people are often seen as audiences of alternative or counter-messaging efforts, leaving unrecognized that they can be key in delivering messages against violent extremism (e.g., Hedayah & ICCT, 2014; RAN, 2015; Richardson, 2013). As argued by Rieger[8]:

> the key audiences you want to prevent from being radicalized are adolescents and young adults. [...] Having this key audience in mind, it is may be more persuasive or more successful if you launch counter messages that will have the same target group as protagonists, as senders, or as distributors of a message, sending or posting a video or message, creating a hashtag or forwarding a hashtag.

Kruglanski[9] puts forward a similar point, arguing that peer influence tends to be high in the age groups that are vulnerable in radicalization.

Beyond merely acting as a messenger, young people are likely good at developing content that is relevant to and grounded in the lived experiences of their peers (RAN, 2015). One example of is the earlier mentioned

---

Box 4.7 Family members as a source

One example in which family members play a role, is the 'Open Letter' campaign, which was launched by the Mothers for Life Network – a network coordinated by the German Institute on Radicalization and De-radicalization Studies (GIRDS) which brings together mothers who have experienced violent radicalization in their families. The campaign revolves around two open letters that were designed by GIRDS in cooperation with mothers from countries around the world. Both letters urge sons and daughters in Syria and Iraq to come home, making use of citations from Islamic scripture. To illustrate with a passage from the first letter:

> We did not want you to leave. We want you to return. We want you to live. Even if you think death will give you that 'better' life, remember that even the Prophet Muhammad (peace and blessings be upon him) said: 'Paradise lies at the feet of your mother' [Musnad Ahmad, Sunan An-Nasâ'i, Sunan Ibn Mâjah]. By leaving us against our will to give up your own life and take those of others, you have put our struggle, pain and honour under your feet and walked over it. Abdullah ibn Amr related that the Messenger of Allah said: The major sins are to believe that Allah has partners, to disobey one's parents, to commit murder, and to bear false witness (Bukhari, Muslim).
>
> Someone told you that we do not have the true faith, and your brothers and sisters in Syria and Iraq are more important than your brothers and sisters here at home. But we need you most. Our bond was, and is, above all others and it is eternal. We will always remain your mothers. We will always *wait in vain for your return, left alone in this life.*
>
> (Mothers for Life, 2015, p. 2)

The letters were disseminated through social media. The website of GIRDS does not provide much detail about the effect of their efforts. However, it does point out that the first letter managed to attract quite some attention, it was reported on by news outlets 1785 times; shared 7000 times on Facebook; translated into eight languages, and responded to by ISIS within three and a half hours after publishing it. Furthermore, mothers from many more countries have since reached out for help and become members of the network 2016 (GIRDS, n.d.-a). The website doesn't provide any details regarding the second letter.

P2P project (see Box 2.2; Chapter 2), which aims to engage college and university students from all over the world to create alternative and counter-messaging campaigns on social media. Many of these campaigns appear to be focused on positive messaging, for instance to promote tolerance and understanding (Szmania & Fincher, 2017).

It has also been suggested that youth may be reluctant to act as messengers when campaigns are framed in terms of counter-radicalization or countering violent extremism. As such, it may perhaps be more suitable to solicit their participation in online efforts that have 'CVE-*relevant*' goals, such as those that are more generally related to issues of social cohesion or political activism, rather than 'CVE-*specific*' goals (RAN, 2015). Arguably, this may hold for other potential messengers as well.

4.4.2.3 Other community actors

There is a wide variety of other community actors that could potentially bear weight with different target audiences (e.g., valued community leaders and organizations, popular figures such as athletes or artists, respected journalists). In particular, religious leaders and associations have often been identified as potential credible sources (Hedayah & ICCT, 2014; Weimann, 2015; Zeiger, 2016). For instance, van Ginkel (2015, p. 11) suggests that these actors may carry the religious expertise and authority to provide "alternative interpretations of the Koran and other religious texts in response to extremist interpretations of Islam." She further suggests that "these actors can moreover directly counter the extremist jihadist narrative" and "could fulfil a role in explaining the values of Western society [...] and the ways in which these values can be respected while still living the life of a devout Muslim" (van Ginkel, 2015, p. 11). Kruglanski[10] adds that that they could potentially make clear that those who become involved with extremism do exactly the opposite of what their religion requires. However, it is essential these sources carry religious authority and charismatic weight among the target audience. Identifying such sources for those that may sympathize with extremist groups proves to be a challenge, and it may well be the case that such actors are outside traditional structures of religious authority in Islam (Zeiger, 2016).

In sum, messages are more likely to strike a chord when they stem from a credible source. But the level of fit also matters. Furthermore, it is evident that the assessments of credibly in the online environment is much more complex than in previous media contexts. Researchers assume that messengers that stem from the grassroots are particularly effective. Commonly mentioned candidates include former extremists, victims of violence, peers, and family, as well as key members of communities and civil society actors. It is also important to point out that those well suited to act as messengers often require training and empowerment to be able to effectively carry out this role (see Chapter 6). In the next section, we discuss via which channel a message might best be disseminated.

4.4.3 *Choose the mode of dissemination*

Logically, a message is unlikely to resonate when it does not reach the target audience. Hence, selecting appropriate channels for message dissemination is generally considered to be of vital importance. When selecting the mode of dissemination one needs to carefully consider the campaign's scope, aims and target audience. In regard to the latter, a rather straightforward, but not important observation is that it is sensible to relay the message through social media channels that are used frequently by the audience(s) one intends to reach. This once more points to the importance of audience research. One needs to gain insight in the target audience's media preferences and consumption patterns (e.g., what social media does the target audience use, how does it use them, when does it use them) (Thackeray, Neiger, & Keller, 2012). Fortunately, today there are a number of tools available to ease this process for digital media. Importantly, the social media landscape is constantly in flux, thus continuous audits will be necessary (Stevens, 2010). It follows that those undertaking counter-messaging efforts should be flexible and able to adapt.

Furthermore, social media encompass a diverse spectrum of tools and technologies. Different social media channels may have distinct advantages and drawbacks that make them more or less suitable for particular communication purposes (e.g., they may be more or less suitable for (spreading) particular content). It is advised that program planners consider the distinct qualities of different platforms when choosing appropriate communication channels (Atkin & Salmon, 2012; Noar, 2011; Thackeray, Neiger, & Keller, 2012). In addition to capacity to reach the intended audience, channels may vary on characteristics such as specialization, interactivity, personalization, meaning modalities, depth capacity, accessibility, decodability, and credibility (Atkin & Salmon, 2012).

Some scholars suggest that utilizing multiple complementary social media channels at the same time will be beneficial to a program, as it may contribute to greater reach and exposure and may help reinforce messages (Korda & Itani, 2013; Levac & O'Sullivan, 2010). However, it is important that communication activities across communication channels are aligned with each other so that they complement in each other in delivering the message (e.g., Kaplan & Haenlein, 2010; Noar, 2011). In any case, it is once again imperative that one takes into account the target audience. Running a program well across a few relevant social media channels through which one can actually reach and engage the target audience makes more sense than taking a broad scatterplot approach (Freeman et al., 2015). Program planners may want to take into account the available resources. As suggested earlier in this chapter (see Section 4.4.3), running a campaign effectively requires adequate technical expertise and skills. Moreover, while social media can often be used for free or against limited costs, running a campaign requires resources that may be costly. Of course, such investments are likely to increase when program planners intend to use multiple channels (Freeman et al., 2015; Gold et al., 2012).

Furthermore, while the current report aims to specifically focus on how social media might be used for a campaign, the question of whether social media is in fact the appropriate channel to reach the audience should be carefully considered. The literature indicates that not all potential target audiences, towards whom communication efforts might be directed, are necessarily engaged with social media (Ingram & Reed, 2016; Levac & O'Sullivan, 2010; Reed, 2017b; Stevens, 2010). As suggested by Reed (2017b, p. 3): "An over-reliance on social media means that messages can only be directed at those who use social media, excluding parts of the population that do not do so, or those who do not have access to them." In some cases, internet access may also be restricted. Hence, it may well be that audience members may be more effectively reached through other means, such as traditional media (e.g., television or radio broadcasts, print media), interpersonal (i.e., face-to-face) communication or events (Ingram & Reed, 2016; Zeiger, 2016). Various scholars across different fields suggest that rather than focusing solely on social media campaigns, utilizing a coordinated set of communication activities across different communication channels may be more effective (e.g., Heldman, Schindelar, & Weaver, 2013; Ingram & Reed, 2016; Levac & O'Sullivan, 2010; Noar & Head, 2011; Reed, 2017b). Such an approach does not only expand opportunities to expose target audiences to messages, it may also compensate for the respective limitations of any single delivery method in isolation (Ingram & Reed, 2016). Of course, here it also holds that one needs to have the capacity (budget, time, expertise) to do this.

Some reports suggests that combining online efforts with offline actions can be particularly beneficial, among other things, because it can help to bring attention to a campaign (e.g., Taylor, 2012; RAN, 2015). Including an offline face-to-face component may be especially important when a program targets those most vulnerable to the extremist message (Richardson, 2013), given that online campaigns are not very likely to steer people away from violent paths in and by themselves. Furthermore, Richardson (2013) puts forward that those who are most motivated to engage with online extremist propaganda and settings are unlikely to be active and enthusiastic consumers of counter-messages. As such, she argues that interpersonal strategies are likely to be far more effective in both reaching and influencing these individuals. Furthermore, as suggested earlier, even when counter-messages reach and resonate with such individuals, it may be important to provide them with something they can actually get involved in offline (Hamid, 2018).

To summarize, selecting channels for one's campaigns includes answering the question of how one's program can best reach and engage the intended audience, and taking into account issues of access as well as what one aims to achieve. It is also vital to look at the strengths and weaknesses of different communication channels, taking into account the message strategy as well as the available resources. Importantly, social media may not be appropriate in all circumstances, and should perhaps be considered a supplement to other program approaches and channels. Linking online with offline activities is also suggested to be important, in particular in case of 'at risk' groups.

4.5 Implementing a campaign

The implementation phase of a communication campaign involves disseminating the message (Section 4.5.1). Furthermore, in considering dissemination issues, one should be consciously aware of the possible risks and limitations in launching a counter-messaging initiative, in particular, adverse actions from those being countered (Section 4.5.2). In the following, we describe what can be learnt in this respect from previous research and the various 'grey' literatures.

4.5.1 Disseminating the message

In addition, to giving consideration to *where* the message will be distributed, program planners should also consider *how* they will effectively distribute messages in order to reach the intended audience through selected (social media) channels. It may be difficult to effectively break through the social media clutter. What the most effective strategy will be to disseminate messages, once again depends on the scope, purpose and target audience of the campaign. Furthermore, it is important to take into consideration possible drawbacks. Below we will propose several issues worth considering.

First, timing is an important aspect to consider when thinking about a dissemination strategy, as it may impact the reach of a message. If messages are posted at a time at which the intended audience is not active on social media, exposure to a campaign message is likely to be low. In line with this, taking into account when audience members are active on social media could potentially increase exposure to messages (Noar, 2011; Fairlie, 2016). Beyond mere exposure, the frequency of exposure also matters for message resonance. An adequate volume of posts may contribute to reach as well as frequency of exposure. However, post too frequently and one may risk annoying the target audience. Yet, when one posts too infrequently a message may not cut through the clutter and get in front of the target audience to begin with (Fairlie, 2016). Using hashtags may be helpful. Often, hashtags can be used on social media platforms to tag content under a specific category, making it easier for others to search for it. For instance, as suggested in Chapter 2, on Twitter, users can use the hashtag symbol (#) before a relevant keyword or phrase to tag those tweets under a category. This helps them show more easily in Twitter searches and may boost impressions. By creating a unique hashtag it is also possible for those engaging in a campaign to track conversations that are directly related to them or track those on another topic of their choosing. It should be noted that created hashtags belong to the public and may be hijacked or co-opted by others. For instance, in Chapter 2 we discussed how ISIS hijacked popular hashtags such as those related to the 2014 World Cup, to spread its message. On the other hand, campaigners could also take a page out of the ISIS playbook, and engage in hijacking or co-opting pre-existing hashtags. When such hashtags already have a following, it may be a way to increase reach and exposure. In order to so effectively, however, it is important to persistently use the hashtag in the messaging as well as to encourage a large number of other users to do so as well (Fairlie, 2016). Of course, one needs to carefully consider whether using this strategy is in fact appropriate, as it may well backfire.

Furthermore, it can be useful to partner up with people and organizations who have already established a strong social media presence and may be able to reach the intended audience (i.e., influencers). People and organizations that are well connected with the target audience may be willing to promote and support a program and could potentially influence others to further share content or to connect with the initiative (Freeman et al., 2015; Tuck & Silverman, 2016). It may also be a strategy to contact established online outlets that have a following among the target audience, and ask them to feature the program or share program material (Tuck & Silverman, 2016). News media coverage through both mainstream and online channels could also help to get the word out about a social media campaign (Freeman et al., 2015).

Another way to get the message out is to leverage targeted digital advertising (Gold et al., 2012; Tuck & Silverman, 2016). Ads on social media provide opportunities to directly reach out to specific audiences on the basis of selected targeting criteria. Tuck & Silverman (2016, p. 31), who provide a starters guide for developing counter-messaging campaigns, set out some advantages of using targeted advertising. Key advantages include: (1) it allows campaigners to narrowly target audiences; (2) it allows one to compete in the same spaces as extremist content circulates (e.g., by targeting specific channels, videos, keywords, followers of specific users, etc.); (3) it can help build momentum for a campaign and contribute to 'engagement' (see below); (4) it gives access to more in-depth social media analytics and metrics, which can be used for evaluation; and (5) it allows for the testing of different types of content with comparison trials and control groups (points (4) and (5) are further discussed in Chapter 5). However, these authors also proposed several drawbacks. Perhaps most importantly, audiences tend to be less trusting of advertised content than content that is delivered 'organically.' Furthermore, other authors have suggested that perceptions of intrusiveness could yield negative judgments of the message's quality and credibility. Braddock and Morrison (2018) argue it may lead to annoyance, which may cause individuals to dismiss the message outright, or worse, induce a backfire effect. Also, it may be time-intensive to start with targeted advertising and it requires sufficient resources (Tuck & Silverman, 2016). An interesting example of an initiative that leverages targeted advertising tools is the 'Redirect Program,' although the methods applied are clearly beyond the capacities of most actors who engage in counter-narrative work (see Box 4.8).

Box 4.8 The Redirect Program

In September 2016, Jigsaw, a Google technology incubator and think-tank (previously called Google Ideas), announced a pilot program called the 'Redirect Program' (The Redirect Method, n.d.-a), which was established in cooperation with Moonshot CVE, Quantum Communications, the Gen Next Foundation and a team of researchers. The program uses AdWord targeting tools to connect those who are actively searching for ISIS-related extremist material to curated YouTube videos that present a countervailing voice. The basic idea is as follows: targeted text, image and video advertisements appear alongside results that are based on search queries that contain terms and phrases that were identified as being suggestive of positive sentiment towards ISIS. These ads link to Arabic and English-language YouTube channels with themed playlists that feature pre-existing videos that are believed to be capable of debunking the ISIS narrative. The videos in these playlists are not necessarily well-known, and are oftentimes not explicitly designed to challenge jihadi propaganda. Rather, they were selected because program developers believed them to be objective in appearance and credible to the specific audience segment. Examples of videos include testimonials of Isis defectors, statements of religious scholars that explain the disconnection between Islam and Isis, and citizen journalists' footage that highlights the suffering of civilians, and the failure of the governance structure in Isis controlled territory. According to Google, the campaign was quite promising – over the course of eight weeks, more than 320,000 people viewed the anti-ISIS YouTube channels and people stayed on these channels longer in comparison with regular viewing patterns. It was also found that the click through rate was considerably higher than the click through rate of all ads that ran against similar search terms 12 months prior the launch of the pilot (The Redirect Method, n.d.-b). The actual offline impact of these efforts is, however, once more unclear. Furthermore, while this initiative may be more targeted in terms of getting counter-messages to the right audience, audience members are not necessarily presented with a message that is suitable for them.

As we suggested earlier in this chapter, in some cases it may be important that message dissemination is carried out in a highly precise fashion. In this regard, we can learn a great deal from political campaigning (Reed, 2017b). Political campaigning is increasingly moving in the direction of micro-targeting. In political campaigns, data-mining techniques are used to draw in whatever information is available on individual voters. Such information is combined with demographic, geographic and marketing data about these individuals and used to build statistical models that can predict attitudes and behaviors of individuals for whom such information is unavailable or not known. This information can then be used to precisely target individuals with tailored adverts through social media: "two individuals living in the same house may get different messages targeted at them when they use the internet" (Reed, 2017b, p. 7). Besides enabling highly precise targeting, it may enable "targeted messaging that is much more context-specific and addresses the radicalising levers of the individuals" (Reed, 2017b, p. 7).

Rather than simply broadcasting messages in the hope that the intended audience will pick it up or share it, it may be beneficial to embrace the social component of social media and actively encourage audience engagement (e.g., Heldman, Schindelar, & Weaver, 2013; Korda & Itani, 2013; Lovejoy & Saxton, 2012; Neiger, Thackeray, Burton, Giraud-Carrier, & Fagen, 2012; Taylor, 2012; Veale et al., 2015). Engagement can be understood as an active process of interaction between a campaign or a campaign-generated message and members of the audience, for instance, in the form of liking, sharing, commenting, etc. (Dahl, 2014). As argued by Taylor (2012, p. 14):

> Engagement is core to campaigning via social media, because it not only encourages followers to move from support to action, but an individual's involvement is visible on their social network profiles and on the feeds of their connections, which enhances the reach of the campaign.

The broader literature discusses a variety of techniques which are argued to enhance user engagement with campaigns. In addition to seeding compelling content and scheduling regular posts, these include being responsive to user feedback, encouraging interaction and conversations by posing questions, soliciting user-generated content (e.g., sharing personal stories, uploading videos or photos), giving acknowledgment for audience members' support, engaging directly with members of the audience through individual responses, including linking online communication with offline action (Heldman et al., 2013; Taylor, 2012; Veale et al., 2015). As we have suggested in the previous chapter, the latter may be relevant for other reasons as well. In any case, which techniques will be appropriate will depend on the purpose and target audience of the campaign (Tuck & Silverman, 2016). Moreover, effective engagement necessitates careful monitoring and listening to what is happening on social media channels (see next section). In addition, real-time engagement requires social media efforts to be flexible, adaptable, and, ideally, able to respond to (real world) events as they happen (Taylor, 2012).

4.5.2 Risk and challenges

Several risks and challenges related to counter-messaging campaign have already been proposed. However, there are several others that deserve consideration, and should be factored in when developing and implementing a social media effort. Below we will provide an outline of different risks and challenges.

In general, those undertaking a campaign should be wary of potential unintended harmful side-effects. Messages intended for specific audiences often end up being viewed by other audiences as well (Atkin, 2004; Egner, 2009; Fink & Barclay, 2013), and there is limited control over how messages are interpreted (Atkin, 2004). Messages that may be effective with a specific intended audience, may be ineffective or even counter-productive with another (Egner, 2009; Freeman et al., 2015; Fink & Barclay, 2013). For instance, as suggested earlier, counter-narrative messages aimed at dissuading people from supporting Salafi-Jihadi groups may cause alienation or be perceived as offensive when they reach people that are not at-risk of falling in the orbit of these groups (Berger, 2016; Reynolds & Tuck, 2016), or may in fact trigger curiosity towards extremist groups and the views they espouse (Berger, 2016).

In addition, when choosing social media for a counter-narrative campaign, the risk of losing control over the message should be considered. As has been noted by Heldman et al. (2013, p. 10), in the context of campaigns that leverage social media, "concerns about negative comments, misdirecting and reshaping the message and conversation or 'online incivility' are valid." The authors point out that it is important that these concerns are considered at the outset of a program, and are factored into the social media engagement strategy. As we suggested earlier, this point may be particularly important for counter-messaging campaigns, which could well evoke negative responses (e.g., hate speech; see Ernst et al., 2017). In fact, it may even be the case that entire counter-narrative campaigns are turned around and used by the adversary in a counter campaign (Briggs & Frenett, 2014).

Anne Aly (interview, February 25, 2016) argues that this is exactly what happened to the 'Say No To Terror' (see Box 2.1) and the 'Think Again, Turn Away' (see Box 4.9) campaigns:

The counter campaign became Say Yes to Jihad. And in fact, the counter campaign messages, and the counter campaign videos outnumber the Say No to Terror videos. That's the first risk, that there'll be a counter campaign. The Think Again, Turn Away had counter campaigns within half a day.

Conversely, Diana Rieger (interview, May 19, 2016) puts forward

we just tried to do an analysis on the hashtag "notinmyname" which was built as a counter-voice. But in Germany at the moment, it is caught up by right wing groups which say 'all these refugees, this is not happening in our name,' like they all use the hashtag "notinmyname," it's covered with right wing extremist messages.

As such, this may well lead people to come across extremist content, which could potentially increase curiosity into violent extremist groups rather than suppress it. These examples highlight the importance of thinking about such adverse unintended options and learning from others before one launches a campaign.

Related to this, it is vital that appropriate precautions are taken to ensure the personal safety and well-being of those who work on or contribute to an online counter-messaging program. Involvement in such work could lead individuals or groups to be targeted by violent extremist groups and receive hate mails. Those engaging in such efforts may for instance

---

Box 4.9 #Thinkagainturnaway

US State Department's Center for Strategic Counterterrorism Communications (CSCC; replaced by the Global Engagement Center (GEC) in 2016) is particularly well-known for its now retired public diplomacy initiative #Thinkagainturnaway. Launched in December 2013, the campaign was designed to challenge Salafi-Jihadi extremist groups in their ability to accumulate cultural and political capital, and focused on refuting ideological claims (Richards, 2016). The campaign aimed to do so in two ways: by providing counter-narrative material in response to online Salafi-jihadi propaganda; and entering in direct conversations with jihadist accounts (van Ginkel, 2015). The campaign has received substantial criticism. In part, because of its second approach of directly addressing and engaging with jihadi accounts. For instance, Rita Katz (2014), director of the SITE Intelligence Group think tank, has argued that trivial exchanges with Jihadi accounts have frequently served extremist groups, providing them with legitimacy and a stage on which to air their views.

---

face (online) harassment or threats, or may even become targeted psychologically (Briggs & Frenett, 2014; Hedayah & ICCT, 2014). Former extremists may well be seen as traitors and could quickly become targets if their safety is not guaranteed (Hedayah & ICCT, 2014). Moreover, victims could potentially face abusive reactions and harassment, leading them to be victimized once more. For both of the above examples, it is also vital to keep in mind that recounting distressing events could also evoke strong emotions and may cause psychological damage (Briggs & Feve, 2013; Hedayah & ICCT, 2014). As such, facilitators should ensure that appropriate support and assistance is in place.

In addition, individuals may be reluctant to engage in counter-messaging work, because they fear they may be perceived as a security threat and become the subject of law enforcement investigation when they engage with those that may be supportive of violent extremism (Beutel et al., 2016). Hence, it has been suggested that it is important that governments promote a 'legal space' that allows those interested in becoming involved in such work to do so without being perceived as a security threat (Hedayah & ICCT, 2014).

Given the sheer speed and real-time nature of communication, social media campaigns need to be flexible, responsive, and ready to adapt (Taylor, 2012; Hedayah & ICCT, 2014). However, this may pose a challenge for organizations. Freeman et al. (2015) explain that multi-tier-approval processes in organizations can severely impede the ability to respond to and engage with audience members in a timely fashion. This challenge is further exacerbated when one takes into account that organizations may ultimately be legally responsible for all content posted on one's social media page, including content and comments generated by members of the audience. This once again points to the importance of having adequate human resources available when engaging in such activities.

Lastly, another difficulty in implementing social media campaigns is to demonstrate the value and effect of such social media efforts. While it is possible to gain insight into the online impact, measuring the offline impact of a counter-narrative is notoriously challenging (e.g., Adewuyi & Adefemi, 2016; Heldman et al., 2013; Taylor, 2012). The difficulties in measuring the effects of a specific social media campaign will be examined in more detail in the next chapter.

4.6 Summary

In this chapter, we sought to uncover some of the principles of an effective counter-narrative campaign via social media. In general, a social media counter-narrative program will not be highly effective among those who have already passed through the first stage of radicalization (see Chapter

3). Therefore, the current chapter addressed research question 4 by focusing on a targeted audience, because a counter-narrative program may prevent opinions and beliefs becoming a fertile ground for radical thoughts to take root. Thus, counter-narrative programs may be effective in preventing radical messages resonating among a targeted audience. However, for a small portion of those in the second stage of radicalization, mainly those who already have doubts about the group, counter-narratives could potentially have a limited effect.

We examined some of the key principles that may guide the development and implementation of a counter-narrative program as addressed in the extant literature to guide an effective communication campaign. Key principles for such a counter-narrative are therefore derived from the general literature on mass communication, health campaigns and persuasion.

By and large, from a wide array of theories addressing smaller aspects and elements of communicating a message for attitude or behavior change, we derived several key principles that appear relevant in a counter-narrative program, preferably aired via social media. We derived three stages in developing and implementing a communication campaign, each including several aspects to consider. Each of these (sub)sections describes what can be learnt in this respect from previous research in view of the effectiveness of a counter-campaign.

Stage 1 is "Research and planning" (Section 4.3), which includes the importance of using theory as a starting point. This includes theory about the causes and triggers of radicalization, as well as theories of how to change the unwanted behavior. In addition, in order to have clearly defined goals and objectives for the counter-narrative campaign, it is vital that audiences are clearly defined, segmented and understood.

In stage 2, "Program development and design" (Section 4.4), first, the content of the message is important in that it should be tailored to the diverse motivations behind radicalization (i.e., people might be motivated to find identity, significance, justice or sensation via the group). Messages that use the narratives have the advantage of using subtle ways to influence people. Moreover, they may overcome various forms of resistance. In addition, double-sided messages (in which one side is being discredited), coupled with a strong emotional appeal may have a persuasive advantage. Finally, relatively simple messages may be more effective than more complex messages.

In addition, at this stage, it is of great importance how to select credible sources as messengers in the development of an effective campaign. Commonly mentioned candidates are former extremists, victims of violence, peers and family, as well as key members of communities and civil society actors. The potential of the government to serve as a credible source might be limited.

Stage 3 "Implementation of a communication campaign" (Section 4.5) includes consciously considering which dissemination channels to choose and how to disseminate the message as well as being aware of possible risks and limitations in launching a counter-narrative, in particular adverse actions from those countered. It is important to closely monitor potential risks, challenges and limitations when developing a communication campaign, for example losing control of the message, having the message 'stolen' and used in another counter-campaign by opponents and, as such, creating unintended adverse effects. In addition, possible threats to the safety of those who feature in social media counter-narratives should be guarded against.

Selected channels should be frequently utilized by the audience one intends to reach. Using multiple channels is suggested to be beneficial. The strengths and weaknesses of different channels of delivery should also be considered, taking into account the communication and message strategy as well as the available resources. Importantly, social media may not be appropriate in all circumstances, and should perhaps at best be considered a supplement to other program approaches and channels. Linking online with offline activities is suggested to be particularly important.

It is important to think about the strategy for message dissemination, as it may be hard to cut out the clutter on social media. Among other things, consideration should be given to the frequency and timing of postings, as these may impact the reach of a message. Using hashtags may help generate more impressions. Also, it may be beneficial to partner with people and organizations who have already established a strong social media presence and are popular among the target audience. Conversely, it may also be useful to ask established online (news) outlets to share the message. Furthermore, it is may be important to create opportunities for audience engagement. Digital advertisements could also help to get the message out. What methods will be most suitable will depend on the campaign.

In general, mass communication theories appear to rely quite strongly on traditional one-directional sender-message-receiver models, each directed at some aspect of the sender-message-receiver/audience chain, and oftentimes only addressing just one element of a message (e.g., one- or two-sided messaging). Of course, these theories have their value and provide important guidelines. However, today's media environments require more dynamic and interactive models, including feedback loops and the agency of both sender and receiver to do justice to communication processes via social media. In considering such feedback loops and dynamics, the risks of potential adverse effects (e.g., from opponents) also become clearer. These should be taken into consideration before launching a campaign.

An important limitation of a counter-narrative program via social media is that it is notoriously difficult to demonstrate the effectiveness of such social media efforts. This is the topic of the next chapter.

Notes

1 Diana Rieger, interview, May 19, 2016.
2 Arie Kruglanski, interview, March 8, 2016.
3 Other message factors they looked into were the format of posts (e.g., video, photos, and text) and the content of posts. The found that photos and content in the form of questions and commentary were most likely to generate interactions with users. In addition, they also looked into the most popular content on right-wing populist pages. In this context, it was found that the most popular tone was celebratory (i.e., commemorating, war dead or patriotic pride) followed by angry. In three countries, the most popular format was photos. Comparing both counter-speech and right-wing populist pages, they found the latter were way more effective in sharing content beyond their network of followers and were generally more active (Bartlett & Krasodomski-Jones, 2015).
4 Martine Bouwman, interview, April 15, 2016.
5 Diana Rieger, interview, May 19, 2016.
6 Arie Kruglanski, interview, March 8, 2016.
7 Maarten van de Donk, interview, April 19, 2016.
8 Diana Rieger, interview, May 19, 2016.
9 Arie Kruglanski, interview, March 8, 2016.
10 Arie Kruglanski, interview, March 8, 2016.

5

DETERMINING THE POTENTIAL EFFECTIVENESS OF A COUNTER-MESSAGING PROGRAM

5.1 Introduction

In this chapter, we provide an answer to research question 6, namely "how can the potential effectiveness of a counter-messaging program be determined?" This question thus concerns campaign evaluation. Evaluation has been described as the: "the systematic application of research procedures to understand the conceptualization, design, implementation, and utility of interventions" (Valente & Kwan, 2012, p. 83). This definition is particularly relevant as it highlights the importance of engaging evaluation activities throughout the development and implementation program (not just at the end), and points out that research procedures should be used. Furthermore, it indicates that evaluation is not just about measuring effectiveness, but also about gaining insight into why and how a program works, which can inform the design and development of future programs (Valente & Kwan, 2012, p. 83). Generally speaking, the effectiveness of any measure or policy against violent extremism can be extremely difficult to assess (e.g., Noordegraaf, Douglas, Bos, & Klem, 2016). This is no different for counter-messaging efforts. Measuring changes in attitudes and beliefs is notoriously difficult, whereas measuring prevention (i.e., measuring a negative or a non-event) is virtually impossible (RAN, 2017).

In Section 5.2, we describe the types of evaluations that are generally recommended in the communication literature (formative, process and summative types). In addition we will describe the realist evaluation paradigm. In Section 5.3, we present the manners in which it is possible to monitor and analyze social media data or metrics, which are often used as an indicator for campaign effectiveness. Section 5.4 describes other online and offline tools and techniques that can be used in the summative evaluation as well as earlier evaluation phases such as focus groups, interviews, surveys, sentiment analysis and social network analysis. Finally, in Section 5.5 we summarize the most important points from this chapter.

5.2 Types of evaluation

As argued above, program evaluation should not be thought of as a one-time activity planned and tackled at the end of a communication effort. As we argued earlier, in the literature on communication campaigns, the evaluation process is commonly subdivided into three distinct phases: formative evaluation, process evaluation (also referred to as monitoring), and summative evaluation (e.g., Coffman, 2002; Macnamara, 2017; Noar, 2011; Paul, Yeats, Clarke, Matthews, & Skrabala, 2015; Valente & Kwan, 2012). Formative evaluation occurs at an early stage (or prior to) development and design process. While the campaign is being implemented, process evaluation in the form of monitoring activities is carried out. Lastly, an outcome evaluation is conducted, ideally on the basis of data collected before, during and after a campaign. In the subsequent sections, we shortly outline each of these phases. While they are presented as sequential phases, they involve a set of interwoven activities that inform each other (Noar, 2011; Paul et al., 2015). Each of them requires some degree of planning at the outset of a campaign in order to execute them properly (Paul et al., 2015).

5.2.1 Formative evaluation

Formative evaluation is the collection of information that can inform program planning and shape campaign design (Coffman, 2002). It involves activities that define the nature and scope of the problem, gather data on potential program strategies, and learn about the audience and factors that could potentially interfere with program implantation (Valente & Kwan, 2012). These data enable one to set sound goals and objectives, specify the logic of a campaign and provide baseline values for *ex post* comparison (Macnamara, 2017; Paul et al., 2015). They also inform the communication strategy (i.e., channel selection and message design). Formative research also involves pre-testing concepts, messages and other dimensions of the communication strategy (Macnamara, 2017). Message pre-testing may, for instance, provide insight into how well a message captures the attention of an audience, is comprehended, is perceived to be relevant, and elicits (un)intended consequences (Atkin & Freimuth, 2012). This aspect of formative evaluation shares characteristics of both process and summative research, as it can be utilized to "examine both the simulated delivery and the effects of a communication strategy and its tactics" (Freimuth, Cole, & Kirby, 2011, p. 80). As such, it can help to assess whether elements in the mix contribute to program objectives and correspond with the information needs of the intended audience. Of course, it differs in the sense that it is carried out before final production and the implementation of a program (Freimuth et al., 2011, p. 80).

5.2.2 Process evaluation

Process evaluation starts with the program launch and is carried out as the program unfolds. It involves progressive tracking and monitoring to discern whether milestones are being met or not (Macnamara, 2017). As such, it involves activities to determine whether a program is delivered as intended and to assess output measures (e.g., reach and exposure). Process evaluation is considered to be valuable, as it may help to identify problems in program delivery, reasons that underlie those problems, as well as potential solutions. This allows those undertaking the program to make adjustments (Paul et al., 2015). Process evaluation is a recommended precursor to summative evaluation, as it can be difficult to interpret why a program did or did not produce expected outcomes without some knowledge of the levels and conditions of implementation (Flay, 1987).

5.2.3 Summative evaluation

Summative evaluation is conducted after the program has been implemented and involves what is arguably most often considered to be 'evaluation' (Atkin & Freimuth, 2012; Coffman, 2002; Macnamara, 2017). Summative evaluation consists of activities to identify outcomes that can be attributed to the program and to establish whether the effort has achieved its objectives (Freimuth et al., 2011; Macnamara, 2017; Paul et al., 2015). Authors have further distinguished between assessments of short-term outcomes (i.e., 'outcome evaluation') as well as long-term impacts, "measures of the ultimate aggregate results of the campaign's outcomes" (i.e., 'impact evaluation'; see Coffman, 2002, p. 24).

5.3 Social media monitoring and analytics

Digital footprints left by campaign audiences have become popular indicators of the impact of campaigns on social media (Shi, Poorisat, & Salmon, 2016). Such measurements center on the analysis of metrics that can be collected real-time from social media platforms that are used in a campaign (Reynolds & Tuck, 2016; RAN, 2015). Many social media platforms provide associated social media analytics services that allow for the real-time tracking and monitoring of social media data at no costs or limited costs. More professional analytics tools have also been developed by third parties, although their level of sophistication is generally reflected in the price tag (usually a subscription fee) (Neiger, Thackeray, Van Wagenen et al., 2012). Importantly, though, it is not always clear how these services log and define the metrics they present, thus they can be misleading. Hence, one should be certain to gain insight into what a particular metric represents (Tuck & Silverman, 2016).

There are a wide variety of quantitative metrics that can be analyzed. However, many of these metrics do not help us make decisions or meaningfully gauge performance on key outcomes (e.g., so-called 'vanity metrics') (Paul et al., 2015). Therefore, it is vital to establish at the outset of a campaign what the program objectives are and what you want to learn, to identify the key metrics that are considered to be central for success or can help to answer key evaluation questions, as well as how they should be analyzed (Reynolds & Tuck, 2016). Authors from the Institute for Strategic Dialogue (Reynolds & Tuck, 2016; Silverman, Stewart, Birdwell, Amanullah, 2016) have provided some suggestions as to what metrics that may be worth tracking when one aims to gauge the performance of a program. They distinguish between several categories of metrics.

The first category consists of *awareness* metrics. These essentially provide an indication of the number of people that were exposed to a campaign, viewed campaign material, and provide a crude picture of the demographics and geography of the audience. Reynolds & Tuck (2016) offer several examples of commonly measured quantitative metrics related to awareness, although it should be noted that the definitions of each can vary between different platforms (this holds for engagement metrics as well). Examples include the number of impressions, reach, video views etc. Awareness metrics can also include aggregate data related self-reported audience demographics and characteristics (e.g., gender, age, language, interests, etc.) and geographic location. The extent to which platforms and services allow one to gain insight in such data varies. There are also privacy-related limitations: it is, for instance, impossible to gain insight into details of individual audience members. Awareness metrics alone are inherently limited in their utility, as they provide no indication of whether any substantial and meaningful engagement with a campaign has taken place (Reynolds & Tuck, 2016).

Engagement metrics can provide some additional insights in that regard. Engagement metrics provide an indication of the volume, types and quality of user interactions with a campaign. This includes quantitative metrics such as the amount of likes, shares, viewer retention rates, comments and interactions. Generally speaking, actions that require more effort of the audience can be regarded as more substantial forms of engagement than those that require less effort (Reynolds & Tuck, 2016; also see Freeman et al., 2015; Neiger, Thackeray, Van Wagenen et al., 2012). Several forms of engagement provide qualitative data, which can be monitored and allow for further analyses. When campaigns spark comments and conversations, audience-generated messages can be coded and analyzed for sentiment or tone, key themes and topics. This can give an indication of what people think or feel about the program and its content, and what themes and topics participants are most likely to engage with (Reynolds & Tuck, 2016). This can be done through manual analysis or more sophisticated approaches using data mining techniques and natural language processing (see Section 5.4.6.).

It is suggested that awareness and engagement metrics can come together to provide an indication of the online, short-term impact of a campaign as defined in the objectives (Reynolds & Tuck, 2016), and can potentially provide useful insights to improve targeting and communications. Of course, engagement in the form of likes, shares, comments does not necessarily indicate that potential extremists have been redirected – whether it actually has reached the intended target audience and has changed people's attitudes or behaviors (Kim, Lee, Marguleas, & Beyer, 2016). As argued earlier, establishing an offline impact on attitudes and behaviors is extremely difficult. The anonymity that the internet provides often makes it impossible to establish precisely who engages with the campaign. Furthermore, disengagement and de-radicalization processes are complex, and may take place over a longer period of time. According to Silverman et al. (2016), 'impact metrics' such as sustained engagement (i.e., longer interactions) or people reaching out to campaigners for assistance may perhaps provide the clearest indication that a campaign is having any impact, at least on a personal level.

5.4 Other evaluation tools and techniques

While basic social media metrics are often used as indicators of the impact of campaigns on social media, developing a better understanding of the relationship between online and offline interaction requires the triangulation of methods (RAN, 2015). There are a wide range of online and offline qualitative and quantitative tools that can help, and may provide valuable information that can improve a campaign. Below we describe several qualitative and quantitative approaches that are outlined in the literature.

5.4.1 (Online) focus groups and interviews

A focus group is a "planned discussion led by a moderator who guides a small group of participants through a set of carefully sequenced (focused) questions in a permissive and nonthreatening conversation" (Krueger & Casey, 2015a, p. 506). They are commonly conducted with groups of approximately five to 12 respondents (smaller groups are recommended for sensitive topics) who have something in common that relates to the topic of conversation. In relation to counter-messaging campaigns, this might for instance be individuals who are representative of segments of the intended audience or subject-matter experts (also see Section 5.4.8.1). The discussion is facilitated by a skillful moderator who encourages participants into discussing the topic in greater detail using focused questions, keeps the discussion on track, ensures there is a permissive environment in which participants feel comfortable sharing their views freely and that every participant receives the opportunity to do so (Kreuger & Casey, 2015a, 2015b). They are often used to garner information in the formative evaluation phase, but can be useful in later stages as well. To name a just few purposes, they can be used to garner insight in the problem situation (e.g., to understand the audience's perspective on a particular problem or issue) and garner other input that can inform the program design. Focus groups are also frequently used to pilot-test various dimensions of the communication and message strategy, for instance to check whether messages are understandable and appealing (Kreuger & Casey, 2015b; Valente, 2002). However, the utility of focus groups is not limited to the formative evaluation. For instance, they can also be used to conduct when the program is up and running. For instance to gain insight into how the program can be improved and what does and does not work. Focus groups can also be set up to discuss the campaign and its effects and can be used to interpret and contextualize quantitative data gathered for summative evaluation (Kreuger & Casey, 2015a, 2015b; Weinreich, 2011).

Focus group sessions have several benefits. They are a relatively cost-friendly, quick, socially oriented and have face validity (Valente, 2002). Moreover, they provide a rather flexible research method; whilst they can be conducted in a laboratory setting, they can also be carried out 'on location' (e.g., a convenient environment, or an environment in which participants feels safe), or via telephone, and online (Atkin & Freimuth, 2012). However, they also have drawbacks. For starters, results are difficult to analyze and outcomes can be unpredictable (Krueger & Casey, 2015b; Valente, 2002). The primary risk, however, is that focus groups can provide misleading information: the group may be overly influenced by one or several people, people may experience normative pressures that may make them reluctant to deviate from group standards, or the topic of conversation may be too distant from audience members to generate opinions (Valente, 2002). Furthermore, as with any other described qualitative method (e.g., interviews), results lack generalizability. Hence, one should be wary not to quantify results (Atkin & Freimuth, 2012). Another challenge is that they might be particularly difficult to arrange. This may hold in particular in the context of a counter-messaging effort. Individuals targeted by counter-messaging activities may be hard to reach and reluctant to participate in focus groups, for instance because they want to remain anonymous (Dawson, Edwards, & Jeffray, 2014; Reynolds & Tuck, 2016). Furthermore, soliciting participation of the target audience may not be possible depending on where they are situated on the radicalization spectrum (RAN, 2015).

In this regard, online focus groups may offer some advantages over their face-to-face counterparts. Such focus groups can be conducted using synchronous (e.g., instant messaging, chat-rooms, or video-conferencing) and asynchronous communication methods (e.g., online discussion boards or forums). Depending on the communication method being utilized, online focus groups allow for greater anonymity than face-to-face groups (Atkin & Freimuth, 2012; Krueger & Casey, 2015b; Morgan, King, & Ivic, 2011; Stewart & Shamdasani, 2014). This could potentially make people more willing to participate, and could make them feel more at ease, which can result in greater disclosure (Morgan et al., 2011). There are several additional benefits. Besides the fact that they are particularly resource-friendly, they also make it possible to interact with hard-to-reach populations, in part because they do not suffer from geographical restrictions. In relation to online settings that allow for asynchronous communication, it has also been observed that they allow participants more time to reflect and reply at a time that is convenient for themselves (Krueger & Casey, 2015b; Morgan et al., 2011; Stewart & Shamdasani, 2014). When focus-groups discussions are text-based, it also provides an instant transcript (Atkin & Freimuth, 2012).

Unfortunately, there are also drawbacks. Online focus group sessions typically reduce the in-depth emotional information that can be obtained when one is physically in one location with participants (Atkin & Freimuth, 2012). When the moderator and participants do not see or hear each other, information present in facial expressions and tone-of-voice, etc., are lost. Reliability of the quality of recruited participants may be questionable given the absence of face-to-face interactions and a lack of screening (Stewart & Shamdasani, 2014). Owing to increased anonymity, it may be difficult to establish who did and did not participate in online focus groups (Morgan et al., 2011). In addition, certain text-based communication methods may favor participants who type and reply quickly, allowing some to 'dominate' the conversation (Krueger & Casey, 2015b). Synchronous focus groups in particular, may require access to good bandwidth, which may be a problem in some cases and locations (Stewart & Shamdasani, 2014).

5.4.2 One-on-one interviews

One-on-one, in-depth interviews with target audiences can be a rich source of information for evaluators. They can be used for similar purposes as focus groups, for instance, to learn about the context in which the program's messages and materials were received and how they were interpreted (Weinreich, 2011). Interviews can be conducted face-to-face, via telephone or through online means (e.g., Skype). During an in-depth interview, an interviewer essentially asks a series of open-ended questions about a particular topic, utilizing a more or less structured format. These interview questions are open-ended in order to give respondents freedom in answering questions, allowing them to express views that relate to the topic of interest (Valente, 2002).

One-on-one interviews can be particularly useful to discuss sensitive topics people might feel uncomfortable discussing in a group or that require deep probing (Atkin & Freimuth, 2012). Face-to-face interviews can potentially increase access and can make it easier to build rapport with respondents. In part, because they can be conducted in locations that are convenient and comfortable to the respondents. Of course, in the context of counter-messaging, interviews may still face similar challenges to focus groups when it comes to soliciting the participation of target audiences.

A benefit of interviews in comparison with focus groups is that they avoid the earlier mentioned challenges associated with normative pressures and other undesirable influences related to group dynamics (Freimuth et al., 2011). However, it should be noted that group dynamics do help people to explore and clarify views in ways that would be less easily accessible in the context of a one-on-one interview (Kitzinger, 1995). Amongst the drawbacks of interviews are that they may be time-consuming and resource-intensive (Atkin & Freimuth, 2012).

5.4.3 (Online) surveys

Surveys are a useful and efficient means for gathering formative evaluation data for multiple purposes. Among other things, they can be used to obtain a quantitative estimate of important (theoretical) variables (i.e., current attitudes, perceptions, behavior, etc.), establish baseline data that permits the measurement of the effects (or lack of effect), and to pre-test concepts and draft versions of messages (Atkin & Freimuth, 2012; Paul et al., 2015). They can also be used in later evaluation stages to gain insights into the proximal effects of a campaign (Reynolds & Tuck, 2016). A survey can contain both closed and open-ended questions and can be used to gather both quantitative and qualitative data (Atkin & Freimuth, 2012; Reynolds & Tuck, 2016).

Surveys can be conducted in various ways – each method has various advantages and disadvantages. One way is through online means. Such a method commonly makes it easier and relatively cheap to produce and distribute a survey, and online surveys can be used to reach and gain insights from geographically dispersed respondents, and they have the *potential* for fast data-collection and turnaround (Atkin & Freimuth, 2012; Austin & Pinkleton, 2015; Sue & Ritter, 2012; Wright, 2005). During the implementation stage of a program, they can also be easily promoted through links embedded in material, allowing for data-collection as the program unfolds. Furthermore, social media also allows for the delivery of surveys through social media advertising, which enables targeting particular audiences (Austin & Pinkleton, 2015; Reynolds & Tuck, 2016).

However, online surveys also have well-documented limitations (e.g., see Austin & Pinkleton, 2015; Bethlehem, 2010; Eysenbach & Wyatt,

2002; Wright 2005). For instance, one limitation is that online surveys frequently suffer from a self-selection bias. Many online surveys rely on respondents selecting themselves for a survey, which means respondents may not be representative of the members of the audience (Bethlehem, 2010; Reynolds & Tuck, 2016, Wright, 2005). To illustrate, it may be the case that those who respond may be particularly inclined to do so, and may generally have more favorable attitudes towards the topic. Others may be unwilling to share their views on a topic as sensitive as counter-messaging campaigning, or may be inclined to respond negatively. Those who are further along the pathway of radicalization, may arguably be difficult to reach. In addition, in relation to counter-messaging campaigns, potential respondents may not want to share any personal information (Reynolds & Tuck, 2016). Of course, one could offer the option to fill in surveys more or less anonymously. However, this may also increase the likelihood of hoax responses (Eysenbach & Wyatt, 2002).

Low response and high non-completion rates are other well-known concerns when conducting online surveys (Austin & Pinkleton, 2015; Eysenbach & Wyatt, 2002; Wright, 2005) and can lead to a sample being unrepresentative of the audience. While participation in a survey can be incentivized – for instance through a price draw (Reynolds & Tuck, 2016), incentives may however also impact on the representativeness of the sample (Eysenbach et al., 2002). Furthermore, efforts to increase participation may also increase the amount time and resources necessary to conduct a survey, which will be reflected in additional cost (Austin & Pinkleton, 2015).

In sum, while online surveys can potentially provide a useful tool to gathering a greater depth of data during different stages of evaluation, they pose a variety of methodological problems. Consequently, online surveys should be used carefully and results should be interpreted with care (Austin & Pinkleton, 2015).

5.4.4 Experiments

Essentially, an experiment is an examination of a cause-and-effect relationship between an independent and a dependent variable. The basic purpose of an experiment is to determine causation. In a conventional type of experiment the influence of an independent variable on a dependent variable is typically examined by making an explicit comparison between at least two similar groups (of individuals): one group (the treatment group) is exposed to an experimental stimulus, while the other group receives no stimulus or perhaps a meaningless one (the control group). The impact of the stimulus can then be assessed by comparing what happens when it is present to what happens when it is not present (Ackland, 2013; Baxter & Babbie, 2004).

Experiments can roughly be classified into two categories depending on whether they are conducted in the laboratory or in the field. For example, in a laboratory experiment, one group of people could be subjected to a counter-message coming from a former radical, while another group of people do not receive a counter-message at all. Subsequently, people's radical attitudes are assessed. This design can test whether presenting a counter-message or not (the independent variable) has an effect on the radical attitudes (the dependent variable).

In order to be able to draw causal conclusions, two elements are crucial: first, people have to be randomly allocated to one of the conditions and, second, it is important that the independent variable differs only on the dimension of interest, and does not co-vary with another variable. Thus, for example, it is not possible to draw causal inferences from a comparison between a message sent by former radical male and a message sent by a female victim of a terrorist attack, because the properties of this message differs on two dimensions at the same time (i.e., gender and "status": former radical versus victim).

In field experiments, researchers use existing groups and test differences. For example, people in Amsterdam receive a different message from people in Rotterdam. You can still test whether people react differently to the two messages, but the strength of the conclusion is hampered by the fact that people from Amsterdam and Rotterdam may have differed from each other before the message. Thus, the ability to draw strong causal conclusions from a field experiment is limited.

Interestingly, it is also possible to do experiments online. Several computer programs offer this option (e.g., Qualtrics, M-Turk, etc.). In addition, some research companies offer online samples via "panels," sometimes even representative of a more general population (for a discussion of the quality of the data see Goodman, Cryder, & Cheema, 2013; Mason & Suri, 2012; Paolacci & Chandler, 2014).

This has several advantages for the current question. It makes it possible to test materials online, for example inspecting the number of views of a message, or by asking people's responses to certain materials (i.e., pilot testing of materials).

The down side of online experiments is that the researcher has no (or limited) control over the situation in which the respondent answers the questions. For example, it might be possible that people get distracted during the study (e.g., their telephone rings, they make a cup of coffee, etc.). In addition, someone might be doing the study together with someone else, who might influence their responses and thus the assumption of independence of the answers is violated. For these reasons, it is usually advised to have higher number of participants in online studies than in offline studies.

5.4.5 Netnography

'Netnography,' a contraction of internet and ethnography, is essentially ethnography adapted for the analysis of social media and allows for in-depth study of smaller online communities (Bartlett & Reynolds, 2015; Kozinets, Dolbec, & Earley, 2014). Netnography utilizes elicited and – more frequently – non-elicited data, which are typically obtained through observation of and/or participation with people as they interact in regular online and social media environments and activities (Kozinets et al., 2014). However, ethnographies may also employ a range of other data collection methods – including many of those outlined in this chapter (although manual methods are most commonly used and numerical measurement or quantification of social media data is typically avoided) (Bartlett & Reynolds, 2015; Kozinets 2015). Data collected and analyzed may take a wide variety of forms, ranging from words, images, audio, video, etc. (Kozinets, 2015). In marketing and consumer research, the field of origin, ethnography is typically used in formative evaluation to develop a deep understanding of online groups and communities. For instance, it can gain insight into attitude formation, behaviors, conversations, and interaction and discursive styles of specific online consumer groups. Such information can subsequently inform strategy development and message design (Belk & Kozinets, 2017; Kozinets, 2015). It could potentially also be useful in later evaluation states, for instance to gain insight into how audiences respond to communications (Belk & Kozinets, 2017).

Netnography shares several characteristics of traditional ethnographic research, such as being immersive and naturalistic. However, it is less time-consuming, simpler, less expensive and treats online communities as a primary fieldwork site (Kozinets, 2010). Netnography is claimed to have various merits. For instance, netnography has the *potential* to be less obtrusive than other qualitative data-collection techniques such as focus groups and interviews, as it is conducted within a context that is not fabricated and because it allows for the collection of data without making one's presence visible (Kozinets, 2002; Kozinets et al., 2014). Therefore, ethnography is particularly useful for studying personally and politically sensitive or controversial topics and illegal acts discussed in online communities by users who prefer to conceal their personal identities (Costello, McDermott, & Wallace, 2017). Perhaps, therefore, netnography is increasingly viewed as a valuable method to gain insight into extremist communities (Bartlett & Reynolds, 2015; Conway, 2016). A study by Hegghammer (2014), which explores the effects of trust issues on jihadi internet discussion forums, provides one example in which this method is applied.

Alas, there are also drawbacks. For instance, Robert V. Kozinets (2002, p. 3) asserts that "the need for researcher interpretive skill, and the lack of informant identifiers present in the online context leads to difficulty generalizing results to groups outside the online community sample." Furthermore, netnography may draw on data that are not given explicitly and in confidence to netnographers. In some cases, this may raise ethical and legal concerns. Hence, it important to give consideration to regulatory and legal requirements and ethical issues such as privacy, anonymity, informed consent and risk of harm. Of course, in general, it is important to consider potential ethical and legal issues resulting from evaluation design decisions. Perhaps, in particular, when they involve social media research (see Moreno et al., 2013; Zimmer, 2010).

5.4.6 Sentiment and content analysis

Storage and retrieval of information on social media, along with datamining techniques, make analyses of a huge amounts of audience-generated messages possible. Automated sentiment analysis techniques can be used to analyze such data and infer the sentiments of social media users towards some topic. Sentiment analysis, also referred to as opinion mining, deals with "the computational treatment of opinion, sentiment, and subjectivity in text" (Pang & Lee, 2008, p. 10). It makes use of computational linguistics, natural language processing (NLP) and other methods of text analytics to automatically detect and extract people's sentiments towards certain entities (e.g., issues, events, individuals, groups, organizations) and their attributes from text sources (e.g., in the context of social media, comments, tweets, blog posts, etc.). While still in its infancy, it has become an increasingly popular way for companies to determine what sentiments and opinions are expressed in response to their products, services, brands, and campaigns (Cohen, Johansson, Kaati, & Mork, 2014). Sentiment analysis can provide insight into how a campaign is received and perceived by those who engage with it, adding quantitative insight to other data that have been gathered as part of the evaluation process (Reynolds & Tuck, 2016).

A basic purpose of sentiment analysis is to identify opinions, identify the sentiments they express, and then classify polarity or opposing views (Medhat, Hassan, & Korashy, 2014). That is, to classify any given text as either positive, negative or neutral, the software needs keywords to search for relevant text and to assess such differentiation. In general, before starting the automatic analyses, specific analyses of the messages' content are done manually to identify those keywords and check coverage and classification. This process is iterative as it needs improvement to reach good inter-coder reliability as well as reliability once automatized (e.g., precision and recall; Riff, Lacy, & Fico, 2014). Recent options for sentiment analyses also go beyond polarity; for instance, it may be employed to detect and analyze specific emotions carried by a text. Sentiment analysis can be conducted at different levels of granularity, including the document, sentence, word, and aspect/feature level (Medhat et al., 2014). Of course, social media contain many forms of multimedia, and sentiment may arguably not only be conveyed through words. For instance, it could be expressed in photos or emoticons. More research is being conducted on how to analyze sentiment that is not directly being expressed in texts (Hui, 2016).

As an example, consider an analysis of how Muslims were portrayed in the news for which seven Dutch newspapers, 14 news broadcasts on television, and six relevant websites were coded for positively and negatively toned content (Konijn et al., 2010). Several thousands of messages have been searched by means of automatic content analyses using hundreds of search terms, in several steps, starting with mapping the past years for news about immigration and integration (from 1998 until 2008). The results showed how the focus had shifted over time since the attack on September 11, 2001. Then, the debate took a turn and the tone hardened. Terrorism became the leading item on the media agenda and became associated with Islam. Interestingly, since 2006 the attention on terrorism decreased, but from 2007 the media attention on political anti-immigration parties in the Netherlands increased considerably. Furthermore, findings from comparing seven digitally available newspapers (from October 2006 until December 2008) showed that Islamic residents and immigrants were often related to terrorism, criminal acts, war violence, and ideological extremism, in those news messages. In addition, the results of a comparison of six web fora (popular among primarily Moroccan Muslim youth) showed that the topics of these web fora clearly follow each other in showing quite some overlap. The discussions on the web closely followed the debate in Dutch news media. Finally, (manual) analyses of 14 television news and information programs (focusing on a specific Muslim-related event over seven weeks) showed how a specific selection of facts colored the news within a specific frame (e.g., problematic youth 'terrorize' the neighborhood; 'street terror') showing a negative tone of the debate.

Although automated sentiment analysis is a hot research topic, it is still in an early stage of development. There are several important challenges. Perhaps most importantly, there are currently few proven methodologies for extracting and analyzing social media content. Although technological know-how is improving, extracting relevant texts for analysis from huge amounts of data remains a significant challenge. In general, there are several operational and practical challenges and limitations when it comes to collecting social media data, this includes issues related to matters such as volume, access, and, as earlier mentioned, ethics (see Hui, 2016, for a general overview). The informal nature of online communication also poses difficulties. For instance, some problems with sentiment analysis are related to 'noisy' texts (e.g., slang, spelling, grammatical errors, problematic and missing punctuation) and the presence of implicit sentiments (e.g., sarcasm, irony), and identifying entities and context (Hui, 2016).

Still, despite the difficulties, some efforts have been made to establish a method via sentiment analysis to find radical people online. For example, Scrivens, Davies, and Frank (2017) present what they label a 'Sentiment-based Identification of Radical Authors,' which entails a combined score for a user's percentile average sentiment score, volume of negative posts, severity of negative posts, and duration of negative posts. Another example is provided by Bermingham, Conway, McInerney, O'Hare, and Smeaton (2009) who use sentiment analysis alongside social network analysis (next section) to explore online radicalization. Given the fact that these techniques differ in their focus, it is challenging to directly combine them, rather than treat them as two separate outcomes of two separate analyses. Furthermore, more thorough research is needed to establish the predictive value of such sentiment analyses to find radical people via their online activities.

Related to sentiment analysis is conducting more complex content analyses, for example, to study the dominant 'frames' in a discussion on social media, or to get an impression how a campaign is discussed by its followers. Such analyses provide richer details about the content of their responses than merely positive or negative content. A relevant example is an extensive content analysis of blog posts of a Dutch website where Moroccan youth and (young) adults often discuss Islam-related issues (i.e., Marokko.nl) (Mann, Doosje, Konijn, Nickolson, Moore, & Ruigrok, 2015). In applying four types of qualitative and quantitative content analyses (i.e., bottom-up and top-down, both manually and automatically), posts could be identified as either representing an 'extremist radical frame' or a 'counter-frame' based on its features referring to a specific 'frame.' In the initial stages (mainly by manual content analyses), seven frames were identified, four of which characteristic extremist messages/posts (e.g., 'hate against the West frame'; a pro-Islamic State frame; a 'fight for Syria' frame) and three frames were characteristic of a counter-message of offering resistance against radical and violent accounts (e.g., a democracy frame; an unacceptability of ISIS-acts frame).

The results of the analyses showed, among others, that the posts on the web forum Marokko.nl in large part contained messages within a counter-frame relative to posts expressing a radical-extremist frame (in an overall corpus of 149,394 posts from 15 September, 2013 to 15 September, 2014; Mann et al., 2015). Based on the relative percentages of extremist and counter-frames, a so-called resilience index could be calculated, per week or per month, to show changes over time (see Figures 5.8. and 5.9 in Mann et al., 2015). It shows, for example, that the extremist voices clearly increased in July 2014, while the counter-voices showed more fluctuations throughout with a dip during the last week of July 2014. In this month, the resilience index showed a reversed pattern in the debate; the amount of extremist posts was larger than the amount of posts from counter-frames.

Results such as these need more follow-up research to allow more solid interpretations as well as to increase the reliability of the automatic content analyses.

For the automatic content analyses, Mann et al. (2015) used the Amsterdam Content Analysis Toolkit (AmCAT, van Atteveldt, 2008). Although this software has been extensively tested, for example on news texts, intensive manual and qualitative analyses are still needed for such 'loose' language use as expressed on social media (e.g., including a lot of slang, typos, unusual terminology), including many repetitions that should be filtered out. A drawback of the automatic content analyses, specifically with such materials, is its lower reliability (cf. standards in Stryker, Wray, Hornik, & Yanovitzky, 2006). To increase the reliability of results, deleting mere repetitions, but also separate older posts from newly added responses and posts, would help. However, this requires time and human labor, and thus financial resources. Related to this, analyses can be restricted to the newly added posts alone. Alternatively, one might select the most active individuals and specifically analyze their posts over time as well as how others respond specifically to this individual. Manual and automatic analyses might further be applied in selecting those who mostly post within extremist frames in comparison to persons typically posting within a counter-frame. Such a dialogue may provide valuable input for designing a counter-message on social media.

5.4.7 Social network analysis

Social network analysis (SNA) is all about relationships, and relationships are at the core of social media. SNA refers to a set of theories, methods and techniques that can be used for the collection and analysis of network data (i.e., relational data), which has been described as "information on the connections and relationships among and between entities" (Valente & Pitts, 2017, p. 104). Correspondingly, basic units of analysis are 'entities' – also referred to as 'nodes' or 'actors' – and 'ties,' which represent connections or relationships between entities. These entities can be people, but they may also be groups, organizations and other connected entities. Ties can represent friendship, common interest, transaction, interaction, and affiliation, among others (Wasserman & Faust, 1994). Network data can be gathered online, offline, and combined. Advances in computing technology and the rise of social media have increased opportunities for social network analysis and have made it easier and cheaper to derive social network datasets at scale (Hui, 2016; Valente & Pitts, 2017). Social network analysts use numerous mathematical techniques and a variety of tools to provide quantitative and visual representations of the properties of a network and the entities that comprise it (Bartlett & Reynolds, 2015). Various measures have been developed over time, for example, to represent interaction among actors, identify how influential each actor is, detect subgroups and communities, examine strong or weak ties and find the network topology and strength (Choudhary & Singh, 2015).

A commonly examined notion is 'centrality' which gives insight into "the extent a person occupies a prominent or important position in the network" (Valente et al., 2015, p. 4). Several measures have been developed to arrive at descriptions of centrality, including, 'degree centrality,' 'betweenness centrality,' and 'closeness centrality' (Choudhary & Singh, 2015). 'Degree centrality' counts the number of direct links of an entity to other entities. Put differently, it helps identify the persons with the greatest number of connections, which often are key influencers in a network. 'Betweenness centrality' measures the proximity of an entity to other entities in a network. High-betweenness nodes may indicate the person is an important gatekeeper or 'bridge' that connects disparate regions of a network, and may therefore have a high degree of control over the flow of information users in a specific part of the network. Finally, 'closeness centrality' is measured as the mean length of distances between an entity and all other entities in a network. Low-closeness may indicate it may be difficult to communicate (Bartlett & Reynolds, 2015; Choudhary & Singh, 2015).

Social media SNA may be a promising tool for a variety of evaluation purposes. To give just a glimpse, SNA techniques can be used alongside other methods to identify and develop an understanding of online communities that are supportive of violent extremism and how the communities evolve (Fairlie, 2016; Marcellino, Smith, Paul, & Skrabala, 2017; van der Hulst, 2008). They can be used to gain insight in how and what information flows among people in a network, and can help to reveal the structure through which influence is exerted (Waldman & Verga, 2016). The use of SNA may also provide information that can help distinguish within the target audience, for instance to separate those that are more engaged with extremist groups from those that are merely curious in extremist material, which may benefit targeting (Berger, 2016). Likewise, SNA techniques may help to discern the most influential members in a network. In this regard, a relevant example is provided by Carter, Maher, and Neumann (2014) who used an approach grounded in SNA to identify the most prominent sources of information and influence among Western foreign fighters. Similarly, it could be used to identify those most capable of swaying supporters away from extremist groups and to discern other roles in social networks such as 'bridges' (Fairlie, 2016; Marcellino et al., 2017).

SNA is an emerging field and applying it to social media presents a variety of challenges. One of these challenges is defining the boundary of the network: "Analysts need to make informed decision in determining which links, seed accounts or websites are to be targeted for analysis, for this is where the nature of the network in question is hinged" (Hui, 2016, p. 333). Furthermore, as suggested in the previous section, there are several other operational and practical challenges and limitations when it comes to collecting relational data from social media (Hui, 2016, p. 333).

5.4.8 Other evaluation methods

5.4.8.1 Expert and gatekeeper reviews

It is often helpful to elicit input and judgement from subject-matter experts, professionals in the field, and intermediary organizations. Experts could, for instance, include those with considerable knowledge of the intended audience and the subject matter of violent extremism, those with expertise and experience in fields such as communications and technology, or people who have experience in counter-messaging campaigns. Eliciting expert judgment can take a variety of forms in different phases. One area in which experts can fruitfully contribute is pre-testing. Expert reviews are argued to be particularly beneficial as they often help to shed light on an issue and trouble spots that may not be identified with other forms of pre-testing (Weinreich, 2011).

Eliciting input from gatekeepers may also prove advantageous (Atkin & Freimuth, 2012; Weinreich, 2011). Gatekeepers are those actors that can act as intermediaries towards intended audiences. For instance, because they control distribution channels that are frequently visited by the target audience. As such, their approval or disapproval of messages and materials could potentially impact upon program success. Besides providing further insights, soliciting their involvement in pre-testing may be contribute to enhanced cooperation, and hence, may benefit the execution of a program (Atkin & Freimuth, 2012).

5.4.8.2 Anecdotes and testimonials

The stories and testimonials of individual people can provide insight into the effects of a campaign at *a personal level*. For instance, these stories might come from members of the target audience that directly reach out in response to a campaign. Interviews with 'formers' – especially those radicalized in the past few years – could potentially also shed light on the role of counter-messaging in their process of disengagement or de-radicalization (RAN, 2015). In and by themselves, such anecdotal evidence does not prove anything about the program. However, it can be used to give meaning or color to quantitative measures and bring to life the people behind the statistics (Weinreich, 2011; Paul et al., 2015).

5.5 Summary

In this chapter, we have addressed the question of how to measure the effectiveness of online counter-messaging programs (research question 6). While in general it is very difficult to establish an effect of a policy or measure in CVE (e.g., Noordegraaf et al., 2016), we have specified various methods that can be employed to at least gain some insight into the potential effectiveness of a counter-messaging campaign. In doing so, it is important to distinguish between the formative evaluation (is the program well-designed, opening the black box: how is the program supposed to work and is it theoretically driven?), the process evaluation (has the program been skillfully executed?) and the summative evaluation (does it result in the desired effect?).

In terms of online monitoring, a combination of awareness (e.g., reach and views) and engagement metrics (e.g., clicks, likes, shares, comments and emoji responses) can provide some insight into the extent to which a counter-messaging campaign achieved its desired *online* effect, as defined in the goals and objectives in terms of reaching and engaging an audience (Reynolds & Tuck, 2016), which can or cannot be related to *offline* behavior.

Several other, more traditional, research techniques can give further insight in the potential effectiveness of a counter-messaging campaign. First, interviews and focus groups can provide important (often qualitative) information about the reception of online materials (useful in the formative phase), but can also provide input into the interpretation of quantitative data in the summative evaluation phase. Second, while online surveys may offer quick results, they may not always reach the intended audience, partly due to the self-selection bias (i.e., only those with a vague interest will participate in a study). Third, experiments (either offline or online) may provide good insight into the cause-and-effect-relationship (e.g., do people respond differently to message A compared with message B?). Fourth, "netnography" is a form of ethnography adapted for the analysis of social media and online communities: it makes use of data usually obtained from observations of people in their regular social media environments. This non-obtrusive manner of collecting data can be useful for sensitive issues, such as counter-messages. Fifth, sentiment analysis is a method to distract the overall evaluation or sentiment towards a counter-messaging campaign (via Natural Language Processing – NLP). A more elaborated content analysis also picks up the specific frames or ideas that were put forward in a particular online setting or community. Finally, social network analyses may give insight into the structure of a group (i.e., who plays a central role?) and potentially how this might change over time, possibly due to a counter-messaging campaign; however, it is difficult to reliably relate an outcome to the counter-messaging campaign, as it always possible that another factor has caused the change in the structure of the social network.

Thus, while at the moment it is still very difficult to establish with great certainty the effect of an online counter-messaging campaign, we do believe that some of the research methods that we have outlined may contribute at least to a better understanding of how (some elements of) a campaign may be perceived and responded to by (individuals in) an audience.

6

THE ROLE OF THE
GOVERNMENT

In this chapter, we examine the following research question: what can the role of the government be in relation to counter-messaging efforts? Before we do so, we shortly discuss the measures that governments have available to counter Salafi-Jihadi propaganda online (Section 6.1). Subsequently, we address this question by examining the potential role of the government in counter-messaging (Section 6.2). We will also discuss other steps governments may take, including developing and streamlining its own strategic communications (Section 6.3), fostering public–private partnerships (Section 6.4), supporting efforts at the grassroots level (Section 6.5.), building capacity (Section 6.6), stimulating evaluation and research (Section 6.7) and encouraging and supporting educational initiatives (Section 6.8). We summarize the main points of this chapter in Section 6.9.

6.1 Negative and positive measures

In terms of the online means that governments have available to counter the influence of Salafi-Jihadi and other violent extremist groups on the internet and social media, we can distinguish between 'negative' and 'positive' measures (Brown & Pearson, 2018; Davies et al., 2016; Neumann, 2012). Negative measures are aimed at reducing and restricting the supply of violent extremist content on the internet and social media (Neumann, 2012). These include efforts to "block, filter, take-down or censor extremist content" (Hussain & Saltman, 2014, p. 10). 'Positive' measures are aimed at reducing the appeal of and demand for such content. Counter-messaging can be put forward as one example (Neumann, 2012).

Negative measures such as 'takedowns' have been an important component of Western governments' strategies to curb the online influence of violent extremists groups and their supporters. For instance, in 2010, the British government opened the Counterterrorism Internet Referral Unit (CTIRU) which seeks to remove extremist content from websites hosted in the UK (Brown & Pearson, 2018; Brocato, 2015; Logan, 2016). In 2015, the European Union mandated Europol to establish a similar initiative, the EU

Box 6.1 EU Internet Referral Unit

In July 2016, Europol established a dedicated unit to address terrorist propaganda and related violent extremist activities on the internet (Europol, 2015). The EU Internet Referral Unit, which is based at Europol's European Counter Terrorism Centre (ECTC), was set up to act as: "as a central service for all EU Member States and third party cooperation partners, helping to reduce terrorist propaganda content on the Internet, while building partnerships with the private sector (to promote 'selfregulation' by online service providers" (Europol, 2016, p. 3).

When it comes to countering violent extremist influence on the internet, it describes its core tasks as: providing strategic and operational analysis to support member states; detecting and flagging relevant online content and sharing it with online service providers and other partners; and carrying out and supporting referral processes in cooperation with the industry.

According to its own figures of December 2017, the unit has assessed in total 42,066 pieces of content since its establishment. This triggered in total 40,714 decisions for referral across over 80 platforms in multiple languages. The content flagged for referrals has been removed in 86 percent of the cases (Europol, 2018).

Internet Referral Unit (EU IRU; see Box 6.1), to address terrorist propaganda on the internet and social media (Europol, 2015). Governments in Europe (including the British, the German, and the French governments) have also sought to hold private companies such as Facebook, Twitter and YouTube responsible for hosting violent extremist content (Rocca, in press). To illustrate, Germany issued the Network Enforcement Act – also known as 'NetzDG' – which came into effect on January 1, 2018. Under this law, social media platforms face fines of up to €50 million when they systemically fail to delete illegal content (Echikson & Knodt, 2018).

Negative measures have their limitations and problems (Briggs & Feve, 2013; Brocato, 2015; Brown & Pearson, 2018; Davies et al., 2016; Reed, Ingram, & Whittaker, 2017; Rocca, in press). For instance, the amount off Salafi-Jihadi content online is so large it is impossible to sift through it all. In addition, it is a game of 'whack-a-mole,' as social media accounts and websites that are taken down will simply reappear (elsewhere). Finally, negative measures may lead Salafi-Jihadi groups to migrate to other, more privacy-enhanced platforms, which may be more difficult to monitor by government and intelligence agencies. Of course, the latter can be viewed more positively, as these platforms do not have as big a reach as mainstream platforms such as Twitter. Besides this, there are issues around civil liberties (e.g., free speech) and with identifying what exactly constitutes extremist content.

Despite these issues, some authors have shown that negative measures can have an impact. For instance, Berger and Morgan (2015, p. 56) found preliminary evidence that Twitter's take down of ISIS-affiliated accounts "limited the ISIS network's ability to grow and spread." Berger and Perez (2016) found that those who repeatedly established new accounts after suspension suffered significant reductions in their follower counts. They also found that networks were disrupted by suspension, and that amount of pro-ISIS content available on Twitter was limited as, typically, all of a user's tweets were deleted after suspension. A more recent study (Conway et al., 2018, p. 12) suggests that take downs of pro-ISIS accounts

> severely affected IS's ability to develop and maintain robust and influential communities on Twitter. As a result, pro-IS Twitter activity has largely been reduced to tactical use of throwaway accounts for distributing links to pro-IS content on other platforms, rather than as a space for public IS support and influencing activity.

Yet, Conway et al. (2018) also found that other Jihadist accounts were subject to much less pressure and disruption and point out that ISIS and other Salafi-Jihadi groups remain active on a wide range of platforms.

In any case, it seems clear that governments should not limit their attention to negative measures. Rather, we suggest that countering the influence of Salafi-Jihadi groups and their supporters online requires a multifaceted approach that involves both negative and positive measures (e.g., Reed et al., 2017; Rocca, in press). One of the positive measures that many governments and intragovernmental organizations have embraced and promoted is counter-messaging.

Governments across the world have established their own websites and engaged in social media campaigns to negate the messaging of Salafi-Jihadi and other violent extremist and terrorist groups and promote their own 'national values' (Brown & Pearson, 2018). The earlier mentioned 'Stop Jihadism,' 'Say no to Terror,' and 'Think Again, Turn Away' campaigns are only three examples of efforts that have been undertaken by governments. Yet, as we will discuss in the next section, governments should act with caution if they aim to directly counter violent extremist messaging.

6.2 Counter-messaging by the government

Although government agencies have engaged in direct forms of counter-messaging, they are not well-positioned to do so because they typically lack the necessary credibility among relevant audiences (e.g., Aistrope, 2016; Briggs & Feve, 2013; RAN, 2015; van Ginkel, 2015; Waldman & Verga, 2016). In this regard, there was also general consensus among the experts interviewed for this study. For instance, Kruglanksi[1] proposed that "The government has very little credibility. So, you know, to the extent that these videos are presented as coming from the government, this undermines their credibility." Based on a similar notion, Aly[2] asserts, "It can't be done by government. The minute government wants to do it, everyone will run away."

One of the problems that plagues their counter-messaging efforts is that governments tend to suffer from a so-called 'say-do gap' (Aistrope, 2016; Briggs & Feve, 2013; Cheong, 2018; Ingram & Reed, 2016; Reed, 2017b; Romaniuk, 2015). The say-do gap refers to the perceived incongruities between what governments say and what they do (e.g., Reed et al., 2017; Romaniuk, 2015). This gap may not only render counter-messaging ineffective, but may also lead efforts to backfire. The say-do gap is often leveraged in Salafi-Jihadi propaganda against the West (Ingram & Reed, 2016). For instance, Ingram and Reed (2016, p. 7) suggests that:

> throughout the so-called War on Terror, it was often the West's perceived say-do gap – whether the use of torture in Abu Ghraib and Guantanamo Bay, the trumped up case for the war in Iraq or 'redlines' in Syria not backed up by military action – that was leveraged in propaganda by Al-Qaeda and its affiliates.

It should also be noted that some experts have argued that past government attempts to challenge Salafi-Jihadi messaging in a confrontational manner have actually served to embolden and dignify them. In fact, it is even posited that Salafi-Jihadi have been able to leverage these efforts to reach a broader audience. In this regard, the 'Think Again, Turn Away' campaign of the US state department is often mentioned as a primary example (e.g., Edelman, 2014; Katz, 2014; see Box 4.9, Chapter 4).

On a more practical level, bureaucratic and operational constraints as well as low risk tolerance may make it difficult for government actors to communicate timely, responsively and assertively, and hence, effectively (Bole & Kallmyer, 2016; Briggs & Feve, 2013). For instance, Briggs and Feve (2013, p. 10) suggest that "the need for institutional sign-off on communications often means that governments are slow to respond and unable to make the kinds of bold statements that are more likely to have an impact with the intended target audiences."

Thus, the ability of governments to directly engage in counter-messaging is described as limited at best and counterproductive at worst. If they do want to address extremist discourses directly, which, according to some authors, may in some cases be appropriate (e.g., Briggs & Feve, 2013; van Ginkel, 2015), they must be careful that they are not backed in a defensive stance or forced into rebuttals that may reinforce the extremist discourse (Briggs & Feve, 2013). Furthermore, they should avoid creating, and aim to minimize, the 'say-do gap,' otherwise such efforts may well be undermined and could backfire (Reed et al., 2017).

6.3 Developing and streamlining government strategic communications

While government actors may not be well placed to confront violent-extremist messaging head on, they can develop and streamline their own strategic communications regarding issues of relevance to countering violent extremism (e.g., Briggs & Feve, 2013; Davies et al., 2016; van Ginkel, 2015; Waldman & Verga, 2016). Of course, in complex governmental systems, different branches do not always speak with the same voice. Governments should strive to develop and implement a coherent and consistent strategic communication policy (Briggs & Feve, 2013). Among other things, to ensure that their "positions and policies are clearly articulated and directed to the right audiences," and "actions that are especially helpful in building relationships with key constituencies are amplified" (Briggs & Feve, 2013, p. 11). So what kind of practical suggestions have been proposed in this area?

Governments are recommended to clearly and proactively communicate and explain their own foreign policy choices in relation to sensitive topics, such as their involvement in conflict zones (e.g., Briggs & Feve, 2013; Briggs & Silverman, 2014; Hussain & Saltman, 2014; Russel & Rafiq, 2016; van Ginkel, 2015). It has been suggested that anger about what is (alleged to be) happening in these conflict zones as well as empathy with the people being affected may play a role in radicalization processes and can be a driver for foreign fighter travel (Frenett & Silverman, 2016; see also Bakker & Grol, 2015; Briggs & Silverman, 2014; Neumann, 2015). In this regard, other advice is that governments make more visible what they are doing in terms of humanitarian aid and assistance to populations in conflict zones such as Syria, Iraq and the like (Bakker & Grol, 2015; Briggs & Silverman, 2014; Cheong, 2018). Furthermore, governments may want to identify and communicate practical and legal alternatives for those who are moved to help (Bakker & Grol, 2015; Briggs & Silverman, 2014).

It is also advised that policies and measures adopted to address national security risks are brought to attention (Russel & Rafiq, 2016; van Ginkel, 2015). For instance, in relation to the foreign fighter phenomenon, there are indications that youngsters expect to find thrills and adventure, but the risks involved with travelling, as well as the grim reality of the terrorist lifestyle, are underplayed. Some authors have therefore suggested that (national and local) governments should communicate and specify what the legal consequences are for travelling, in addition to pointing out the risks involved (Briggs & Silverman, 2014).

Another recommendation that can be made is that authorities communicate that they are committed to tackling extremist violence and terrorism generally, and minimize the perception that policies to counter violent extremism are exclusively attuned to (a cross-section of) Muslim communities. (Berger, 2016; Waldman & Verga, 2016). As we have suggested in Chapter 4, sending the opposite signal may feed the discourse that Muslims are a threat, and could contribute to feelings of stigmatization and alienation among the Muslim populations (Berger, 2016).

Related to this, governments may want to consider distinguishing programs from each other when they communicate what they are doing (Waldman & Verga, 2016; Romaniuk, 2015). Programs that may serve preventative purposes, such as community and relationship-building initiatives, may be undermined when they are branded or framed as efforts to counter violent extremism (CVE). Doing so may give targeted communities the impression that they are 'suspect,' leading to feelings of stigmatization, and may discourage community members from engaging with such initiatives. As pointed out by Romaniuk (2015, p. 181): "there is a need to elaborate measures without isolating the very communities whose engagement is sought, including through considering alternatives to the CVE label, which has sometimes been a positive liability."

In addition to developing and streamlining their own communications, some authors contend that governments can fruitfully engage in alternative messaging in order to reinforce values that stand in opposition to violent extremism (e.g., freedom, democracy, tolerance; Briggs & Feve, 2013; Davies et al., 2016). However, as indicated earlier, governments should be aware these efforts may also suffer from a perceived 'say-do gap' by audiences (Berger, 2016). Messages promoting values such as democracy may, for instance, be difficult to reconcile with the fact that Western governments have engaged and collaborated with various authoritarian regimes around the world. Indeed, projecting a message is not enough when it is not backed up by deeds, or worse, if deeds actually contradict what is being proclaimed (van Ginkel, 2015).

6.4 Fostering public-private partnerships

Community-based organizations and grassroots networks are better positioned to act as agents for messaging activities than governments. Specifically, such organizations are likely to be more aware of what goes on with (vulnerable) members of a given community, may be better able to judge what types of communications are likely resonate, inspire, and mobilize others to become active in challenging the online influence of Salafi-Jihadi and other violent extremist groups (RAN, 2015). Waldman and Verga (2016, p. 14) concur, and also argue they are:

more likely to be trusted and invested with moral authority by community members, making them better able to take conversations with individuals offline where they are more likely to be effective. Communities may also be better able to cultivate nuanced relationships with non-violent extremists whom governments might not want to be seen as endorsing.

Yet these actors often lack recourses (e.g., funding and capacity), expertise and competencies to carry out counter-messaging activities effectively (Briggs & Feve, 2013, RAN, 2015). Moreover, it has been noted that their counter-messaging efforts are frequently based on noble intentions, but not on solid and rigorous research (Russel & Rafiq, 2016). While governments may be ill-positioned to engage in alternative and counter-messaging work themselves because of the credibility gap, they do have necessary resources and may be motivated to support the work of such actors (RAN, 2015). In addition, there are many academics that possess valuable expertise that could be leveraged for counter-narrative work. They could give a helping hand in mediating between governments and communities, developing original counter-messaging programs and monitoring their effects. Yet it has been argued that the number of academics who have been invited to do so is limited (Holtmann, 2013). Furthermore, private sectors parties, such as technology and social media firms, and advertisement and marketing specialists, could lend valuable skills, expertise, funds, services, and access to tools that could enable civil society actors to be more effective in their work. However, these parties often lack knowledge of violent extremism and may have (reputational) concerns about working in this particular area. Moreover, their primary focus will be on their core business, which could be reflected in a lack of time or investments in this domain (RAN, 2015).

Given the complementary roles these different actors could potentially play, it is frequently argued that governments can fulfill a particularly valuable function by encouraging and brokering partnerships between civil society and the private sector. Governments may establish an infrastructure to streamline and sustain such partnerships, and may provide funding or other in-kind support to such partnership initiatives (Briggs & Feve, 2013; Briggs & Frenett, 2014; Neumann, 2012; RAN, 2015; Helmus, York, & Chalk, 2013; Russel & Rafiq, 2016; Waldman & Verga, 2016). Importantly though, we suggest that governments should remain at arms-length, and should try to repress any urge to front such initiatives or influence the content that is developed and relayed through such efforts. Moreover, it is vital that developed funding models and infrastructures do not 'contaminate' any efforts undertaken, as endorsement of (or association with) the government may well serve as a 'kiss of death,' in the sense that it may serve to discredit such initiatives (RAN, 2015).

This is a position echoed by various experts that were interviewed for this book as well. For instance, Kruglanski[1] argues that the extent to which campaign content is associated with the government will undermine its credibility. While he acknowledges that the government can potentially facilitate with providing an infrastructure as well as support, training, and funding, "the government has to remain in the shadow [...] the sponsorship of the government is not an advantage, it is a disadvantage." In line with this, the RAN issue report concludes that governments essentially "need to help to create an infrastructure that is community-owned and operated, but that is non-governmental in how it operates" (RAN, 2015). Conversely, Aly[2] argues: "the best thing governments can do is, to help build the civil society structures and infrastructure to deal with this, but they have to be prepared to walk away and do it at arm's length."

6.5 Empowering effective messengers

Counter messages and alternative messages are assumed to be most effective when they stem from credible messengers. In Chapter 4, we pointed out that various actors at the grassroots level are commonly assumed to be effective messengers. These include youth, family members, former violent extremists and survivors. Therefore, it may potentially be worthwhile for governments to encourage efforts that solicit involvement of these actors.

Young people in particular are often mentioned as actors who may be able to act as efficient messengers, mentioned in the literature as well as by some of our interviewees.[3,4] Furthermore, it is suggested young people may well be able to create content that resonates with their peers. Hence, facilitating initiatives for youth engagement may be beneficial (RAN, 2015). In addition, they can also look into ways to support community and/or youth-generated online initiatives that are already out there and may be popular among relevant target audiences (e.g., Briggs & Feve, 2013; Helmus et al., 2013; Richardson, 2013). However, grassroots actors – youth in particular – may feel reluctant to work on campaigns when they are framed in terms of 'countering violent extremism' as well as to associate themselves with the government (RAN, 2015). Hence, it is argued that it would be more suitable to solicit their participation in campaigns that may be relevant for countering violent extremism, such as those related to issues such as social cohesion or non-violent political activism (which may in fact be government critical) (Helmus et al., 2013; RAN, 2015). Furthermore, as argued earlier, it is vital that governments limit their involvement and allow for operational independence.

Governments can also support efforts that solicit the involvement of formers and survivors. However, as mentioned in Section 4.4.2.1, there are numerous practical and (in the case of formers, legal) challenges that stand in the way of soliciting their participation in initiatives. For instance, formers may not want to have public profiles or may want to leave that part of their life behind them (Hedayah & ICCT, 2014). Those that are in fact willing to contribute to efforts, often do not have the time, competencies or resources to effectively do so. Hence, governments may want to consider ways in which they can incentivize and facilitate formers and survivors to play a role (Briggs & Feve, 2013; RAN, 2015). For instance, the ISD suggests assisting formers on an 'ad hoc basis.' For instance, "through the provision of contacts to expand their reach, help in unlocking independent funds for specific project-based activities, or brokering offers of in-kind support" (Briggs & Feve, 2013, p. 19).

Of course, governments should make certain that the necessary checks and balances and accountability mechanisms are in place before deciding upon supporting or funding projects involving formers (Briggs & Feve, 2013, p. 19). In this regard, it is important that formers are carefully vetted and selected, before they are supported in engaging in any work in this area (Zeiger, 2016). In addition, it is important these actors themselves are made aware of the potential personal risks involved (Briggs & Feve, 2013; Waldman & Verga, 2016). Lastly, governments should take notice that supporting formers may give rise to contention among parts of the general population (QIASS, 2013).

6.6 Building capacity

A barrier that may stand in the way of grassroots actors who want to get involved in or set-up their own initiatives is a gap in skills and expertise. As such, governments could lend support to capacity building, for instance by establishing or seeding training programs (e.g., Briggs & Feve, 2013; Briggs & Frenett, 2014; Hedayah & ICCT, 2014; Helmus et al., 2013; RAN, 2015; van Ginkel, 2015; Waldman & Verga, 2016).

In developing training programs, governments are advised to involve private sector parties such as technology and social media firms, marketing and advertising companies, and other parties with experience in relevant domains which could contribute to the value and effectiveness of the programs (Briggs & Feve, 2013; Briggs & Frenett, 2014; Hedayah & ICCT, 2014; Helmus et al., 2013; Waldman & Verga, 2016). Private sector organizations could lend help with providing (technical) guidance on such things as search-engine optimization techniques, marketing and crowd-sourcing strategies, and digital media-making. These training programs are ideally delivered by community-based organizations in order to ensure that these are optimally attuned to the needs of key audiences (Briggs & Feve, 2013). In addition, once such training programs have been established, it would be worthwhile that efforts focus on training the trainers (Hedayah & ICCT, 2014).

In recent years, several such training programs have been established. One example is the Civil Society Empowerment Program of the European Union's Internet Forum, which aims to support "civil society, grass roots organisations and credible voices" in its counter-messaging efforts. This program, which was rolled out across Europe in 2017, is intended to provide participants "with the skills needed to design and implement an effective, convincing and credible online campaign, and to ensure it reaches the target audience" (DG HOME, 2019a, "how?," para. 2). Some of its training material has been made available in multiple languages on the European directorate-general for migration and home affairs website.

Related to this, governments could collect and disseminate information and best practices regarding existing programs and campaigns to those interested in counter-messaging. There are already various interesting online 'resource hubs' that house valuable documents and materials, many of which have been supported by governments (some examples are included in Box 6.2). Supporting the translation of key resources and providing assistance to getting these to relevant audiences is another area in which governments can assist (Briggs & Feve, 2013).

6.7 Supporting evaluation and research

While many of the recommendations that have been put forward in regard to counter-messaging appear reasonable, we would like to emphasize the approach still lacks thorough grounding research. "There is little evidence to support the effectiveness of counternarratives and many of its underlying assumptions have been called into question" (Reed et al., 2017, p. 8). There are hardly any thorough evaluations available (e.g., Berger, 2016; Beutel et al., 2016; Ferguson, 2016; Lee, 2018; Waldman & Verga, 2016). Already in 2013, Von Behr et al. (2013, p. 35) argued that

> the absence of a robust, comprehensive evaluation of counter-narrative work online is a concern – not least because it is not clear whether the work is well targeted or effective in changing the attitudes or behaviours of those vulnerable individuals engaging with radicalizing material online.

Three years later, Berger (2016, p. 8) concluded: "There is no shortage of literature discussing the need for metrics to evaluate CVE success, but that has not translated into the implementation of actual evaluation on any significant scale." We believe that this still is the case. As we have argued, this makes it difficult to come to valid pre-requisites for an effective counter-messaging initiative. While it may be difficult to measure 'effect' (see Chapter 5), if any new activities in this realm are to be supported, governments should encourage that they are consistently and thoroughly

Box 6.2 Online resources

The Radicalization Awareness Network

The Radicalization Awareness Network (RAN) was created by the European council to serve as an "umbrella network connecting people involved in preventing radicalisation and violent extremism throughout Europe" (DG HOME, 2019b, "RAN Working Groups," para. 1). The RAN connects over 3000 people across Europe, including teachers, youth workers, civil society representatives, healthcare professionals, academics, local authorities and those working in the criminal justice system. The RAN is structured around a number of thematic working groups. Among them, the 'Communication and Narratives' working group focuses "on the delivery of both on- and offline communication that offers alternatives or that counters extremist propaganda and/or challenges extremist ideas" (DG HOME, 2019c, "Communication and Narratives Working Group (RAN C&N)," para. 1). It gathers insights on counter-messaging content, its target audiences, credible messengers, and ways of dissemination. The working group has released a range of papers through which gathered knowledge has been shared. "The Preventing Radicalisation to Terrorism and Violent Extremism: Approaches and Practices" collection is one of the main products of the broader network. It provides an elaborate overview of various insights, lessons learned and practices that have come out of various working groups.

The Institute for Strategic Dialogue's Counter-Narrative Toolkit

An important aim of the London-based Institute for Strategic Dialogue (ISD) is to empower civil society networks committed to tackling violent extremism (ISD, 2018). "The Counter-Narrative Toolkit" is one example of their work, an online resource that offers a free online step-by-step guide for any individual or organization looking to engage in counter-messaging. According to the website it is not intended to be comprehensive, yet it provides a very useful and accessible beginners' guide for those with little or no experience in campaigning. Besides offering general insights in some 'best practices,' it provides video-tutorials, and offers a detailed downloadable 'counter-narrative handbook' (Tuck & Silverman, 2016), as well as several case studies that can serve as an inspiration. The toolkit was funded by Facebook. It was inspired by an earlier pilot project with Jigsaw (formerly Google Ideas), who also funded some of its video content (Counter-Narrative Toolkit, n.d.).

VOX-Pol Network of Excellence

VOX-Pol Network of Excellence (NoE) is a European Union Framework Programme 7 (FP7)-funded academic research network focusing on researching violent online political extremism. It aims to provide an "establishment of a robust partnering, research, training, and dissemination network that has as its core function comprehensive research, analysis, debate, and critique of topics in and issues surrounding Violent Online Political Extremism" (VOX-pol, 2019, "VOX-Pol: An Introduction," para. 1). The dedicated website provides a comprehensive and regularly updated collection of publications related to various aspects of online violent political extremism which can be used as an educational and research resource.

Hedayah's Counter Narrative Library

The Hedayah Center, which is based in Abu Dhabi in the UAE, was set up to act as a "premier international hub for CVE policy makers, practitioners and researchers to enhance understanding and share good practices to build the capacity of CVE actors across the globe to promote tolerance, stability and security" (Hedayah, 2019a, "strategic Significance," para. 1). One of the initiatives the center has launched to encourage counter-messaging is the Counter-Narrative Library. The library provides a portal where governments, civil society actors and frontline practitioners can access content, toolkits, and documentation on good practices (Hedayah, 2019b).

Against Violent Extremism network

As mentioned in Chapter 4, Against Violent Extremism (AVE) is a private sector partnership between the Institute for ISD, Jigsaw (formerly Google Ideas), the Gen Next Foundation and Rehabstudio and is managed by ISD in London. Its official aim is to "prevent the recruitment of 'at risk' youths and encourage the disengagement of those already involved" (Against Violent Extremism, n.d.-b, "about the Against Violent Extremism ..." para. 1), and is dedicated to countering all forms of violent extremism (e.g., far-right, far-left, Al-Qaeda-linked or inspired, and gangs). It intends to leverage lessons, experiences and networks of individuals who have dealt first-hand with extremism, such as formers and victims. Through a dedicated website and YouTube channel, members can connect, exchange information, ideas and perspectives, find potential partners and investors, and project their messages to a wider audience.

monitored and evaluated. As has been noted elsewhere, whenever possible, these evaluations should be made publicly available in order to facilitate comparison and analysis so they can inform future initiatives (Romaniuk, 2015). Ideally, outcomes are shared in a way that is operationally useful to citizens and groups interested in engaging in such efforts (Waldman & Verga, 2016).

At the same time, it may be worthwhile for governments to support further research and (online) experimentation to identify meaningful measures or proxies of success in changing attitudes and/or behaviors of specific target audiences (Waldman & Verga, 2016) or, more generally, meaningful approaches to come to these measures. Also, gaining a deeper understanding of the

> [t]he process by which terrorists' [or extremists'] audiences make meaning from the violent extremist narrative and the variables – demographic, contextual, individual and group related – that effect these meanings could help ensure that counter-narratives are equally as effective as the violent extremist narrative appears to be.
>
> (Aly, 2016, "Conclusion," para. 1)

Hence, more contextualized research on how audiences engage with, interpret, and reproduce extremist messaging online and how this relates to violent radicalization could inform future efforts in the field of counter-messaging. These are by no means the only topics that deserve attention; a recent list compiled by Schmid and Forest (2018) of 150 un- and under-researched topics in the study of terrorism and counter-terrorism puts forward a variety of relevant issues that deserve further attention, among which, perhaps not unsurprisingly, is "Counter-messaging and counter-narratives – does it work and how?" (Schmid & Forest, 2018, p. 75).

6.8 Increasing resilience through education

While not directly related to counter-messaging, we want to propose that there is another area in which the government could play an important role. Bartlett and Miller (2010, p. 38) of the British think-thank Demos argue that: "While government cannot tell people what to think, they can help teach people how to think." Several studies and reports point to the importance of strengthening people's ability to critically appraise the online (sources of) information they encounter through educational programs (e.g., Briggs & Feve, 2013; Hussain & Saltman, 2014; Miller & Bartlett, 2012; Neumann, 2013b; Reynolds & Scott, 2016). It is often difficult to distinguish between legitimate and false information in the digital world. While young people may be adept in using the internet and social media, they frequently lack the appropriate skills to thoroughly evaluate and judge the content they consume and share in these spaces. This could potentially make them vulnerable to negative online influences (e.g., conspiracy theories, misinformation, and scams), including radicalizing influences (Miller & Bartlett, 2012). In enhancing children's and young people's digital literacy and critical consumption skills, schools and various community actors can play an important role. Government efforts could perhaps focus on promoting and supporting the development, implementation, and evaluation of undertakings in this area (in Box 6.3, we discuss an example of such an initiative). Also, in this case, the government could act as a hub in collecting and disseminating information and best practices, as well as supporting academic research in this area.

Box 6.3 'Digital Citizens: Countering Extremism Online'

A report from the United Kingdom think-tank Demos (Reynolds & Scott, 2016), which sets out the findings of a pilot project involving a digital citizenship intervention developed in cooperation with Bold Creative provides some indication that developing young people's critical thinking and digital literacy skills can prove effective in improving their resilience to online extremist influences. The pilot, which was conducted under the UK's Home Office's 'Prevent' Innovation Fund, involved developing, testing, and evaluating new resources to help schools tackle online radicalization.

The design of the intervention was informed by interviews with 11 key stakeholders and a review of nine higher quality evaluations and meta-evaluations of similar CVE interventions from the UK, US, and Australia (Reynolds & Scott, 2016). Rather than focusing on countering the ideologies underlying extremism, the intervention sought to increase resilience to online radicalization through a skills-based teaching approach (Demos, 2016). More specifically, it intended to "teach young people how to recognise online propaganda and manipulation, understand how social media change how we communicate, and develop a sense of responsibility over their online social network" (Reynolds & Scott, 2016, p. 12).

Four schools took part in a pilot of the intervention. The post-pilot evaluation revealed it had produced statistically significant improvements on all three focus areas mentioned above. Moreover, the intervention was evaluated favorably by both teachers and participants. Although the results are promising, the report also points out that participants and comparison group members were not selected randomly and that the sample size was small. As such, the report argues that it is difficult to draw any general conclusions about the effectiveness of this pilot project (Reynolds & Scott, 2016).

Related to this, Davies (2018) provided a useful review of educational initiatives aimed at preventing violent extremism. She proposes various other ways in which educational initiatives can play a role in increasing resilience to violent extremism influences among young people, providing a typology and review of myriad interventions that take place in schools and higher education, and through extra-curricular activities for youth. She highlights a range of principles that may be taken into account when developing such initiatives. Among them, is that such initiatives do well to "focus less on what [youth] should not become and more on what they actively become" (Davies, 2018, p. 49). Furthermore, rather than being moralizing or prescriptive, programs should stimulate independent thinking and reflection on ethical dilemmas and concerns. She also pointed towards the importance of integrating efforts into the broader framework of schools: "The myriad interventions and workshops [aimed at preventing violent extremism], interesting though the students find them, are less than effective in providing permanent resilience unless they are part of a broader framework in the school." In her view, schools can best contribute to preventing violent extremism when strategies to do so are firmly embedded in their permanent safeguarding policies, curriculum structures and teachers' working practices. She argues that the main focus should be on "building a permanent culture in schools where resilience to extremism is just one aspect of a fuller learning of rights, history, religious and ethnic conflict, and community dynamics" (Davies, 2018, pp. 49–50). Governments have a role to play in encouraging, stimulating and facilitating schools to do this.

6.9 Summary

Governments have two categories of measures available to counter the online influence of Salafi-Jihadi groups and their supporters: 'positive' and 'negative' measures. Whilst some authors have questioned the effectiveness of negative measures such as take-downs, other scholars have demonstrated that taking down extremist accounts on platforms such as Twitter can have an impact. Notwithstanding, governments should adopt a multifaceted approach to tackle propaganda of violent extremists online, and not limit themselves to negative measures. Counter-messaging is one of the positive measures that governments have embraced.

Attempts by Western governments to engage in confrontational counter-messaging have been criticized for being ineffective and offering Salafi-Jihadi groups a stage to spread their message. Furthermore, many authors agree that governments lack the necessary credibility to engage in counter-messaging. In part, this is because they often suffer from the so-called 'say-do gap,' which is in fact a primary target of Salafi-Jihadi propaganda against the West. Hence, the ability of governments to engage in counter-messaging is described as limited at best and counterproductive at worst.

While government agencies may not be well-positioned to engage in counter-messaging, it is argued they do have a role to play. First, governments can fruitfully engage in developing and streamlining their own strategic communications. Among other things, it is important that they explain their own actions locally and in an international context. In addition, the government may be able to play a valuable role by facilitating and supporting grassroots and community actors who may be better placed to engage in counter-messaging activities. They can do this by brokering public–private partnerships, and establishing an infrastructure to streamline and sustain them. In addition, they can stimulate efforts at the grassroots level with funding (albeit the government should remain in the shadows), training and expertise.

Importantly though, there is only limited evidence regarding the usefulness of online counter-messaging efforts. Hence, if any new initiatives are to be supported, the government should encourage monitoring and evaluation. At the same time, further research to identify meaningful measures or proxies of success in changing attitudes and/or behaviors of specific target audiences is needed, and governments could play a role in supporting those efforts. Likewise, more exhaustive research is necessary on the way audiences engage, interpret and reproduce extremist messaging online and how it relates to violent radicalization, in order to inform meaningful counter-strategies.

Finally, government efforts could focus on promoting and supporting the development and implementation of educational initiatives, such as programs in the area of strengthening digital literacy and critical consumption skills. This can be achieved by encouraging efforts and evaluation, as well as stimulating knowledge sharing and development, in this area.

Notes

1 Arie Kruglanski, interview, March 8, 2016.
2 Anne Aly, interview, February 25, 2016.
3 Anne Aly, interview, February 25, 2016.
4 Diana Rieger, interview, May 19, 2016.

7

SUMMARY, CONCLUSIONS, LIMITATIONS, AND FUTURE DIRECTIONS

7.1 Introduction

In this report, we have examined the extent to which counter-messaging initiatives via social media can be effective in preventing people from radicalization or can de-radicalize people. We have done so by studying the literature in combination with conducting interviews and focus groups with academics, field workers, young social media experts and some former radical people. In Section 7.2, we present a summary of our answers to the main research questions posed in Chapter 1, the Introduction. In Section 7.3, we discuss more generally the findings from our analysis. In Section 7.4, we describe the most important limitations of the current study. Finally, in Section 7.5, we sketch some potential future directions.

7.2 Summary of answers to research questions

In Chapter 1, we formulated the following research questions and we now present the following answers to these questions:

1   Why and in what manner have Salafi-Jihadi groups exploited social media to spread their propaganda?

The main aim of Salafi-Jihadi propaganda is to convince audiences it adopt a 'competitive system of meaning' or worldview, with the ultimate aim to stimulate behavior that is conducive to their interests. In terms of distribution of their propaganda messages, social media have become highly important in recent years. Messaging has been achieved using mainly YouTube, Twitter, and Facebook. Social media offer various advantages to extremist groups: they are cheap, easy to use, facilitate broad dissemination of messages, and allow them to be part of the mainstream. Furthermore, social media allow them to circumvent interference of intermediaries, such as news agencies. Social media also enable them to reach out to their audience directly and engage them in a conversation. In addition, social media make it easier for audiences to reach out to them. Lastly, social media enable anyone to take part in the production and dissemination of propaganda, allowing them reach audiences outside of their traditional orbit.

2   What is the relation between consumption of violent extremist propagandistic content and radicalization into violent extremism?

The exact nature and extent of the influence of Salafi-Jihadi propaganda on radicalization processes is not yet clear and deserves further study. Nevertheless, the literature suggests propaganda in and by itself is unlikely to lead to radicalization into extremism. However, it may contribute to the process.

3   How can we conceptualize counter-messaging and how has it been used via social media?

For counter-messaging on social media, we identify three domains: (1) counter-messaging (e.g., activities that challenge extremist messages head on); (2) alternative messaging (e.g., activities that aim to provide a positive alternative to extremist messages); and (3) strategic communication by the government (e.g., activities that provide insight into what the government is doing).

4   How feasible is it to prevent or counter violent radicalization with counter-messaging? And for whom may it be effective?

Based on our analysis, we argue that to the extent that people have become more radical, they are less likely to be persuaded by a counter-messaging campaign. They may not pay attention to these messages or even may adopt a stronger attitude in the other direction than intended as a reaction to this persuasive attempt. This may be particularly the case when the aim is to directly confront. Thus, we argue that a counter-messaging campaign might best be used for prevention purposes for a well-defined target group. Specifically, it is best to focus on those individuals who can be identified to show some curiosity or sympathy for extremist groups, but are not yet active supporters.

In addition, we have raised the question whether or not such counter messaging efforts may have some effect on the individuals from radical groups who show a glimpse of doubt about their group. For such individuals, a counter-message may fall on fertile ground and a seed may be planted – although this is highly speculative at the moment and more research is needed to support this notion.

5   What principles can inform the development of a counter-messaging campaign?

In developing a campaign and determining the communication strategy, it is important to give consideration to theory, the audience, extremist messages, goals and objectives, available resources, the message, the message source, channels, methods of dissemination, and the potential risks and limitations of a strategy. First, the application of relevant *theory* is an important strategy to increase the effectiveness of campaigns. Beyond borrowing from existing theory, program planners do well to develop a sound theory of change that explicates how campaign efforts are going to lead to the desired result. With respect to the *audience*, this should be narrowly defined and segmented on the basis of meaningful variables. This can only be done effectively when the target audience is thoroughly examined and understood, hence rigorous audience analysis is necessary.

In addition to studying the audience, it is important to develop an in-depth understanding of the *extremist messages* one aims to counter. This holds in particular in relation to counter-messages. When deciding upon which elements of the Salafi-Jihadi message one aims to counter, we argue it is also important to consider why members of the target audience in question may be drawn to these messages. For example, different motives of radical people may require different content of counter-messages. This is related to the point that, at the outset of a campaign, *goals and objectives* should be delineated that clearly specify which change one aims to achieve in terms of audience knowledge, attitudes or behaviors. Well-defined objectives are specific, measurable, achievable, relevant, and time-bound. Running an effective social media effort also requires adequate *resources* (time, finances, human capital) which should be assessed at the outset of a program, taking into account all relevant stages of a campaign.

Furthermore, *messages* that use narratives have the advantage of using subtle ways to influence people. Moreover, they may overcome various forms of resistance. In addition, double-sided messages (in which one side is being discredited), coupled with a strong emotional appeal may prove to be persuasive. In terms of *sources*, it is clear that they need to be perceived as credible to function as trustworthy messengers. Most likely candidates are former extremists, victims of violence, peers and family, as well as key members of communities and civil society actors. The potential of the government to serve as a credible source might be limited.

In terms of selected *channels*, obviously they should be frequently utilized by the audience one intends to reach. Using multiple channels is argued to be beneficial. Importantly, social media may not be appropriate in all circumstances, and should be considered in combination with offline activities. In terms of *message dissemination*, it is important to think about the timing and frequency with which one posts messages. Also, depending on the purpose of the campaign, it may be beneficial to partner with people and organizations that have already established a strong social media presence and are popular among the target audience. Conversely, it may also be useful to ask established online (news) outlets to share the message. Furthermore, it may be important to create opportunities for audience engagement. Digital advertisements could also help to get the message out, but this also has important limitations.

Finally, we argue it is important to assess the potential risks, challenges and limitations when developing a communication strategy. These might include losing control of the message, counter-campaigns, threats to safety and well-being of messengers, and multi-tier approval processes that hamper campaign efforts, as well as the notoriously difficulty of demonstrating the effect of social media efforts.

6   How can the potential effectiveness of such an effort be determined?

Generally speaking, it is not easy to establish an effect of a policy or measure in CVE (e.g., Noordegraaf et al., 2016). For the potential effectiveness of a counter-message campaign, it is important to distinguish between a formative evaluation, a process evaluation, and a summative evaluation.

Specifically tailored at online interventions, we argue that a combination of awareness (e.g., reach and views) and engagement metrics (e.g., clicks, likes, shares, comments, and emoji responses) can provide some insight into the extent to which a counter-messaging campaign achieved its desired effect in terms of reaching and engaging an audience. More traditional research techniques such as interviews and focus groups can give further insight into the reception of online materials (thus are useful in the formative phase), but can also provide input in the interpretation of quantitative data in the summative evaluation phase. Experiments (either offline or online) offer insight in the cause-and-effect-relationship, while "netnography" makes use of data usually obtained from observations of people in their regular social media environments. Sentiment and content analyses are methods to distract the overall evaluation towards a counter-messaging campaign as well as the specific messages that were put forward in a particular online community. Finally, social network analyses can give insight into the structure of a network, the spread of messages within communities, as well as potential changes in the network.

7   What can be the role of government in relation to counter-messaging efforts?

As argued before, government actors are not well-positioned to act as counter-message producers or messengers, as they lack credibility.

However, they do have an important role to play. First, governments can fruitfully engage in streamlining their own strategic communications in terms of explaining their own actions locally and in an international context. Second, the government can play a valuable role by facilitating grassroots and civil society actors best placed to act as counter-narrative messengers. They can do so by sponsoring such efforts (providing help, expertise, or financial support) as well as by establishing an infrastructure to support these initiatives. Third, they could stimulate thorough monitoring and evaluation, as there is only limited evidence for the effectiveness of counter-messaging efforts. Finally, government efforts could focus on supporting the development of educational programs. For instance, in the area of strengthening digital literacy and critical consumption skills.

7.3 Discussion

Taking into account the insights derived from our literature study, in combination with our interviews, we can draw several conclusions. First, we argue that, in general, the development and implementation of online counter-messages are still in their infancy phases. This seriously undermines the potential to draw any firm conclusions from our analysis at this moment. As such, the arguments presented here need to be treated with caution and deserve further examination at a later date when there is more empirical research available on which to base our arguments.

Second, we argue that the domain of counter-messages is severely hampered by a lack of strong empirical research and thorough evaluations. This is perhaps partly due to the difficulties of doing research with radical people, because they are not easy to recruit as participants. In general, it is also extremely difficult to measure changes in attitudes and beliefs (which may take place over a long term), let alone measuring the effectiveness of any strategy aimed at prevention, because the expected outcome (of prevention) is a non-event. More specifically related to online efforts, the anonymity that the internet provides often makes it impossible to establish precisely who engages with a campaign on social media. This leads to the conclusion that it is virtually impossible to establish a direct connection between counter-messaging campaigns and the prevention of extremism.

Third, given the fact that people increasingly make use of social media, it makes it all the more likely that people may be influenced by them, and also in terms of radicalization. As such, this makes it crucially important to have a thorough understanding of the techniques and strategies employed by radical groups and how they are capable of reaching out to their audiences. However, there are limitations in the use of counter-messages to influence people. In particular, to the extent that radical groups use ideological messages about perceived grievances to stir up feelings of resentment, which are rooted in deep experiences (e.g., in terms of everyday experiences of discrimination of one's group), counter-messages may fail, as they do not directly impact on these actual everyday experiences.

Fourth, our analysis shows that presenting online counter-messages may be most fruitful when used in a prevention context, in which people may still be willing to process the message. Alternatively, in terms of de-radicalization, it might be possible to explore the options to expose individuals who have demonstrated some doubts about their group to specific counter messages. However, ideally, this is not done in an online context, but in an offline context, in order to directly monitor the reactions of the individuals.

7.4 Limitations of the current study

We have tried to answer the research questions using a literature study in combination with interviews and focus groups with experts on radicalization and social media – academics, field workers, social media students, and some former radicals. While this has given us a solid and broad scope of the domain, this study (like any study) has its limitations.

First, because the domain of narratives is covered in various disciplines, such as, amongst others, media studies, history, and psychology, we have drawn from a large body of studies and have tried to present an integration of the ideas from these fields. However, we acknowledge we might not have covered all there is to be found in the scientific literature terms of messages and counter-messages.

In addition, another limitation from the current study is that it has been done while the field is in flux. This means that the current state of affairs, as presented in this report, most likely will be outdated in the near future. As such, the analysis presented here has a "limited warranty" in terms of the time that it is relevant and valid.

Another limitation concerns the fact that there is a great deal of "grey literature": studies or reports by semi-commercial agencies about their own product. We have tried to limit our use of such materials, but in cases where we had few other materials we occasionally had to base our analysis on this grey literature. A further limitation concerns the people we have interviewed and invited for our focus groups. While we have tried to gather a strong line-up of people, including Skype interviews with international experts, as always such a selection is limited given the time and resources available for this study. This means that if we had included more people, we would have broadened our scope. Of course, this could have led to more specific, and slightly different, insights.

Moreover, some people we interviewed were commercially involved in the production of counter-narrative campaigns. While such people are experts in the ins-and-outs of counter-messaging, for them it is also a matter of utmost importance. Arguably, this may undermine their objective focus and impartial judgment on this topic.

Finally, much of the literature on counter-messages is focused on countering Jihadist propaganda and radical groups with a Salafi-Jihadi signature. We should be cautious in generalizing the findings derived from this literature to other groups (e.g., extreme right-wing groups). Furthermore, given that there is hardly any strong empirical research available on many issues related to the subject matter, we had to base some of our analysis on the general literature on persuasion and communication campaigns, as well as some "grey literature." This undermines the options to draw strong conclusions from the current analysis, as one might question the extent to which it is possible to generalize from the general field of persuasion to this particular area of interest. Furthermore, the "grey literature" included studies or reports by semi-commercial agencies that are involved in counter-narrative work. While we have tried to limit our use of such materials, we occasionally had to base our analysis on this grey literature.

7.5 Future directions

In the domain of counter-messaging initiatives via social media, an underlying assumption is that (a) people become radical via radical propaganda messages, and that (b) presenting people with counter-messages is a fruitful manner to undermine this. Both assumptions can be questioned. There is little hard evidence from which causal inferences can be made that interaction with extremist content on social media leads to participation in violent extremism. Furthermore, "The theory that the messages, myths, promises, objectives, glamour and other enticements propagated via violent extremism narratives can be replaced with, or dismantled by, an alternative set of communications is an assumption that remains unproven" (Ferguson, 2016, p. 16). Partly, this is because radicalization is a complex process that may involve a variety of factors and influences and can be triggered by various motives. For example, based on a literature review, Feddes et al. (2015) distinguish between four motives that people can possess:

1   Need for *certainty*: people who feel uncertain may search for groups with a clear identity and focus (i.e., radical groups; Hogg, 2014);
2   Need for *significance/meaning*: people who experience a loss in significance are more open to radical groups (e.g., Kruglanski et al., 2014);
3   Need for *sensation*: people who have a high need for sensation and adventure are more likely to feel attracted to radical groups because this is exciting and might involve weapons, etc. (e.g., Bjørgo, 2011);
4   Need for *justice*: some people search for justice for their group; ideology can play an important role in their radicalization process.

Thus, if one wants to use the method of a counter-message program, one should decide on the goals in terms of which aspect one primarily wants to focus on. It can be any of the four above or any combination of them, because the needs in this list can combine. Thus, for example, a focus solely on undermining an ideology by presenting a counter-message, in terms of this ideology, may not be sufficient to de-radicalize a person who is mostly attracted to the radical groups because of a need for sensation.

At the same time, a distinction between different motives may inform first-line workers involved in de-radicalization. If one discovers a person has become radical mainly due to, for example, an attraction for sensation (rather than due to strong ideological motives), a program to de-radicalize this person may include elements to fulfill this attraction in another manner (rather than containing a strong anti-ideological component).

As indicated in the chapter about the role of the government (Chapter 6), another future direction might be a focus on curriculum development in support of children and young people's resilience to negative online influences, including extremist propaganda – for instance, by examining existing and developing new teaching approaches for media literacy and critical thinking. At the same time, it may be worthwhile looking into methods that aim to foster competencies for teaching media literacy and critical thinking.

With regard to this suggestion, it has been examined in other domains at what age children are "advertisement-wise," in that they understand what advertisements aim to do (i.e., changing their attitudes and behavior) and how they aim to reach these goals (e.g., Rozendaal, Buijzen, & Valkenburg, 2011; Rozendaal, Opree, & Buijzen, 2016; Valkenburg, Peter, & Walther, 2016).

Generally speaking, the understanding of advertisement by children is related to age. Three developmental phases can be distinguished: early childhood (up to five years old), middle childhood (six to nine years old) and late childhood (10 to 12 years old). In early childhood, advertisement knowledge is limited. In middle childhood, this knowledge is clearly increasing and most of these children understand that an advertisement is trying to persuade them. By the age of 10–12 years, children also under-stand how this persuasion might work (Rozendaal et al., 2011). While radical propaganda differs from advertisements in a number of ways, we argue that it is possible to make a direct comparison in terms of the aim of influencing another (young) person with regard to their attitudes and/or behavior. This might be a fruitful area of future research to examine closely. At what age do children become aware of how propaganda might work? Is it possible to increase this awareness and as such strengthen their resilience? Which factors might be involved in this process?

One idea is that inoculation might work: in this view, it should be pos-sible to stimulate resilience in children by exposing them to a mild form of radical narrative (without violence or blood) and help them to refute this propaganda (i.e., provide them with a potential counter-message). Subsequently, when they are confronted with "real propaganda," they should be able to recognize the common elements of propaganda, and be able to come up with counter-narrative arguments themselves. While the strength of the inoculation theory has been tested in other domains among youth (alcohol, cigarette smoking), the potential of this theory for strengthening resilience against extremist messaging has not been studied.

Another potential future direction might be to examine what happens to messages and counter-messages in a virtual world running in computer simulations, for example in terms of social network analyses. These simulations might inform us how messages and counter-messages could evolve in the long run. However, critically, in order to arrive at reliable estimates of such processes over time in computer simulations, we need to have a clear understanding of the most important factors at play in this context. At the moment, unfortunately, this understanding is far from complete. As such, such computer simulations may be fruitfully explored in a (near) future when this understanding is more advanced.

We conclude that, although presenting online counter-messages intuitively appears to be an appealing strategy to employ, our analysis shows that this may not be an ideal option to de-radicalize people. It might be more fruitful to use counter-messages in a prevention context, in which people's minds may still be open enough to register and process the information presented. Alternatively, it might be possible to explore the options to expose known individuals (e.g., convicted prisoners) with specific counter-messages – ideally in an offline, not an online, context – in order to directly monitor the reactions of the individuals and to build the necessary trust.

APPENDIX
Method

This research relied predominantly on a literature review. Data from the literature were supplemented by subject-matter expert interviews.

The literature study has been done using Google Scholar for scientific literature and Google for other "grey literature." Owing to the multifaceted nature of the research questions, we have searched for scientific literature in various disciplines, including psychology, political science, communication science, health science, and computer science. In addition, we have made use of the "grey literature," such as research reports, policy papers, working papers, evaluations and recommendations. Sometimes this involved documents of private companies involved in counter-messaging work, which we have treated with some caution, for obvious reasons. We have used search terms related to persuasion, narratives, counter narratives, online, social media, radicalization, terrorism, as well as effectiveness, test, approach, and method. In addition, we have used the search backward method (i.e., checking the citations in an article) as well as the search forward method (i.e., checking online who has cited this article).

Based on engagement with our area of interest, we have conducted interviews ($n = 8$) with experts with roles in academia and industry. We have used the following inclusion criteria when selecting the mix of people in our study:

- People who have direct expertise in or an academic understanding of the use of counter-messaging.
- People with a thorough academic understanding of radicalization processes.
- People who work on practical matters related to radicalization, such as trainers or advisors.
- People with academic or practical understanding of strategic communication, persuasion and online campaigns.

The interviews were audiotaped and transcribed in full. After analysis key findings were integrated in the report.

REFERENCES

Ackland, R. (2013). *Web social science: Concepts, data and tools for social scientists in the digital age*. London: Sage.

Adewuyi, E. O., & Adefemi, K. (2016). Behavior change communication using social media: A review. *International Journal of Communication and Health*, 9, 109–116. Retrieved from http://communicationandhealth.ro/upload/number9/EMMANUEL-O-ADEWUYI.pdf.

Against Violent Extremism. (n.d.-a). *About Against Violent Extremism*. Retrieved from www.againstviolentextremism.org/about.

Against Violent Extremism. (n.d.-b). *FAQ*. Retrieved from www.againstviolentextremism.org/about.

Aistrope, T. (2016). Social media and counterterrorism strategy. *Australian Journal of International Affairs*, 70(2), 121–138. doi:10.1080/10357718.2015.1113230.

Al Raffie, D. (2012). Whose hearts and minds? Narratives and counter-narratives of Salafi Jihadism. *Journal of Terrorism Research*, 3(2), 13–31. doi:10.15664/jtr.304.

Allen, M. (1991). Meta-analysis comparing the persuasiveness of one-sided and two-sided messages. *Western Journal of Speech Communication*, 55(4), 390–404. doi:10.1080/10570319109374395.

Allen, M. (1998). Comparing the persuasive effectiveness of one-and two-sided messages. In M. Allen & R. W. Preiss (Eds), *Persuasion: Advances through meta-analysis* (pp. 87–98). Cresskill, NJ: Hampton Press.

Aly, A. (2016). Brothers, believers, brave Mujahideen: Focusing attention on the audience of violent jihadist preachers. In A. Aly, S. MacDonald, L. Jarvis, & T. Chen (Eds), *Violent extremism online: New perspectives on terrorism and the internet*. London, UK: Routledge. Retrieved from www.taylorfrancis.com/books/e/9781315692029/chapters/10.4324/9781315692029-8. doi:10.4324/ 9781315692029.

Aly, A., Macdonald, S., Jarvis, L., & Chen, T. M. (2016). Introduction to the special issue: Terrorist online propaganda and radicalization. *Studies in Conflict & Terrorism*, 40(1), 1–9. doi:10.1080/1057610X.2016.1157402.

Aly, A., Weimann-Saks, D., & Weimann, G. (2014). Making 'noise' online: An analysis of the say no to terror online campaign. *Perspectives on Terrorism*, 8(5), 33–47. Retrieved from www.terrorismanalysts.com/pt/index.php/pot/article/view/376.

Appiah, O., Knobloch-Westerwick, S., & Alter, S. (2013). Ingroup favoritism and outgroup derogation: Effects of news valence, character race, and recipient race on selective News Reading. *Journal of Communication*, 63(3), 517–534. doi:10.1111/jcom.12032.

Ashour, O. (2011). Online de-radicalization? Countering violent extremist narratives: message, messenger and media strategy. *Perspectives on Terrorism*, 4(6), 15–19. Retrieved from www.terrorismanalysts.com/pt/index.php/pot/article/view/128/html.

Atkin, C. (2004). Media intervention impact: evidence and promising strategies. In R. J. Bonnie & M. E. O'Connell (Eds), *Reducing underage drinking: A collective responsibility* (pp. 565–597). Washington: The National Academies Press.

Atkin, C. K., & Freimuth, V. (2012). Guidelines for formative evaluation research in campaign design. In R. E. Rice & C. K. Atkin (Eds), *Public communication campaigns* (4th edn, pp. 53–68). Thousand Oaks, CA: Sage.

Atkin, C. K., & Rice, R. E. (2012). Theory and principles of public communication campaigns. In R. E. Rice & C. K. Atkin (Eds), *Public communication campaigns* (4th edn, pp. 3–20). Thousand Oaks, CA: Sage.

Atkin, C. K., & Salmon, C. T. (2012). Persuasive strategies in health campaigns. In J. P. Dillard & L. Shen (Eds), *The SAGE handbook of persuasion: Developments in theory and practice* (pp. 278–295). Thousand Oaks, CA: SAGE Publications. doi:10.4135/9781452218410.n17.

Austin, E. W., & Pinkleton, B. E. (2015). *Strategic public relations management: Planning and managing effective communication campaigns* (3rd edn). New York: Routledge.

Bakker, E., & Grol, P. (2015, July). *Motives and considerations of potential foreign fighters from the Netherlands* [Policy Brief]. Retrieved from International Centre for Counter-Terrorism Website www.icct.nl/wp-content/uploads/2015/07/ICCT-Bakker-Grol-Motives-andConsiderations-of-Potential-Foreign-Fighters-from-the-Netherlands-July2015.pdf.

Banas, J. A., & Miller, G. (2013). Inducing resistance to conspiracy theory propaganda: Testing inoculation and metainoculation strategies. *Human Communication Research*, 39(2), 184–207. doi:10.1111/hcre.12000.

Banas, J. A., & Rains, S. A. (2010). A meta-analysis of research on Inoculation Theory. *Communication Monographs*, 77(3), 281–311. doi:10.1080/0363775 1003758193.

Baray, G., Postmes, T., & Jetten, J. (2009). When I equals we: Exploring the relation between social and personal identity of extreme right-wing political party members. *British Journal of Social Psychology*, 48(4), 625–647. doi:10.1348/014466608X389582.

Bartlett, J., Birdwell, J., & King, M. (2010). *The edge of violence: A radical approach to extremism* [Interim Research Report]. Retrieved from the Demos website www.demos.co.uk/files/Edge_of_Violence_-_full_-_web.pdf?1291806916.

Bartlett, J., & Krasodomski-Jones, A. (2015, October). *Counter-speech: Examining content that challenges extremism online* [Research Report]. Retrieved from the Demos website www.demos.co.uk/wp-content/uploads/2015/10/Counter-speech.pdf.

Bartlett, J., & Miller, C. (2010, August). *The power of unreason: Conspiracy theories, extremism and counter-terrorism*. Retrieved from the Demos website www.demos.co.uk/files/Conspiracy_theories_paper.pdf.

Bartlett, J., & Reynolds, L. (2015). *The state of the art 2015: A literature review of Social Media intelligence capabilities for counter-terrorism* [Research Paper]. Retrieved from the Demos website www.demos.co.uk/wpcontent/uploads/2015/09/State_of_the_Arts_2015.pdf.

Baxter, L. A., & Babbie, E. R. (2004). *The basics of communication research.* Belmont, CA: Wadsworth/Thomson Learning.

Bazarova, N. N., Walther, J. B., & McLeod, P. L. (2012). Minority influence in virtual groups. *Communication Research, 39*(3), 295–316. doi:10.1177/009365 0211399752.

Belk, R. W., & Kozinets, R. V. (2017). Videography and netnography. In K. Kubacki & S. Rundle-Thiele (Eds), *Formative Research in Social Marketing: Innovative Methods to Gain Consumer Insights* (pp. 265–279). Singapore: Springer Singapore.

Berger, J. M. (2014, June 15). How ISIS games Twitter. *The Atlantic.* Retrieved from *The Atlantic* website www.theatlantic.com/international/archive/2014/06/isis-iraq-twitter-social-media-strategy/372856.

Berger, J. M. (2016, May). *Making CVE work: A focused approach based on process disruption* [Research Paper]. The Hague, NL: International Centre for Counter-Terrorism. doi:10.19165/2016.1.05.

Berger, J., & Milkman, K. L. (2012). What makes online content viral? *Journal of Marketing Research, 49*(2), 192–205. doi:10.1509/jmr.10.0353.

Berger, J. M., & Morgan, J. (2015, March). *The ISIS Twitter census: Defining and describing the population of ISIS supporters on Twitter* (The Brookings Project on US Relations with the Islamic World Analysis Paper No. 20). Retrieved from The Brookings Institution website www.brookings.edu/wp-content/uploads/2016/06/ISIS_twitter_census_berger_morgan.pdf.

Berger, J. M., & Perez, H. (2016, February). *The Islamic State's diminishing returns on Twitter: How suspensions are limiting the social networks of English-speaking ISIS supporters* [Occasional Paper]. Retrieved from George Washington University Program on Extremism website https://extremism.gwu.edu/sites/extremism.gwu.edu/files/downloads/JMB%20Diminishing%20Returns.pdf.

Bermingham, A., Conway, M., McInerney, L., Hare, N. O., & Smeaton, A. F. (2009). *Combining social network analysis and sentiment analysis to explore the potential for online radicalisation.* Paper presented at the 2009 International Conference on Advances in Social Network Analysis and Mining. Retrieved from http://doras.dcu.ie/4554/.

Bethlehem, J. (2010). Selection bias in web surveys. *International Statistical Review, 78*(2), 161–188. doi:10.1111/j.175823.2010.00112.x.

Beutel, A., Weine, S. M., Saeed, A., Mihajlovic, A. S., Stone, A., Beahrs, J. O., & Shanfield, S. B. (2016). Guiding principles for countering and displacing extremist narratives. *Journal of Terrorism Research, 7*(3), 35–49. doi:10.15664/jtr.1220.

Bijvank, M. N., Konijn, E. A., Bushman, B. J., & Roelofsma, P. H. M. P. (2009). Age and violent-content labels make video games forbidden fruits for youth. *Pediatrics, 123*(3), 870–876. doi:10.1542/peds.200601.

Bilandzic, H., & Busselle, R. (2012). Narrative persuasion. In J. P. Dillard & L. Shen (Eds), *The SAGE handbook of persuasion: Developments in theory and practice* (pp. 200–219). Thousand Oaks, CA: SAGE Publications. doi:10.4135/9781452218410.n13.

Bindner, L. (2018). *Jihadists' grievance narratives against France* [Policy Brief]. The Hague, NL: The International Centre for Counter-Terrorism. doi:10.19165/2018.2.01.

140

Bjørgo, T. (2011). Dreams and disillusionment: Engagement in and disengagement from militant extremist groups. *Crime, Law and Social Change*, 55(4), 277–285. doi:10.1007/s1061128.

Bole, R., & Kallmyer, K. (2016). Combatting the Islamic State's digital dominance: Revitalizing U.S. communication strategy. *The Washington Quarterly*, 39(1), 29–48. doi:10.1080/0163660X.2016.1170478.

Borum, R. (2011). Radicalization into violent extremism I: A review of social science theories. *Journal of Strategic Security*, 4(4), 7–36. doi:10.5038/194472.4.4.1.

Boslaugh, S. E., Kreuter, M. W., Nicholson, R. A., & Naleid, K. (2005). Comparing demographic, health status and psychosocial strategies of audience segmentation to promote physical activity. *Health Education Research*, 20(4), 430–438. doi:10.1093/her/cyg138.

Brachman, J. M. (2009). *Global jihadism: Theory and practice*. London: Routledge.

Brachman, J. M., & Levine, A. N. (2011). You too can be Awlaki. *Fletcher Forum of World Affairs*, 35(1), 25–46. Retrieved from https://static1.squarespace.com/static/579fc2ad725e253a86230610/t/57ec9034f7e0abf8c055c74b/1475121204759/Brachman-Levine_3.pdf.

Braddock, K. (2014). The talking cure?: Communication and psychological impact in prison de-radicalisation programmes. In A. Silke (Ed.), *Prisons, Terrorism and Extremism: Critical Issues in Management, Radicalization and Reform* (pp. 60–74). Abingdon, Oxon/New York: Routledge.

Braddock, K., & Dillard, J. P. (2016). Meta-analytic evidence for the persuasive effect of narratives on beliefs, attitudes, intentions, and behaviors. *Communication Monographs*, 83(4), 1–22. doi:10.1080/03637751.2015.1128555.

Braddock, K., & Horgan, J. (2016). Towards a guide for constructing and disseminating counternarratives to reduce support for terrorism. *Studies in Conflict & Terrorism*, 39(5), 381–404. doi:10.1080/1057610X.2015.1116277.

Braddock, K., & Morrison, J. F. (2018). Cultivating trust and perceptions of source credibility in online counternarratives intended to reduce support for terrorism. *Studies in Conflict & Terrorism*, 1–25. doi:10.1080/1057610X.2018.1452728.

Brannon, L. A., Tagler, M. J., & Eagly, A. H. (2007). The moderating role of attitude strength in selective exposure to information. *Journal of Experimental Social Psychology*, 43(4), 611–617. doi:10.1016/j.jesp. 2006.05.001.

Brehm, J. W. (1966). *A theory of psychological reactance*. New York: Academic Press.

Brehm, S. S., & Brehm, J. W. (1981). *Psychological reactance: A theory of freedom and control*. New York: Academic Press.

Brewer, M. B. (1991). The social self: On being the same and different at the same time. *Personality and Social Psychology Bulletin*, 17(5), 475–482. doi:10.1177/0146167291175001.

Brewer, N. T., DeFrank, J. T., & Gilkey, M. B. (2016). Anticipated regret and health behavior: A meta-analysis. *Health Psychology*, 35(11), 1264–1275. doi:10.1037/hea0000294.

Briggs, R., & Feve, S. (2013). *Review of programs to counter narratives of violent extremism: What works and what are the implications for government* [Research Report]. Retrieved from The Public Safety Canada website: www.publicsafety.gc.ca/lbrr/archives/cn28580-eng.pdf.

Briggs, R., & Frenett, R. (2014). *Foreign fighters, the challenge of counter-narratives* [Policy Briefing]. Retrieved from The Institute for Strategic Dialogue Counter Extremism website www.counterextremism.org/resources/details/id/683/foreign-fighters-the-challenge-ofcounter-narratives.

Briggs, R., & Silverman, T. (2014). *Western foreign fighters: Innovations in responding to the threat* [Research Paper]. Retrieved from The Institute for Strategic Dialogue website www.isdglobal.org/wpcontent/uploads/2016/02/ISDJ2784_Western_foreign_fighters_V7_WEB.pdf.

Brocato Jr., A. L. (2015). Tackling terrorists' use of the Internet: Propaganda dispersion & the threat of radicalization. In M. N. Ogun (Ed.), *Terrorist use of cyberspace and cyber terrorism: New challenges and responses* (pp. 129–148). Amsterdam: IOS Press. doi:10.3233/97-61492-129.

Brown, K. E. & Pearson E. (2018). Social media, the online environment and terrorism. In A. Silke (Ed.), *Routledge handbook of terrorism and counterterrorism* (pp. 149–164). London, UK: Routledge.

Buijzen, M., & Valkenburg, P. M. (2004). Developing a typology of humor in audiovisual media. *Media Psychology*, 6(2), 147–167. doi:10.1207/s1532785xmep0602_2.

Bunzel, C. (2016). *From paper state to caliphate: The ideology of the Islamic State* (The Brookings Project on US Relations with the Islamic World Analysis Paper No. 19). Retrieved from the Brookings Institution website: www.brookings.edu/wpcontent/uploads/2016/06/The-ideology-of-the-Islamic-State.pdf.

Burgoon, M., Alvaro, E., Grandpre, J., & Voulodakis, M. (2002). Revisiting the theory of psychological reactance: Communicating threats to attitudinal freedom. In J. P. Dillard & M. Pfau (Eds), *The persuasion handbook: Developments in theory and practice* (pp. 213–232). Thousand Oaks, CA: Sage.

Campo, S., Askelson, N. M., Spies, E. L., Boxer, C., Scharp, K. M., & Losch, M. E. (2013). "Wow, that was funny": The value of exposure and humor in fostering campaign message sharing. *Social Marketing Quarterly*, 19(2), 84–96. doi:10.1177/1524500413483456.

Carter, J. A., Maher, S., & Neumann, P. R. (2014). *#Greenbirds: Measuring importance and influence in Syrian foreign fighter networks* [Research Report]. Retrieved from International Centre for the Study of Radicalization and Political Violence website http://icsr.info/wpcontent/uploads/2014/04/ICSR-Report-Greenbirds-Measuring-Importance-and-Infleunce-inSyrian-Foreign-Fighter-Networks.pdf.

Cheong, D. D. (2018). Strategic communication and violent extremism: The importance of state action. *Journal of Asian Security and International Affairs*, 5(2), 129–148. doi:10.1177/2347797018783115.

Choudhary, P., & Singh, U. (2015). A survey on social network analysis for counter-terrorism. *International Journal of Computer Applications*, 112(9), 24–29.

Civettini, A. J., & Redlawsk, D. P. (2009). Voters, emotions, and memory. *Political Psychology*, 30(1), 125–151. doi:www.jstor.org/stable/20447187.

Coffman, J. (2002, May). *Public communication campaign evaluation: An environmental scan of challenges, criticisms, practice, and opportunities* [Research Paper]. Retrieved from the Harvard Family Research Project website: www.hfrp.org/evaluation/publications-resources/public-122-communication-campaign-evaluation-an-environmental-scan-of-challenges-criticismspractice-and-opportunities.

Cohen, J. (2001). Defining Identification: A theoretical look at the identification of audiences with media characters. *Mass Communication and Society*, *4*(3), 245–264. doi:10.1207/S15327825MCS0403_01.

Cohen, J., Tal-Or, N., & Mazor-Tregerman, M. (2015). The tempering effect of transportation: Exploring the effects of transportation and identification during exposure to controversial two-sided narratives. *Journal of Communication*, *65*(2), 237–258. doi:10.1111/jcom.12144.

Cohen, J., Weimann-Saks, D., & Mazor-Tregerman, M. (2017). Does character similarity increase identification and persuasion? *Media Psychology*, 1–23. doi:1 0.1080/15213269.2017.1302344.

Cohen, K., Johansson, F., Kaati, L., & Mork, J. C. (2014). Detecting linguistic markers for radical violence in social media. *Terrorism and Political Violence*, *26*(1), 246–256. doi:10.1080/09546553.2014.849948.

Compton, J. (2012). Inoculation theory. In J. P. Dillard & L. Shen (Eds), *The SAGE handbook of persuasion: Developments in theory and practice* (pp. 220–236). Thousand Oaks, CA: SAGE Publications. doi:10.4135/9781452218410.n14.

Conway, M. (2016). Determining the role of the Internet in violent extremism and terrorism: Six suggestions for progressing research. In A. Aly, S. MacDonald, L. Jarvis, & T. Chen (Eds), *Violent extremism online: new perspectives on terrorism and the internet*. London, UK: Routledge. Retrieved from www.taylorfrancis. com/books/e/9781315692029/chapters/10.4324/9781315692029-8. doi:10.4324/9781315692029.

Conway, M., Khawaja, M., Lakhani, S., Reffin, J., Robertson, A., & Weir, D. (2018). Disrupting Daesh: Measuring takedown of online terrorist material and its impacts. *Studies in Conflict & Terrorism*, 1–20. doi:10.1080/1057610X.2018.151 3984.

Conway, M., & McInerney, L. (2008). Jihadi video and auto-radicalisation: Evidence from an exploratory YouTube study. In D. Ortiz-Arroyo, H. L. Larsen, D. D. Zeng, D. Hicks, & G. Wagner (Eds), *Intelligence and security informatics* (pp. 108–118). Berlin, Germany: Springer Verlag.

Costello, L., McDermott, M.-L., & Wallace, R. (2017). Netnography: Range of practices, misperceptions, and missed opportunities. *International Journal of Qualitative Methods*, *16*(1), 1–12. doi:1609406917700647.

Coull, A., Yzerbyt, V. Y., Castano, E., Paladino, M.-P., & Leemans, V. (2001). Protecting the ingroup: Motivated allocation of cognitive resources in the presence of threatening ingroup members. *Group Processes & Intergroup Relations*, *4*(4), 327–339. doi:10.1177/1368430201004004003.

Counter-Narrative Toolkit. (n.d.). *About*. Retrieved from the Counter-Narrative Toolkit website www.counternarratives.org/about-us.

Dafnos, A. (2014). Narratives as a means of countering the radical right; Looking into the Trojan T-Shirt project. *Journal EXIT-Deutschland*, *3*, 156–188. Retrieved from http://journals.sfu.ca/jed/index.php/jex/article/viewFile/98/126.

Dahl, S. (2014). *Social media marketing: Theories and applications*. Hull University: SAGE Publications.

Dal Cin, S., Zanna, M. P., & Fong, G. T. (2004). Narrative persuasion and overcoming resistance. In E. S. Knowles & J. A. Linn (Eds), *Resistance and persuasion* (pp. 175–191). Mahwah, NJ: Lawrence Erlbaum Associates Publishers.

Dalgaard-Nielsen, A. (2010). Violent radicalization in Europe: What we know and what we do not know. *Studies in Conflict & Terrorism*, *33*(9), 797–814. doi:10.1080/1057610X.2010.501423.

Dalgaard-Nielsen, A. (2013). Promoting exit from violent extremism: Themes and approaches. *Studies in Conflict & Terrorism*, *36*(2), 99–115. doi:10.1080/10576 10X.2013.747073.

Dare to be Grey. (2017). #Dare to be Grey. Retrieved from the Dare to Be Grey website www.dtbg.nl/en.

Davies, G., Neudecker, C., Ouellet, M., Bouchard, M., & Ducol, B. (2016). Toward a framework understanding of online programs for countering violent extremism. *Journal for Deradicalization*, *6*, 51–86. Retrieved from http://journals.sfu.ca/jd/index.php/jd/article/view/43/0.

Davies, L. (2018). *Review of educational initiatives in counter-extremism internationally: What works?* Gothenburg: The Segerstedt Institute. Retrieved from https://segerstedtinstitutet.gu.se/digitalAssets/1673/1673173_review-of-educational-initiatives-180110.pdf.

Dawson, L., Edwards, C., & Jeffray, C. (2014, May). *Learning and adapting: The use of monitoring and evaluation in countering violent extremism* [E-handbook]. Retrieved from the Royal United Services Institute website: https://rusi.org/sites/default/files/201406_bk_learning_and_adapting.pdf.

De Graaf, A., Hoeken, H., Sanders, J., & Beentjes, J. W. J. (2012). Identification as a mechanism of narrative persuasion. *Communication Research*, *39*(6), 802–823. doi:10.1177/0093650211408594.

De Koning, M. de (2013). Between the prophet and paradise: The Salafi struggle in the Netherlands. *Canadian Journal of Netherlandic Studies*, *33*(2)–*34*(1), 17–34. Retrieved from www.researchgate.net/publication/281376874_Between_the_Prophet_and_Paradise_The_Salafi_struggle_in_the_Netherlands.

De Wolf, A., & Doosje, B. (2010/2015). *Aanpak van radicalisme: een psychologische analyse* [Dealing with radicalization: A psychological analysis]. Amsterdam, NL: SWP.

Dean, G. (2016). Framing the challenges of online violent extremism: "Policing-public-policies-politics" framework. In M. Khader, L. S. Neo, G. Ong, E. Tan, & J. Chin (Eds), *Countering violent extremism and radicalisation in the digital era* (pp. 226–269). Hershey, PA: IGI Global. doi:10.4018/97-52215.ch012.

Demant, F., Slootman, M., Buijs, F., & Tillie, J. (2008). *Decline and disengagement: An analysis of processes of deradicalisation*. Amsterdam, NL: Institute for Migration and Ethnic Studies. Retrieved from https://pure.uva.nl/ws/files/1079141/64714_Demant_Slootman_2008_Decline_and_Disengagement.pdf.

Demos (2016). *Pioneering school pilot a breakthrough in building students' resilience to extremism online* [Press release]. Retrieved from the Demos website www.demos.co.uk/press-release/pioneering-school-pilot-a-breakthrough-in-building-students-resilience-to-extremism-online/.

Devichand, M. (2016, 3 January). *How the world was changed by the slogan 'Je Suis Charlie.'* Retrieved on September 7, 2017, from www.bbc.com/news/blogs-trending-35108339.

DG HOME (2019a). *EU internet forum: Civil society empowerment programme*. Retrieved from the European Commission, Migration and Home Affairs Website https://ec.europa.eu/home-affairs/what-we-do/networks/radicalisation_awareness_network/civil-society-empowerment-programme_en.

DG HOME (2019b). *RAN working groups*. Retrieved from the European Commission, Migration and Home Affairs Website https://ec.europa.eu/home-affairs/what-we-do/networks/radicalisation_awareness_network/about-ran_en.

DG HOME (2019c) *Communication and Narratives Working Group (RAN C&N)*. Retrieved from the European Commission, Migration and Home Affairs Website https://ec.europa.eu/home-affairs/what-we-do/networks/radicalisation_awareness_network/about-ran/ran-c-and-n.

Dillard, J. P., Plotnick, C. A., Godbold, L. C., Freimuth, V. S., & Edgar, T. (1996). The multiple affective outcomes of AIDS PSAs. *Communication Research*, 23(1), 44–72. doi:10.1177/009365096023001002.

Dillard, J. P., & Shen, L. (2005). On the nature of reactance and its role in persuasive health communication. *Communication Monographs*, 72(2), 144–168. doi:10.1080/03637750500111815.

Doosje, B., Loseman, A., & Van Den Bos, K. (2013). Determinants of radicalization of Islamic youth in the Netherlands: Personal uncertainty, perceived injustice, and perceived group threat. *Journal of Social Issues*, 69(3), 586–604. doi:10.1111/josi.12030.

Doosje, B., Moghaddam, F. M., Kruglanski, A. W., de Wolf, A., Mann, L., & Feddes, A. R. (2016). Terrorism, radicalization and de-radicalization. *Current Opinion in Psychology*, 11, 79–84. doi:10.1016/j.copsyc.2016.06.008.

Eagly, A. H., & Chaiken, S. (1984). Cognitive theories of persuasion. *Advances in Experimental Social Psychology*, 17, 267–359. doi:10.1016/S006601(08)6012.

Echikson, W., & Knodt, O. (2018, November). *Germany's NetzDG: A key test for combatting online hate* (CEPS Research report No. 2018/09). Retrieved from the CEPS website: www.ceps.eu/publications/germany%E2%80%99s-netzdg-key-test-combatting-online-hate.

Edelman, A. (2014, 16 September). State department's 'embarrassing' 'Think Again Turn Away' Twitter campaign could actually legitimize terrorists: Expert. *New York Daily News*. Retrieved from www.nydailynews.com/news/politics/state-department-embarrassing-turn-twittercampaign-legitimizes-terrorists-expert-article-1.1941990.

EdVenture Partners. (2017). Peer to peer. Retrieved from https://edventurepartners.com/peer2peer.

Edwards, C., & Gribbon, L. (2013). Pathways to violent extremism in the digital era. *The RUSI Journal*, 158(5), 40–47. doi:10.1080/03071847.2013.847714.

Egner, M. (2009). Social-science foundations for strategic communications in the global war on Terrorism. In P. K. Davis, K. Cragin & D. Noricks (Eds), *Social science for counterterrorism: Putting the pieces together* [e-book version] (pp. 323–355). Retrieved from the RAND corporation website www.rand.org/content/dam/rand/pubs/monographs/2009/RAND_MG849.pdf.

Eisend, M. (2009). A meta-analysis of humor in advertising. *Journal of the Academy of Marketing Science*, 37(2), 191–203. doi:10.1007/s11740096-y.

Ellemers, N., Spears, R., & Doosje, B. (2002). Self and social identity. *Annual Review of Psychology*, 53(1), 161–186. doi:10.1146/annurev.psych.53.100901.135228.

Ernst, J., Schmitt, J. C., Rieger, D., Beier, A. K., Vorderer, P., Bente, G., & Roth, H.-J. (2017). Hate beneath the counter speech? A qualitative content analysis of user comments on YouTube related to counter speech videos. *Journal for Deradicalization*, 10, 1–49. Retrieved from http://journals.sfu.ca/jd/index.php/jd/article/view/91.

Escalas, J. E. (2004). Imagine yourself to be the product: Mental simulation, narrative transportation, and persuasion. *Journal of Advertising, 33*(2), 37–48. doi: 10.1080/00913367.2004.10639163.

Esposo, S. R., Hornsey, M. J., & Spoor, J. R. (2013). Shooting the messenger: Outsiders critical of your group are rejected regardless of argument quality. *British Journal of Social Psychology, 52*(2), 386–395. doi:10.1111/bjso.12024.

European Council (2014) http://data.consilium.europa.eu/doc/document/ST-9956-2014-INIT/en/pdf (retrieved on April 26, 2019).

Europol (2015, July 1). *Europol's Internet Referral Unit to combat terrorist and violent extremist propaganda* [Press Release]. Retrieved from the Europol website www.europol.europa.eu/newsroom/news/europol%E2%80%99s-internet-referral-unit-to-combat-terrorist-and-violent-extremist-propaganda.

Europol (2016). *EU Internet Referral Unit: Year one report highlights.* Retrieved from the Europol website www.europol.europa.eu/sites/default/files/documents/eu_iru_1_year_report_highlights.pdf.

Europol (2018). *Europol's Internet Referral Unit – EU IRU: Monitoring terrorism online.* Retrieved from the Europol website www.europol.europa.eu/about-europol/eu-internet-referal-unit-eu-iru.

Evers, C. W., Albury, K., Byron, P., & Crawford, K. (2013). Young people, social media, social network sites and sexual health communication in Australia: "This is Funny, You Should Watch It." *International Journal of Communication and Health, 7*, 63–280. Retrieved from http://ijoc.org/index.php/ijoc/article/download/1106/853.

Eysenbach, G., & Wyatt, J. (2002). Using the internet for surveys and health research. *Journal of Medical Internet Research, 4*(2), e13. doi:10.2196/jmir.4.2.e13.

Fairlie, B. M. (2016). The spread of information via social media. In J. V. Cohn, S. Schatz, H. Freeman, & D. J. Y. Combs (Eds), *Modeling sociocultural influences on decision making: Understanding conflict, enabling stability.* Boca Raton, FL CRC Press.

Farwell, J. P. (2014). The media strategy of ISIS. *Survival, 56*(6), 49–55. doi:10.10 80/00396338.2014.985436.

Feddes, A. R., Nickolson, L., & Doosje, B. (2015). *Triggerfactoren in het radicaliseringsproces* [Trigger factors in the radicalisation process]. Retrieved from the Social Stability Expertise Unit, Dutch Ministry of Social Affairs & Employment website www.socialestabiliteit.nl/documenten/publicaties/2015/10/13/triggerfactoren-in-hetradicaliseringsproces.

Felten, H., Taouanza, I., & Keuzenkamp, S. (2016, June). *Klaar met discriminatie? Onderzoek naar effectiviteit van sociale media-campagnes tegen discriminatie* [Done with discrimination? Research into the effectiveness of social media campaigns against discrimination]. Retrieved from the Kennisplatform Integratie & Samenleving website www.kis.nl/publicatie/klaar-met-discriminatie.

Ferguson, K. (2016, March). *Countering violent extremism through media and communication strategies: A review of the evidence* [Research Report]. Retrieved from the Partnership for Conflict, Crime & Security Research website www.paccsresearch.org.uk/wpcontent/uploads/2016/03/Countering-Violent-Extremism-Through-Media-and-CommunicationStrategies-.pdf

Festinger, L. (1957). *A theory of cognitive dissonance.* Evanston, IL: Row & Peterson.

Fink, N. C., & Barclay, J. (2013, February). *Mastering the narrative: Counterterrorism strategic communications and the United Nations* [Research Report]. Retrieved from The Center on Global Counterterrorism Cooperation website www.globalcenter.org/publications/mastering-thenarrative-counterterrorism-strategic-communication-and-the-united-nations/.

Flay, B. R. (1987). Evaluation of the development, dissemination and effectiveness of mass media health programming. *Journal of Health Education Research*, 2(2), 123–129. doi:10.1093/her/2.2.123.

Fransen, M. L., Smit, E. G., & Verlegh, P. W. J. (2015). Strategies and motives for resistance to persuasion: An integrative framework. *Frontiers in Psychology*, 6, 1201. doi:10.3389/fpsyg.2015.01201.

Freeman, B., Potente, S., Rock, V., & McIver, J. (2015). Social media campaigns that make a difference: What can public health learn from the corporate sector and other social change marketers. *Public Health Research Practice*, 25(2), 2–8. doi:10.17061/phrp2521517.

Freimuth, V., Cole, G., & Kirby, S. (2011). Issues in evaluating mass media-based health communication campaigns. In J. S. Detrani (Ed.), *Mass communication: Issues, perspectives and techniques* (pp. 77–98). Oakville, ON: Apple Academic Press.

Frenett, R., & Dow, M. (2015, September). *One to one online interventions: A pilot CVE methodology* [Research Report]. Retrieved from The Institute for Strategic Dialogue website www.isdglobal.org/wp-content/uploads/2016/04/One2One_Web_v9.pdf.

Frenett, R., & Silverman, T. (2016). Foreign fighters: Motivations for travel to foreign conflicts. In A. de Guttry, F. Capone & C. Paulussen (Eds), *Foreign fighters under International Law and beyond* (pp. 63–76). The Hague, NL: T.M.C. Asser Press. doi:10.1007/97269_5.

Gartenstein-Ross, D. Barr, N., & Moreng, B. (2016, March). *The Islamic State's global propaganda strategy* [Research Paper]. The Hague, NL: The International Centre for Counter-Terrorism. doi:10.19165/2016.1.01.

Geeraerts, S. B. (2012). Digital radicalization of youth. *Social Cosmos*, 3(1), 25–32. Retrieved from https://dspace.library.uu.nl/bitstream/handle/1874/237584/45-PB.pdf%3Bsequence=2.

German Institute on Radicalization and De-radicalization Studies (GIRDS). (n.d.-a). *Open letter to our sons and daughters in Syria and Iraq*. Retrieved from http://girds.org/mothersforlife/openletter-to-our-sons-and-daughters.

German Institute on Radicalization and De-radicalization Studies (GIRDS). (n.d.-b). *A second letter to Abu Bakr al-Baghdadi from the Mothers for Life*. Retrieved from http://girds.org/mothersforlife/a-second-letter-to-abu-bakr-al-baghdadi-from-the-mothers-forlife.

General Intelligence and Security Service (GISS). (2014). *The transformation of jihadism in the Netherlands Swarm dynamics and new strength*. The Hague: General Intelligence and Security Service, Ministry of the Interior Kingdom Relations of the Netherlands. Retrieved from https://english.aivd.nl/publications/publications/2014/10/01/the-transformation-of-jihadismin-the-netherlands.

Gielen, A.-J. (2017). Evaluating countering violent extremism. In L. Colaert (Ed.), *'De-radicalisation': Scientific insights for policy* (pp. 101–118). Brussels, BE: Flemish Peace Institute. Retrieved from www.flemishpeaceinstitute.eu/sites/vlaamsvredesinstituut.eu/files/wysiwyg/de-radicalisation_-_chapter_gielen.pdf.

Glazzard, A. (2017, May). *Losing the plot: Narrative, counter-narrative and violent extremism* [Research Paper]. The Hague, NL: The International Centre for Counter-Terrorism. doi:10.19165/2017.1.08.

Global Counter-Terrorism Forum (GCTF). (2013). *Good practices on community engagement and community-oriented policing as tools to counter violent extremism*. Retrieved from The Global Counter-Terrorism Forum website www.thegctf. org/documents/10162/159885/13Aug09_EN_Good+Practices+on+Community+ Engagement+and+Community-Oriented+Policing.pdf.

Godbold, L. C., & Pfau, M. (2000). Conferring resistance to peer pressure among adolescents. *Communication Research, 27*(4), 411–437. doi:10.1177/009365 000027004001.

Gold, J., Pedrana, A. E., Stoove, M. A., Chang, S., Howard, S., Asselin, J., ... Hellard, M. E. (2012). Developing health promotion interventions on social networking Sites: Recommendations from the FaceSpace project. *Journal of Medical Internet Research, 14*(1), e30. doi:10.2196/jmir.1875.

Goodall, H., Cheong, P. H., Fleischer, K., & Corman, S. R. (2012). Rhetorical charms: The promise and pitfalls of humor and ridicule as strategies to counter extremist narratives. *Perspectives on Terrorism, 6*(1), 70–79. Retrieved from www. terrorismanalysts.com/pt/index.php/pot/article/view/goodall-et-al-rhetorical/html.

Goodman, J. K., Cryder, C. E., & Cheema, A. (2013). Data collection in a flat world: The strengths and weaknesses of Mechanical Turk Samples. *Journal of Behavioral Decision Making, 26*(3), 213–224. doi:10.1002/bdm.1753.

Gouvernement.fr. (2015, 28 January). *#StopJihadism: Everyone on alert and taking action against Jihadism*. Retrieved from www.gouvernement.fr/en/stopjihadism-everyone-on-alert-andtaking-action-against-jihadism.

Grandpre, J., Alvaro, E. M., Burgoon, M., Miller, C. H., & Hall, J. R. (2003). Adolescent reactance and anti-smoking campaigns: A theoretical approach. *Health Communication, 15*(3), 349–366. doi:10.1207/S15327027HC1503_6.

Green, J. (2000). The role of theory in evidence-based health promotion practice. *Health Education Research, 15*(2), 125–129. doi:10.1093/her/15.2.125.

Green, M. C. (2004). Transportation into narrative worlds: The role of prior knowledge and perceived realism. *Discourse Processes, 38*(2), 247–266. doi:10.1207/s15326950dp3802_5.

Green, M. C., & Brock, T. C. (2000). The role of transportation in the persuasiveness of public narratives. *Journal of personality and social psychology, 79*(5), 701–721. doi:10.1037//002514.79.5.701.

Greene, K. J. (2015). *ISIS: Trends in terrorist media and propaganda*. Retrieved from http://digitalcommons.cedarville.edu/international_studies_capstones/3/.

Guadagno, R. E., Rempala, D. M., Murphy, S., & Okdie, B. M. (2013). What makes a video go viral? An analysis of emotional contagion and internet memes. *Computers in Human Behavior, 29*(6), 2312–2319. doi:10.1016/j.chb.2013. 04.016.

Hafez, M., & Mullins, C. (2015). The radicalization puzzle: A theoretical synthesis of empirical approaches to homegrown extremism. *Studies in Conflict & Terrorism, 38*(11), 958–975. doi:10.1080/1057610X.2015.1051375.

Hamid, N. (2018, November 28). *Don't just counter-message; Counter-engage*. Retrieved from the International Centre for Counter-Terrorism website: https:// icct.nl/publication/dont-just-counter-message-counter-engage/.

Hanna, R., Rohm, A., & Crittenden, V. L. (2011). We're all connected: The power of the social media ecosystem. *Business Horizons, 54*(3), 265–273. doi:10.1016/j.bushor.2011.01.007.

Harmon-Jones, E. (2012). Cognitive dissonance theory. In V. S. Ramachandran (Ed.), *The encyclopedia of human behavior* (2nd edn, Vol. 1, pp. 543–549). Cambridge, MA: Academic Press.

Harmon-Jones, E., & Harmon-Jones, C. (2007). Cognitive dissonance theory after 50 years of development. *Zeitschrift für Sozialpsychologie, 38*(1), 7–16.

Harmon-Jones, E., Harmon-Jones, C., & Levy, N. (2015). An action-based model of cognitive-dissonance processes. *Current Directions in Psychological Science, 24*(3), 184–189. doi:10.1177/0963721414566449.

Harmon-Jones, E., & Mills, J. (1999). An introduction to cognitive dissonance theory and an overview of current perspectives on the theory. In E. Harmon-Jones & J. Mills (Eds), *Cognitive dissonance: Progress on a pivotal theory in social psychology* (pp. 3–21). Washington, DC: American Psychological Association.

Harris, K. J. (2011). *Entitativity and ideology: A grounded theory of disengagement.* Paper presented at the 4th Australian Security and Intelligence Conference, Edith Cowan University, Perth, Australia. doi:10.4225/75/57a01cd3ac5c7.

Harris, K., Gringart, E., & Drake, D. (2014, December). *Understanding the role of social groups in radicalisation.* Paper presented at the 7th Australian Security and Intelligence Conference, Edith Cowan University, Perth, Australia. doi:10.4225/75/57a83235c833d.

Harris-Hogan, S., Barrelle, K., & Zammit, A. (2016). What is countering violent extremism? Exploring CVE policy and practice in Australia. *Behavioral Sciences of Terrorism and Political Aggression, 8*(1), 6–24. doi:10.1080/19434472.2015.1104710.

Hedayah (2019a). *Strategic significance.* Retrieved from the Hedayah Centre website www.hedayahcenter.org/what-we-do/77/strategic-significance.

Hedayah (2019b). *Counter-narrative library.* Retrieved from the Hedayah Centre website www.hedayahcenter.org/what-we-do/91/departments/98/research-and-analysis/477/counter-narrative-library.

Hedayah & International Center for Counter-Terrorism (ICCT). (2014). *Developing effective counter narrative frameworks for countering violent extremism* [Meeting Note]. Retrieved from the International Center for Counter-Terrorism website www.icct.nl/download/file/Developing%20Effective%20CN%20Frameworks_Hedayah_ICCT_Report_FINAL.pdf.

Hegghammer, T. (2014). Interpersonal trust on Jihadi internet forums. Norwegian Defence Research Establishment. Retrieved from http://hegghammer.com/_files/interpersonal_trust.pdf.

Heldman, A. B., Schindelar, J., & Weaver, J. B. (2013). Social media engagement and public health communication: Implications for public health organizations being truly "social." *Public Health Reviews, 35*(1), 13. doi:10.1007/bf03391698.

Helmus, T. C., York, E., & Chalk, P. (2013*). Promoting online voices for countering violent extremism* (RAND Publication No. RR-130-OSD) [Research Report]. Retrieved from the RAND corporation website www.rand.org/content/dam/rand/pubs/research_reports/RR100/RR130/RAND_RR130.pdf.

149

Hoeken, H., & Fikkers, K. M. (2014). Issue-relevant thinking and identification as mechanisms of narrative persuasion. *Poetics, 44*, 84–99. doi:http://dx.doi.org/10.1016/j.poetic.2014.05.001.

Hogg, M. A. (2000). Subjective uncertainty reduction through self-categorization: A motivational theory of social identity processes. *European Review of Social Psychology, 11*(1), 223–255. doi:10.1080/14792772043000040.

Hogg, M. A. (2014). From uncertainty to extremism: Social categorization and identity processes. *Current Directions in Psychological Science, 23*, 338–342. doi:10.1177/0963721414540168.

Hogg, M. A., Kruglanski, A., & van den Bos, K. (2013). Uncertainty and the roots of extremism. *Journal of Social Issues, 69*(3), 407–418. doi:10.1111/josi.12021.

Holtmann, P. (2013). Countering al-Qaeda's single narrative. *Perspectives on Terrorism, 7*(2), 142–146. Retrieved from www.terrorismanalysts.com/pt/index.php/pot/article/view/262/html.

Hong, S.-M., Giannakopoulos, E., Laing, D., & Williams, N. A. (1994). Psychological Reactance: Effects of age and gender. *The Journal of Social Psychology, 134*(2), 223–228. doi:10.1080/00224545.1994.9711385.

Horgan, J. (2008). Deradicalization or disengagement? *Perspectives on Terrorism, 2*(4), 3–8. Retrieved from www.terrorismanalysts.com/pt/index.php/pot/article/view/32/html.

Hornsey, M. J. (2008). Social identity theory and self-categorization theory: A historical review. *Social and Personality Psychology Compass, 2*(1), 204–222. doi:10.1111/j.175004.2007.00066.x.

Howe, L. C., & Krosnick, J. A. (2017). Attitude strength. *Annual Review of Psychology, 68*(1), 327–351. doi:10.1146/annurev-psych-1224133600.

Hu, Y., & Sundar, S. (2009). Effects of online health sources on credibility and behavioral intentions. *Communication Research, 37*(1), 105–132. doi:10.1177/0093650209351512.

Hui, J. Y. (2016). Social media analytics for intelligence and counter-extremism. In M. Khader, Loo Seng Neo, G. Ong, E. T. Mingyi, & J. Chin (Eds), *Combating violent extremism and radicalization in the digital era* (pp. 328–348). Hershey, PA: IGI Global. doi:10.4018/97-52215.ch016.

Hussain, G., & Saltman, E. M. (2014). *Jihad trending: A comprehensive analysis of online extremism and how to counter it*. London, UK: The Quilliam Foundation. Retrieved from www.quilliamfoundation.org/wp/wp-content/uploads/publications/free/jihad-trendingquilliam-report.pdf.

Igartua, J. J., & Vega, J. (2015, May). *Identification with characters and cognitive processes in entertainment-education interventions through audiovisual fiction*. Paper presented at the Mass Communication Division of the International Communication Association 65th Annual Conference, San Juan, Puerto Rico. Retrieved from www.researchgate.net/profile/Juan_Jose_Igartua/publication/280314331_Identification_With_Characters_and_Cognitive_Processes_in_Entertainment-_Education_Interventions_Through_Audiovisual_Fiction/links/55b205b008aed621ddfd7a9b.pdf.

Iles, I. A., & Nan, X. (2017). It's no laughing matter: An exploratory study of the use of ironic versus sarcastic humor in health-related advertising messages. *Health Marketing Quarterly, 34*(3), 187–201. doi:10.1080/07359683.2017.1346432.

Ingram, H. J. (2016, June). *A brief history of propaganda during conflict: Lessons for counter-terrorism strategic communications* [Research Paper]. The Hague, NL: The International Centre for Counter-Terrorism. doi:10.19165/2016.1.06.

Ingram, H. J. (2016, November). *A "Linkage-based" approach to combating militant Islamist propaganda: A two-tiered framework for practitioners* [Policy Brief]. The Hague, NL: The International Centre for Counter-Terrorism. doi:10.19165/2016.2.06.

Ingram, H. J. (2017). Learning from ISIS's virtual propaganda war for Western Muslims: A comparison of Inspire and Dabiq. Retrieved from the International Centre for Counter-Terrorism website https://icct.nl/wp-content/uploads/2017/07/INGRAM-nato-chapter-21JUL17.pdf.

Ingram, H. J., & Reed, A. G. (2016). *Lessons from history for counter-terrorism strategic communications* [Policy Brief]. The Hague, NL: The International Centre for Counter-Terrorism. doi:10.19165/2016.2.04.

Institute for Strategic Dialogue (ISD). (2018). *Civil society networks*. Retrieved from The Institute for Strategic Dialogue website: www.isdglobal.org/programmes/grassroots-networks/.

Jacobson, M. (2010). Terrorist drop-outs: One way of promoting a counter-narrative. *Perspectives on Terrorism, 3*(2). Retrieved from www.terrorismanalysts.com/pt/index.php/pot/article/view/66/html.

Jervis, R. (2017). *Perception and misperception in international politics*. Princeton, NJ: Princeton University Press.

Jowett, G. S., & O'Donnell, V. (2012). *Propaganda and persuasion* (5th Ed.). Thousand Oaks, CA: SAGE Publications.

Kaplan, A. M., & Haenlein, M. (2010). Users of the world, unite! The challenges and opportunities of Social Media. *Business Horizons, 53*(1), 59–68. doi:10.1016/j.bushor.2009.09.003.

Katz, R. (2014, September 26). The state department's Twitter war with ISIS is embarrassing. *Time*. Retrieved from http://time.com/3387065/ISIS-twitter-war-state-department.

Keller, P. A., & Lehmann, D. R. (2008). Designing effective health communications: A meta-analysis. *Journal of Public Policy & Marketing, 27*(2), 117–130. doi:10.1509/jppm.27.2.117.

Khalil, J. (2014). Radical beliefs and violent actions are not synonymous: How to place the key disjuncture between attitudes and behaviors at the heart of our research into political violence. *Studies in Conflict & Terrorism, 37*(2), 198–211. doi:10.1080/1057610X.2014.862902.

Khalil, J., & Zeuthen, M. (2016, June). *Countering violent extremism and risk reduction* (Whitehall Report 2–16). London, UK: Royal United Services Institute for Defence and Security Studies (RUSI). Retrieved from https://rusi.org/sites/default/files/20160608_cve_and_rr.combined.online4.pdf.

Khalil, J., & Zeuthen, M. (2018). *The 'disconnect model' of violent extremism*. Retrieved from the PCDN website https://pcdnetwork.org/wp-content/uploads/2018/07/Khalil-Zeuthen-The-Disconnect-Model-of-Violent-Extremism.pdf.

Kim, A., Lee, S., Marguleas, O., & Beyer, J. L. (2016, October 3). *Do counter-narrative programs slow terrorist recruiting?* (JSIS Cybersecurity Report). Retrieved from The Henry M. Jackson School of International Studies website https://jsis.washington.edu/news/jsis-cybersecurity-reportcounter-narrative-programs-stop-terrorist-recruiting-efforts.

Kim, Y. (2015). Exploring the effects of source credibility and others' comments on online news evaluation. *Electronic News of the Association for Education in Journalism and Mass Communication (AEJMC)*, 9(3), 160–176. doi:10.1177/1931243115593318.

Kitzinger, J. (1995). Qualitative research. Introducing focus groups. *British Medical Journal*, 311, 299–302. Retrieved from www.ncbi.nlm.nih.gov/pmc/articles/PMC2550365/pdf/bmj0060031.pdf.

Klausen, J. (2015). Tweeting the Jihad: Social media networks of Western foreign fighters in Syria and Iraq. *Studies in Conflict & Terrorism*, 38(1), 1–22. doi:10.1080/1057610x.2014.974948.

Klausen, J., Barbieri, E. T., Reichlin-Melnick, A., & Zelin, A. Y. (2012). The YouTube Jihadists: A social network analysis of Al-Muhajiroun's propaganda campaign. *Perspectives on Terrorism*, 6(1). Retrieved from www.terrorism-analysts.com/pt/index.php/pot/article/view/klausen-et-al-youtube-jihadists/361.

Knobloch-Westerwick, S., & Hastall, M. R. (2010). Please yourself: Social identity effects on selective exposure to news about in- and out-Groups. *Journal of Communication*, 60(3), 515–535. doi:10.1111/j.146466.2010.01495.x.

Koch, E. J. (2014). How does anticipated regret influence health and safety decisions? A literature review. *Basic and Applied Social Psychology*, 36(5), 397–412. doi:10.1080/01973533.2014.935379.

Koehler, D. (2016). *Understanding deradicalization: Methods, tools and programs for countering violent extremism*. London: Routledge.

Konijn, E. A. (2008). Affects and media exposure. In W. Donsbach (Ed.), *The international encyclopedia of communication* (Vol. 1, pp. 123–129). Oxford: Wiley-Blackwell.

Konijn, E. A., & Hoorn, J. F. (2005). Some like it bad: Testing a model for perceiving and experiencing fictional characters. *Media Psychology*, 7(2), 107–144. doi:10.1207/S1532785XMEP0702_1.

Konijn, E. A., Oegema, D., Schneider, I. K., De Vos, B., Krijt, M., & Prins, J. (2010). *Jong en multimediaal: Mediagebruik en meningsvorming onder jongeren, in het bijzonder moslimjongeren* [Young and multi-media: Media use and information seeking among adolescents and young adults, especially among Muslim youth in the Netherlands]. Amsterdam, NL: Breckfield Hall Publishers.

Konijn, E. A., van der Molen, J. H. W., & van Nes, S. (2009). Emotions bias perceptions of realism in audiovisual media: Why we may take fiction for real. *Discourse Processes*, 46(4), 309–340. doi:10.1080/01638530902728546.

Korda, H., & Itani, Z. (2013). Harnessing social media for health promotion and behavior change. *Health Promotion Practice*, 14(1), 15–23. doi:10.1177/1524839911405850.

Kozinets, R. V. (2002). The field behind the screen: Using netnography for marketing research in online communities. *Journal of Marketing Research*, 39(1), 61–72. doi:10.1509/jmkr.39.1.61.18935.

Kozinets, R. V. (2010). *Netnography: Doing ethnographic research online*. Thousand Oaks, CA: Sage.

Kozinets, R. V. (2015). *Netnography: Redefined*. Los Angeles, CA: Sage.

Kozinets, R. V., Dolbec, P.-Y., & Earley, A. (2014). Netnographic analysis: Understanding culture through social media data. In U. Flick (Ed.), *The SAGE handbook of qualitative data analysis* (pp. 262–276). London, UK: SAGE Publications.

Kreuter, M. W., Green, M. C., Cappella, J. N., Slater, M. D., Wise, M. E., Storey, D., ... Woolley, S. (2007). Narrative communication in cancer prevention and control: A framework to guide research and application. *Annals of Behavioral Medicine, 33*(3), 221–235. doi:10.1007/bf02879904.

Kreuter, M. W., & Wray, R. J. (2003). Tailored and targeted health communication: Strategies for enhancing information relevance. *American Journal of Health Behavior, 27*(1), S227–S232. doi:10.5993/AJHB.27.1.s3.6.

Krueger, R. A., & Casey, M. A. (2015a). Focus group interviewing. In K. E. Newcomer, H. P. Hatry & J. S. Wholey (Eds), *Handbook of Practical Program Evaluation* (4th edn, pp. 506–534). San Francisco, CA: John Wiley & Sons.

Krueger, R. A., & Casey, M. A. (2015b). *Focus groups: A practical guide for applied research* [E-book version] (5th edn). Los Angeles, CA: SAGE Publications.

Kruglanski, A. W., Gelfand, M. J., Belanger, J. J., Sheveland, A., Hetiarachichi, M., & Gunaratna, R. (2014). The psychology of radicalization and deradicalization: How significance quest impacts violent extremism. *Advances in Political Psychology, 1,* 69–93.

Lee, B. J. (2018). Informal countermessaging: The potential and perils of informal online countermessaging *Studies in Conflict & Terrorism*, 1–17. doi:10.1080/10 57610X.2018.1513697.

Lee, E.-J. (2006). When and how does depersonalization increase conformity to group norms in computer-mediated communication? *Communication Research, 33*(6), 423–447. doi:10.1177/0093650206293248.

Lee, E.-J. (2007). Deindividuation effects on group polarization in computer-mediated communication: The role of group identification, public-self-awareness, and perceived argument quality. *Journal of Communication, 57*(2), 385–403. doi:10.1111/j.146466.2007.00348.x.

Lentini, P. (2013). *Neojihadism: Towards a new understanding of terrorism and extremism?* (E-book edn). Cheltenham, UK: Edward Elgar Publishing.

Levac, J. l. J., & O'Sullivan, T. (2010). Social media and its use in health promotion. *Revue interdisciplinaire des sciences de la santé-Interdisciplinary Journal of Health Sciences, 1*(1), 47–53. doi:10.18192/riss-ijhs.v1i1.1534.

Liht, J., & Savage, S. (2013). Preventing violent extremism through value complexity: Being Muslim being British. *Journal of Strategic Security, 6*(4), 44–66. doi:10.5038/194472.6.4.3.

Lindekilde, L. (2012). Introduction: Assessing the effectiveness of counter-radicalisation policies in northwestern Europe. *Critical Studies on Terrorism, 5*(3), 335–344. doi:10.1080/17539153.2012.723522.

Lindekilde, L. (2016). Radicalization, de-radicalization, and counter-radicalization. In R. Jackson (Ed.), *Routledge handbook of critical terrorism studies* (pp. 248–259). Abingdon, UK: Routledge.

Logan, S. (2016). Grasping at thin air: Countering terrorist narratives online. In A. Aly, S. MacDonald, L. Jarvis, & T. Chen (Eds), *Violent extremism online: New perspectives on terrorism and the internet*. London, UK: Routledge. doi:10.4324/9781315692029.

Lovejoy, K., & Saxton, G. D. (2012). Information, community, and action: How nonprofit organizations use social media. *Journal of Computer-Mediated Communication, 17*(3), 337–353. doi:10.1111/j.108101.2012.01576.x.

Mackie, D. M., Gastardo-Conaco, M. C., & Skelly, J. J. (1992). Knowledge of the advocated position and the processing of in-group and out-group persuasive messages. *Personality and Social Psychology Bulletin, 18*(2), 145–151. doi:10.1177/0146167292182005.

Mackie, D. M., Worth, L. T., & Asuncion, A. G. (1990). Processing of persuasive in-group messages. *Journal of Personality and Social Psychology, 58*(5), 812–822. doi:10.1037/002514.58.5.812.

Macnair, L., & Frank, R. (2017). Voices Against Extremism: A case study of a community-based CVE counter-narrative campaign. *Journal for Deradicalization, 10,* 147–174. Retrieved from http://journals.sfu.ca/jd/index.php/jd/article/view/86.

Macnamara, J. (2017). *Evaluating public communication: Exploring new models, standards, and best practice.* London, UK/New York, NY: Routledge.

Mann, L. Doosje, B., Konijn, E. A., Nickolson, L., Moore, U., & Ruigrok, N. (2015). *Indicatoren en manifestaties van weerbaarheid van de Nederlandse bevolking tegen extremistische boodschappen: Een theoretische en methodologische verkenning* [Indicators and manifestations of resilience of the Dutch population against extremist messages. A theoretical and methodological exploration]. Retrieved from The Research and Documentation Centre, Dutch Ministry of Security & Justice website www.wodc.nl/onderzoeksdatabase/2488-de-meetbaarheid-van-deweerbaarheid.aspx.

Marcellino, W., Smith, M., Paul, C., & Skrabala, L. (2017). *Monitoring social media: Lessons for future Department of Defense social media analysis in support of information operations* (RAND Publication no. RR-1742-OSD) [Research Report]. Retrieved from the RAND corporation website www.rand.org/pubs/research_reports/RR1742.html.

Marques, J., Abrams, D., Páez, D., & Martinez-Taboada, C. (1998). The role of categorization and in-group norms in judgments of groups and their members. *Journal of Personality and Social Psychology, 75*(4), 976. doi:10.1037/002514.75.4.976.

Marques, J. M., Abrams, D., Páez, D., & Hogg, M. A. (2001). Social categorization, social identification and rejection of deviant group members. In M. A. Hogg & R. S. Tindale (Eds), *Blackwell handbook of social psychology: Group processes* (pp. 400–424). Oxford, UK: Blackwell Publishers. doi:10.1002/9780470998458.ch17.

Marques, J. M., Yzerbyt, V. Y., & Leyens, J.-P. (1988). The "Black Sheep Effect": Extremity of judgments towards ingroup members as a function of group identification. *European Journal of Social Psychology, 18*(1), 1–16. doi:10.1002/ejsp.2420180102.

Mason, W., & Suri, S. (2012). Conducting behavioral research on Amazon's Mechanical Turk. *Behavior Research Methods, 44*(1), 1–23. doi:10.3758/s1342112.

McCauley, C., & Moskalenko, S. (2014). Toward a profile of lone wolf terrorists: What moves an individual from radical opinion to radical action. *Terrorism and Political Violence, 26* (January), 69–85. Retrieved from www.tandfonline.com/doi/abs/10.1080/09546553.2014.849916#.UtVbJPtfkpo.

McDowell-Smith, A., Speckhard, A., & Yayla, A. S. (2017). Beating ISIS in the digital space: Focus testing ISIS defector counter-narrative videos with American college students. *Journal for Deradicalization*, *10*, 50–76. Retrieved from http://journals.sfu.ca/jd/index.php/jd/article/view/83/73.

McGarty, C., Haslam, S. A., Hutchinson, K. J., & Turner, J. C. (1994). The effects of salient group memberships on persuasion. *Small Group Research*, *25*(2), 267–293. doi:10.1177/1046496494252007.

McGuire, W. J. (1964). Inducing resistance to persuasion: Some contemporary approaches. In L. Berkowitz (Ed.), *Advances in experimental social psychology* (Vol. 1, pp. 191–229). New York: Academic Press.

Medhat, W., Hassan, A., & Korashy, H. (2014). Sentiment analysis algorithms and applications: A survey. *Ain Shams Engineering Journal*, *5*(4), 1093–1113. doi:10.1016/j.asej.2014.04.011.

Metzger, M. J., & Flanagin, A. J. (2013). Credibility and trust of information in online environments: The use of cognitive heuristics. *Journal of Pragmatics*, *59*, 210–220. doi:10.1016/j.pragma.2013.07.012.

Metzger, M. J., & Flanagin, A. J. (2017). Digital media and perceptions of source credibility in political communication. In K. Kenski & K. H. Jamieson (Eds), *The Oxford handbook of political communication*. New York: Oxford University Press.

Metzger, M. J., Flanagin, A. J., & Medders, R. B. (2010). Social and heuristic approaches to credibility evaluation online. *Journal of Communication*, *60*(3), 413–439. doi:10.1111/j.146466.2010.01488.x.

Miller, C., & Bartlett, J. (2012). 'Digital fluency': Towards young people's critical use of the internet. *Journal of Information Literacy*, *6*(2), 35–55. doi:10.11645/6.2.1714.

Miller, C., & Chauhan, L. S. (2017). Radical beliefs and violent behaviours. In L. Colaert (Ed.), *'De-radicalisation': Scientific insights for policy* (pp. 23–46). Brussels: Flemish Peace Institute. Retrieved from www.flemishpeaceinstitute.eu/sites/vlaamsvredesinstituut.eu/files/wysiwyg/de-radicalisation_-_chapter_miller_selig_chauhan.pdf.

Miller, C. H., Burgoon, M., Grandpre, J. R., & Alvaro, E. M. (2006). Identifying principal risk factors for the initiation of adolescent smoking behaviors: The significance of psychological reactance. *Health Communication*, *19*(3), 241–252. doi:10.1207/s15327027hc1903_6.

Miller, C. H., Lane, L. T., Deatrick, L. M., Young, A. M., & Potts, K. A. (2007). Psychological reactance and promotional health messages: The effects of controlling language, lexical concreteness, and the restoration of freedom. *Human Communication Research*, *33*(2), 219–240. doi:10.1111/j.146958.2007.00297.x.

Miron, A. M., & Brehm, J. W. (2006). Reactance theory – 40 years later. *Zeitschrift für Sozialpsychologie*, *37*(1), 9–18. doi:10.1024/004514.37.1.9.

Moghaddam, F. M. (2005). The staircase to terrorism: A psychological exploration. *American Psychologist*, *60*(2), 161–169. doi:10.1037/00066X.60.2.161.

Mothers for Life (2015). *Open letter to our sons and daughters*. Retrieved from the GIRDS website www.girds.org/files/openletter.pdf.

Moran, M. B., & Sussman, S. (2014). Translating the link between social identity and health behavior into effective health communication strategies: An experimental application using antismoking advertisements. *Health Communication*, *29*(10), 1057–1066. doi:10.1080/10410236.2013.832830.

Moreno, M. A., Goniu, N., Moreno, P. S., & Diekema, D. (2013). Ethics of social media research: Common concerns and practical considerations. *Cyberpsychology, Behavior and Social Networking*, 16(9), 708–713. doi:10.1089/cyber.2012.0334.

Morgan, S. E., King, A. J., & Ivic, R. (2011). Using new technologies to enhance health communication research methodology. In T. L. Thompson, R. Parrot, & J. F. Nussbaum (Eds.), *Handbook of health communication* [E-reader version]. (2nd edn). London, UK: Taylor & Francis.

Moyer-Gusé, E. (2008). Toward a theory of entertainment persuasion: Explaining the persuasive effects of entertainment-education messages. *Communication Theory*, 18(3), 407–425. doi:10.1111/j.146885.2008.00328.x.

Moyer-Gusé, E., & Dale, K. (2017). Narrative persuasion theories. In R. Patrick (Ed.), *The international encyclopedia of media effects* (Vol. 3, pp. 1345–1354). Chichester, UK: John Wiley & Sons, Inc. doi:10.1002/9781118783764.wbieme0082.

Moyer-Gusé, E., Mahood, C., & Brookes, S. (2011). Entertainment-education in the context of humor: Effects on safer sex intentions and risk perceptions. *Health Communication*, 26(8), 765–774. doi:10.1080/10410236.2011.566832.

Moyer-Gusé, E., & Nabi, R. L. (2010). Explaining the effects of narrative in an entertainment television program: Overcoming resistance to persuasion. *Human Communication Research*, 36(1), 26–52. doi:10.1111/j.146958.2009.01367.x.

Nabi, R. L. (2015). Emotional flow in persuasive health messages. *Health Communication*, 30(2), 114–124. doi:10.1080/10410236.2014.974129.

Nabi, R. L. (2016). Laughing in the face of fear (of disease detection): Using humor to promote cancer self-examination behavior. *Health Communication*, 31(7), 873–883. doi:10.1080/10410236.2014.1000479.

Nabi, R. L., Moyer-Gusé, E., & Byrne, S. (2007). All joking aside: A serious investigation into the persuasive effect of funny social issue messages. *Communication Monographs*, 74(1), 29–54. doi:10.1080/03637750701196896.

Neiger, B. L., Thackeray, R., Burton, S. H., Giraud-Carrier, C. G., & Fagen, M. C. (2012). Evaluating social media's capacity to develop engaged audiences in health promotion settings. *Health Promotion Practice*, 14(2), 157–162. doi:10.1177/1524839912469378.

Neiger, B. L., Thackeray, R., van Wagenen, S. A., Hanson, C. L., West, J. H., Barnes, M. D., & Fagen, M. C. (2012). Use of social media in health promotion: Purposes, key performance indicators, and evaluation metrics. *Health Promotion Practice*, 13(2), 159–164. doi:10.1177/1524839911433467.

Nelson-Field, K., Riebe, E., & Newstead, K. (2013). The emotions that drive viral video. *Australasian Marketing Journal (AMJ)*, 21(4), 205–211. doi:10.1016/j.ausmj.2013.07.003.

Neo, L. S., Dillon, L., Shi, P., Tan, J., Wang, Y., & Gomes, D. (2016). Understanding the psychology of persuasive violent extremist online platforms. In M. Khader, L. S. Neo, G. Ong, E. Tan, & J. Chin (Eds), *Countering violent extremism and radicalisation in the digital era* (pp. 1–15). Hershey, PA: IGI Global. doi:10.4018/97-52215.ch001.

Neumann, P. R. (2012). *Countering online radicalization in America*. Washington, DC: Bipartisan Policy Center.

Neumann, P. R. (2013a). The trouble with radicalization. *International Affairs*, 89(4), 873–893. doi:10.1111/146346.12049.

Neumann, P. R. (2013b). Options and strategies for countering online radicalization in the United States. *Studies in Conflict & Terrorism*, 36(6), 431–459. doi:1 0.1080/1057610X.2013.784568.

Neumann, P. R. (2015). *Victims, perpetrators, assets: The narratives of Islamic State defectors*. Retrieved from London, UK: http://icsr.info/wp-content/ uploads/2015/09/ICSR-Report-Victims-Perpertrators-Assets-The-Narratives-of-Islamic-State-Defectors.pdf.

Neumann, P. R. (2016). *Radicalized: New jihadists and the threat to the west* [E reader version]. London, UK: I.B. Tauris

Noar, S. M. (2006). A 10-year retrospective of research in health mass media campaigns: Where do we go from here? *Journal of Health Communication*, 11(1), 21–42. doi:10.1080/10810730500461059.

Noar, S. M. (2011). An audience–channel–message–evaluation (ACME) framework for health communication campaigns. *Health Promotion Practice*, 13(4), 481–488. doi:10.1177/1524839910386901.

Noar, S. M., Harrington, N. G., & Aldrich, R. S. (2009). The role of message tailoring in the development of persuasive health communication messages. *Annals of the International Communication Association*, 33(1), 73–133. doi:10.1080/23 808985.2009.11679085.

Noar, S. M., & Head, K. J. (2011). Trends in the research and practice of health communication campaigns. *Sociology Compass*, 5(6), 426–438. doi:10.1111/ j.175020.2011.00379.x.

Noar, S. M., Palmgreen, P., Chabot, M., Dobransky, N., & Zimmerman, R. S. (2009). A 10-year systematic review of HIV/AIDS mass communication campaigns: Have we made progress? *Journal of Health Communication*, 14(1), 15–42. doi:10.1080/10810730802592239.

Noordegraaf, M., Douglas, S., Bos, A., & Klem, W. (2016). *Evaluation Counterterrorism Strategy 2011–2015*. Retrieved from the Research and Documentation Centre, Dutch Ministry of Security & Justice website www.wodc.nl/ onderzoeksdatabase/2608-evaluatie-nationalecontraterrorisme-strategie-201015. aspx.

O'Keefe, D. (1999). How to handle opposing arguments in persuasive messages: A meta-analytic review of the effects of one-sided and two-sided messages. *Annals of the International Communication Association*, 22(1), 209–249. doi:10.1080/2 3808985.1999.11678963.

O'Keefe, D. J. (2016). *Persuasion: Theory and research* (3rd edn). Los Angeles, CA: SAGE Publications.

Pang, B., & Lee, L. (2008). Opinion mining and sentiment analysis. *Foundations and Trends in Information Retrieval*, 2(1–2), 1–135. doi:10.1561/1500000011.

Paolacci, G., & Chandler, J. (2014). Inside the Turk: Understanding Mechanical Turk as a participant pool. *Current Directions in Psychological Science*, 23(3), 184–188. doi:10.1177/0963721414531598.

Paul, C., Yeats, J., Clarke, C. P., Matthews, M., & Skrabala, L. (2015). *Assessing and evaluating Department of Defense efforts to inform, influence, and persuade: Desk reference* (RAND Publication No. RR809/1-OSD) [Research Report]. Retrieved from the RAND corporation website: www.rand.org/content/dam/ rand/pubs/research_reports/RR800/RR809z1/RAND_RR809z1.pdf.

Pauwels, L., Brion, F., Schils, N., Laffineur, J., Verhage, A., De Ruyver, B., & Easton, M. (2014). *Explaining and understanding the role of exposure to new social media on violent extremism: An integrative quantitative and qualitative approach*. Ghent: Academia Press. Retrieved from www.researchgate.net/publication/271511172_Explaining_and_understanding_the_role_of_exposure_to_new_social_media_on_violent_extremism_an_integrative_quantitative_and_qualitative_approach.

Pauwels, L., & Schils, N. (2016). Differential online exposure to extremist content and political violence: Testing the relative strength of social learning and competing perspectives. *Terrorism and Political Violence, 28*(1), 1–29. doi:10.1080/09546553.2013.876414.

Pearson, E. (2018). Online as the new frontline: Affect, gender, and ISIS-take-down on social media. *Studies in Conflict & Terrorism*, 1–25. doi:10.1080/1057610x.2017.1352280.

Pearson, E., & Brown, K. E. (2018). Social media, the online environment and terrorism. In A. Silke (Ed.), *Routledge handbook of terrorism and counterterrorism* (pp. 149–164). London, UK: Routledge.

Perloff, R. M. (2010). *The dynamics of persuasion communication and attitudes in the 21st century* (4th edn). New York: Routledge.

Peters, G.-J. Y., Ruiter, R. A. C., & Kok, G. (2013). Threatening communication: A critical re-analysis and a revised meta-analytic test of fear appeal theory. *Health Psychology Review, 7*(sup1), S8–S31. doi:10.1080/17437199.2012.703527.

Petrosino, A., Turpin-Petrosino, C., & Buehler, J. (2003). Scared straight and other juvenile awareness programs for preventing juvenile delinquency: A systematic review of the randomized experimental evidence. *The ANNALS of the American Academy of Political and Social Science, 589*(1), 41–62. doi:10.1177/0002716203254693.

Petty, R. E., & Cacioppo, J. T. (1986). The elaboration likelihood model of persuasion. *Advances in Experimental Social Psychology, 19*, 123–205. doi:10.1016/S006601(08)6021.

Pfau, M., & van Bockern, S. (1994). The persistence of inoculation in conferring resistance to smoking initiation among adolescents. *Human Communication Research, 20*(3), 413–430. doi:10.1111/j.146958.1994.tb00329.x.

Pfau, M., van Bockern, S., & Kang, J. G. (1992). Use of inoculation to promote resistance to smoking initiation among adolescents. *Communication Monographs, 59*(3), 213–230. doi:10.1080/03637759209376266.

Pfau, M., & Burgoon, M. (1988). Inoculation in political campaign communication. *Human Communication Research, 15*(1), 91–111. doi:10.1111/j.146958.1988.tb00172.x.

Pfau, M., Kenski, H. C., Nitz, M., & Sorenson, J. (1990). Efficacy of inoculation strategies in promoting resistance to political attack messages: Application to direct mail. *Communication Monographs, 57*(1), 25–43. doi:10.1080/03637759009376183.

Postmes, T., Spears, R., Lee, A. T., & Novak, R. J. (2005). Individuality and social influence in groups: inductive and deductive routes to group identity. *Journal of Personality and Social Psychology, 89*(5), 747. doi:10.1037/0022514.89.5.747.

Postmes, T., Spears, R., Sakhel, K., & Groot, D. (2001). Social influence in computer-mediated communication: The effects of anonymity on group behavior.

Personality and Social Psychology Bulletin, 27(10), 1243–1254. doi:10.1177/01461672012710001.

Pyszczynski, T., Abdollahi, A., Solomon, S., Greenberg, J., Cohen, F., & Weise, D. (2006). Mortality salience, martyrdom, and military might: The great Satan versus the axis of evil. *Personality and Social Psychology Bulletin*, 32(4), 525–537. doi:10.1177/0146167205282157.

Qatar International Academy for Security Studies (QIASS). (2013, September). *Countering violent extremism: the counter narrative study*. Retrieved from The Qatar International Academy for Security Studies website. https://qiass.org/wp-content/uploads/2016/05/CVE-Counter-Narrative-Study.pdf.

Quick, B. L., & Considine, J. R. (2008). Examining the use of forceful language when designing exercise persuasive messages for adults: A test of conceptualizing reactance arousal as a two-step process. *Health Communication*, 23(5), 483–491. doi:10.1080/10410230802342150.

Quick, B. L., & Stephenson, M. T. (2008). Examining the role of trait reactance and sensation seeking on perceived threat, state reactance, and reactance restoration. *Human Communication Research*, 34(3), 448–476. doi:10.1111/j.146958. 2008.00328.x.

Rabasa, A., & Benard, C. (2015). *Eurojihad: Patterns of Islamist radicalization and terrorism in Europe*. New York: Cambridge University Press.

Radicalisation Awareness Network (RAN). (2015). *Counter narratives and alternative narratives*. Retrieved from https://ec.europa.eu/home-affairs/sites/home affairs/files/what-we-do/networks/radicalisation_awareness_network/ran-papers/docs/issue_paper_cn_oct2015_en.pdf.

Radicalisation Awareness Network (RAN). (2016). *Handbook: Voices of victims of terrorism*. Retrieved from Retrieved from https://ec.europa.eu/home-affairs/sites/homeaffairs/files/what-wedo/networks/radicalisation_awareness_network/about-ran/ranrvt/docs/ran_vvt_handbook_may_2016_en.pdf.

Radicalisation Awareness Network (RAN). (2017). *Preventing radicalisation to terrorism and violent extremism: Approaches and practices*. Retrieved from https://ec.europa.eu/home-affairs/sites/homeaffairs/files/what-wedo/networks/radicalisation_awareness_network/ran-best-practices/docs/ran_collectionapproaches_and_practices_en.pdf.

Rane, H. (2016). Narratives and counter-narratives of Islamist extremism. In A. Aly, S. MacDonald, L. Jarvis, & T. Chen (Eds), *Violent extremism online: New perspectives on terrorism and the internet*. London, UK: Routledge. doi:10.4324/9781315692029.

Ranstorp, M. (2010). *Understanding violent radicalisation: Terrorist and jihadist movements in Europe*. London, UK: Routledge.

Reed, A. (2017a, March 17). Should we counter the narrative? Retrieved from The International Centre for Counter-Terrorism website: https://icct.nl/publication/is-propaganda-should-we-counter-the-narrative/.

Reed, A. (2017b). *Counter-terrorism strategic communications back to the future: Lessons from past and present*. Retrieved from The International Centre for Counter-Terrorism website: https://icct.nl/wp-content/uploads/2017/07/FINAL-Reed-CTSC-Back-to-the-Future.pdf.

Reed, A., Ingram, H., & Whittaker, J. (2017, November). *Countering terrorist narratives* (PE 596.829). Directorate General for Internal Policies, Study for Committee on Civil Liberties, Justice and Home Affairs. Retrieved from www.europarl.europa.eu/RegData/etudes/STUD/2017/596829/IPOL_STU(2017)596829_EN.pdf.

Reicher, S., Spears, R., & Haslam, A. S. (2010). The social identity approach in social psychology. In M. Wetherell & C. T. Mohanty (Eds), *The SAGE handbook of identities* (pp. 45–62). London, UK: SAGE.

Reynolds, L., & Scott, R. (2016). *Digital citizens: Countering extremism online.* Retrieved from the Demos website www.demos.co.uk/wpcontent/uploads/2016/12/Digital-Citizenship-web-1.pdf.

Reynolds, L., & Tuck, H. (2016). *The counter-narrative monitoring & evaluation handbook.* London: The Institute for Strategic Dialogue. Retrieved from www.isdglobal.org/wp-content/uploads/2017/06/CN-Monitoring-and-EvaluationHandbook.pdf.

Richards, I. (2016). "Flexible" capital accumulation in Islamic State social media. *Critical Studies on Terrorism, 9*(2), 205–225. doi:10.1080/17539153.2015.1125642.

Richardson, R. (2013, December). *Fighting fire with fire: Target audience responses to online antiviolence campaigns* [ASPI Report]. Retrieved from the Australian Strategic Policy Institute website www.aspi.org.au/report/fighting-fire-fire-target-audience-responses-online-antiviolence-campaigns.

Rieger, D., Frischlich, L., & Bente, G. (2013). *Propaganda 2.0: Psychological effects of right-wing and Islamic internet videos.* Köln: Wolters Kluwers Germany.

Rieger, D., Frischlich, L., & Bente, G. (2017). Propaganda in an insecure, unstructured world: How psychological uncertainty and authoritarian attitudes shape the evaluation of right-wing extremist internet propaganda. *Journal for Deradicalization, 10*, 203–229. Retrieved from http://journals.sfu.ca/jd/index.php/jd/article/download/88/78.

Rieger, D., Schmitt, J. B., & Frischlich, L. (2018). Hate and counter-voices in the Internet: Introduction to the special issue. *SCM Studies in Communication and Media, 7*(4), 459–472. doi:10.5771/2190001-459.

Riff, D., Lacy, S., & Fico, F. (2014). *Analyzing media messages: Using quantitative content analysis in research* (3rd edn). New York: Routledge.

Rimal, R. N., & Adkins, A. D. (2003). Using computers to narrowcast health messages: The role of audience segmentation, targeting, and tailoring in health promotion. In T. L. Thompson, A. M. Dorsey, K. I. Miller, & R. Parrott (Eds), *Handbook of health communication* (pp. 497–513). Mahwah, NJ: Lawrence Erlbaum Associates.

Ritzmann, A. (2017). *The role of propaganda in violent extremism and how to counter it.* Barcelona: Euro-Mediterranean Policies Department (IEMed). Retrieved from www.iemed.org/publicacions/historic-de-publicacions/enquesta-euromed/euromed-survey-2017/role_propaganda_in_violent_extremism_how_to_counter_Alexander_Ritzmann_EuromedSurvey2017.pdf.

Rocca, N. M. (in press). *Internet security facing Jihadist propaganda in Europe: The last challenge for society?* Cahiers des IFRE, Fondation Maison des sciences de l'homme. Retrieved from https://hal.archives-ouvertes.fr/hal-01651193.

Roex, I. (2014). Should we be scared of all Salafists in Europe? *Perspectives on Terrorism, 8*(3), 51–63. Retrieved from www.terrorismanalysts.com/pt/index.php/pot/article/download/346/689.

Rogers, R. W., & Mewborn, C. R. (1976). Fear appeals and attitude change: Effects of a threat's noxiousness, probability of occurrence, and the efficacy of coping responses. *Journal of Personality and Social Psychology, 34*(1), 54–61. doi:10.1037/002514.34.1.54.

Romaniuk, P. (2015, September). *Does CVE work? Lessons learned from the global effort to counter violent extremism* [Research Report]. Retrieved from the Global Center on Cooperative Security website www.globalcenter.org/wp-content/uploads/2015/09/Does-CVE-Work_2015.pdf.

Romaniuk, P., & Fink, N. C. (2012). *From input to impact: Evaluating terrorism prevention programs* [Policy Report]. Retrieved from the Center on Cooperative Security website http://globalcenter.org/wp-content/uploads/2012/10/CGCC_EvaluatingTerrorismPrevention.pdf.

Rossmann, C. (2015). Strategic health communication: Theory- and evidence-based campaign development. In A. Z. Derina Holtzhausen (Ed.), *The Routledge handbook of strategic communication* (pp. 409–423). New York: Routledge.

Rozendaal, E., Buijzen, M., & Valkenburg, P. (2011). Children's understanding of advertisers' persuasive tactics. *International Journal of Advertising, 30*(2), 329–350. doi:10.2501/IJA-3-3250.

Rozendaal, E., Opree, S. J., & Buijzen, M. (2016). Development and validation of a survey instrument to measure children's advertising literacy. *Media Psychology, 19*(1), 72–100. doi:10.1080/15213269.2014.885843.

Ruiter, R. A. C., Kessels, L. T. E., Peters, G.-J. Y., & Kok, G. (2014). Sixty years of fear appeal research: Current state of the evidence. *International Journal of Psychology, 49*(2), 63–70. doi:10.1002/ijop.12042.

Russell, J., & Rafiq, H. (2016). *Countering Islamist extremist narratives: A strategic briefing.* Retrieved from https://s3.amazonaws.com/academia.edu.documents/50998161/Countering-islamist-extremist-narratives.pdf?AWSAccessKeyId=AKIAIWOWYYGZ2Y53UL3A&Expires=1551656305&Signature=AAPSnTFlqHn00%2FlUtf55Jbf9v1Y%3D&response-content-disposition=inline%3B%20filename%3DCountering_Islamist_Extremist_Narratives.pdf.

Sageman, M. (2008). *Leaderless jihad: Terror networks in the twenty-first century.* Philadelphia, PA: University of Pennsylvania Press.

Saltman, E. M. (2014). *Online extremism: We need to target causes rather than symptoms* [Blog Post]. Retrieved from https://erinmariesaltman.com/2014/07/09/online-extremism-we-need-to-target-causes-rather-than-symptoms/.

Saltman, E. M., & Frenett, R. (2016). Female radicalization to ISIS and the role of women in CVE. In N. C. Fink, S. Zeiger & R. Bhulai (Eds), *A man's world? Exploring the roles of women in countering terrorism and violent extremism* (pp. 142–162). Retrieved from The Global Center on Cooperative Security website: www.globalcenter.org/wp-140 content/uploads/2016/07/AMansWorld_FULL.pdf.

Sandberg, T., & Conner, M. (2008). Anticipated regret as an additional predictor in the theory of planned behaviour: A meta-analysis. *British Journal of Social Psychology, 47*(4), 589–606. doi:10.1348/014466607X258704.

Sassenberg, K., Boos, M., & Rabung, S. (2005). Attitude change in face-to-face and computer-mediated communication: private self-awareness as mediator and moderator. *European Journal of Social Psychology, 35*(3), 361–374. doi:10.1002/ejsp.254.

Sassenberg, K., & Jonas, K. J. (2009). Attitude change and social influence on the net. In A. N. Joinson, K. Y. A. McKenna, T. Postmes & U.-D. Reips (Eds),

Oxford handbook of internet psychology. New York: Oxford University Press. doi:10.1093/oxfordhb/9780199561803.013.0018.

Schils, N., & Verhage, A. (2017). Understanding how and why young people enter radical or violent extremist groups. *International Journal of Conflict and Violence (IJCV)*, *11*, 473. doi:10.4119/UNIBI/ijcv.473.

Schmid, A. P. (2012, August). *Strengthening the role of victims and incorporating victims in efforts to counter violent extremism and terrorism* [Research Paper]. The Hague: The International Centre for Counter-Terrorism. doi:10.19165/2012.1.07.

Schmid, A. P. (2013, March). *Radicalisation, de-radicalisation, counter-radicalisation: A conceptual discussion and literature review* [Research Paper]. The Hague: The International Centre for Counter-Terrorism. doi:10.19165/2013.1.02.

Schmid, A. P. (2014, January). *Al-Qaeda's "single narrative" and attempts to develop counternarratives: The state of knowledge* [Research Paper]. The Hague: The International Centre for Counter-Terrorism. Retrieved from www.icct.nl/ download/file/Schmid-Al-Qaeda's-Single-Narrative-and-Attempts-to-Develop-Counter-Narratives-January-2014.pdf.

Schmid, A. P. (2014, May). *Violent and non-violent extremism: Two sides of the same coin* [Research Paper]. The Hague: The International Centre for Counter-Terrorism. doi:10.19165/2014.1.05.

Schmid, A. P. (2015, June). *Challenging the narrative of the "Islamic State"* [Research Paper]. The Hague: The International Centre for Counter-Terrorism. Retrieved from https://icct.nl/wp-content/uploads/2015/06/ICCT-Schmid-Challenging-the-Narrative-of-the-Islamic-State-June2015.pdf.

Schmid, A. P., & Forest, J. J. (2018). Research desiderata: 150 un- and under-researched topics and themes in the field of (counter-) terrorism studies – a new list. *Perspectives on Terrorism*, *12*(4), 68–76. Retrieved from www.jstor.org/ stable/pdf/26482979.pdf.

Scrivens, R., Davies, G., & Frank, R. (2017). Searching for signs of extremism on the web: An introduction to sentiment-based identification of radical authors. *Behavioral Sciences of Terrorism and Political Aggression*, 1–21. doi:10.1080/19 434472.2016.1276612.

Sherif, C. W., Sherif, M., & Nebergall, R. E. (1965). *Attitude and attitude change: The social judgment-involvement approach*. Philadelphia, PA: W. B. Saunders.

Sherif, C. W., Kelly, M., Rodgers, H. L., Jr., Sarup, G., & Tittler, B. I. (1973). Personal involvement, social judgment, and action. *Journal of Personality and Social Psychology*, *27*, 311–328.

Sherif, M., & Hovland, C. I. (1961). *Social judgment: Assimilation and contrast effects in communication and attitude change*. New Haven, CT: Yale University Press.

Shi, J., Poorisat, T., & Salmon, C. T. (2016). The use of social networking sites (SNSs) in health communication campaigns: review and recommendations. *Health Communication*, 1–8. doi:10.1080/10410236.2016.1242035.

Sieckelinck, S., & de Winter, M. (2015). Introduction. In S. Sieckelinck & M. de Winter (Eds), *Formers and families: Transitional journeys in and out of extremisms in the United Kingdom, Denmark and The Netherlands* (pp. 15–24), Retrieved from the National Coordinator Security and Counterterrorism (NCTV), Dutch Ministry of Security and Justice website www.nctv.nl/binaries/ end-report-formers-and-families_tcm31-30167.pdf.

Sikkens, E., van San, M., Sieckelinck, S., & de Winter, M. (2017). Parental influence on radicalization and de-radicalization according to the lived experiences of former extremists and their families. *Journal for Deradicalization, 12*, 192–226. Retrieved from http://journals.sfu.ca/jd/index.php/jd/article/download/115/96.

Silverman, T., Stewart, C. J., Birdwell, J., & Amanullah, Z. (2016, August). *The impact of counternarratives. Insights from a year-long cross-platform pilot study of counter-narrative curation, targeting, evaluation and impact.* Retrieved from The Institute for Strategic Dialogue website www.isdglobal. org/wp-content/uploads/2016/08/Impact-of-CounterNarratives_ONLINE_1. pdf *targeting, evaluation and impact.* Retrieved from London: www.isdglobal. org/wp-content/uploads/2016/08/Impact-of-CounterNarratives_ONLINE_1. pdf.

Simon, L., Greenberg, J., & Brehm, J. W. (1995). Trivialization: The forgotten mode of dissonance reduction. *Journal of Personality and Social Psychology, 68*(2), 247–260. doi:10.1037/002514.68.2.247.

Slater, M. D. (1996). Theory and method in health audience segmentation. *Journal of Health Communication, 1*(3), 267–284. doi:10.1080/108107396128059.

Slater, M. D. (2002). Entertainment education and the persuasive impact of narratives. In *Narrative impact: Social and cognitive foundations.* (pp. 157–181). Mahwah, NJ: Lawrence Erlbaum Associates Publishers.

Slater, M. D., Kelly, K. J., & Thackeray, R. (2006). Segmentation on a shoestring: Health audience segmentation in limited-budget and local social marketing interventions. *Health Promotion Practice, 7*(2), 170–173. doi:10.1177/1524839906286616.

Smith, A. N., Fischer, E., & Yongjian, C. (2012). How does brand-related user-generated content differ across YouTube, Facebook, and Twitter? *Journal of Interactive Marketing, 26*(2), 102–113. doi:10.1016/j.intmar. 2012.01.002.

Smith, J. R., & Hogg, M. A. (2008). Social identity and attitudes. In W. Crano & R. Prislin (Eds), *Attitudes and attitude change* (pp. 337–360). New York: Psychology Press.

Snyder, L. B. (2007). Health communication campaigns and their impact on behavior. *Journal of Nutrition Education and Behavior, 39*(2), S32–S40. doi:10.1016/j. jneb.2006.09.004.

Sorrentino, R. M., Bobocel, D. R., Gitta, M. Z., Olson, J. M., & Hewitt, E. C. (1988). Uncertainty orientation and persuasion: Individual differences in the effects of personal relevance on social judgments. *Journal of Personality and Social Psychology, 55*(3), 357.

Spears, R., Lea, M., & Lee, S. (1990). De-individuation and group polarization in computer-mediated communication. *British Journal of Social Psychology, 29*(2), 121–134. doi:10.1111/j.204309.1990.tb00893.x.

Spears, R., Lea, M., & Postmes, T. (2001). Social psychological theories of computer-mediated communication: Social pain or social gain. In *The new handbook of language and social psychology* (2nd edn, pp. 601–623). Chichester, UK: Wiley.

Spears, R., Lea, M., Postmes, T., & Wolbert, A. (2011). A SIDE look at computer-mediated interaction. In Z. Birchmeier, B. Dietz-Uhler, & G. Stasser (Eds), *Strategic uses of social technology: An interactive perspective of social psychology* (pp. 16–39). Cambridge, UK: Cambridge University Press.

Speckhard, A., & Shajkovci, A. (2018). *Challenges in creating, Deploying counter-narratives to deter would-be terrorists.* The International Center for the Study of Violent Extremism (ICSVE). Retrieved from www.researchgate.net/publication/329271529_Challenges_in_Creating_Deploying_Counter-Narratives_to_Deter_Would-be_Terrorists.

Speckhard, A., Shajkovci, A., & Bodo, L. (2018). *Fighting ISIS on Facebook—Breaking the ISIS brand counter-narratives project.* The International Center for the Study of Violent Extremism (ICSVE). Retrieved from www.icsve.org/fighting-isis-on-facebook-breaking-the-isis-brand-counter-narratives-project.

Speckhard, A., Shajkovci, A., Bodo, L., & Fazliu, H. (2018). *Bringing down the digital caliphate: A Breaking the ISIS Brand Counter-Narratives intervention with Albanian speaking Facebook accounts.* The International Center for the Study of Violent Extremism (ICSVE). Retrieved from www.icsve.org/bringing-down-the-digital-caliphate-a-breaking-the-isis-brand-counter-narratives-intervention-with-albanian-speaking-facebook-accounts.

Speckhard, A., Shajkovci, A., Wooster, C., & Izadi, N. (2018a). Mounting a Facebook brand awareness and safety ad campaign to break the ISIS brand in Iraq. *Perspectives on Terrorism, 12*(3), 50–66. Retrieved from www.universiteitleiden.nl/binaries/content/assets/customsites/perspectives-on-terrorism/2018/issue-3/04-mounting-a-facebook-brand-awareness-and-safety-ad-campaign-to-break-the-isis-brand-in-ira.pdf.

Speckhard, A., Shajkovci, A., Wooster, C., & Izadi, N. (2018b). Engaging English speaking Facebook users in an anti-ISIS awareness campaign. *Journal of Strategic Security, 11*(3), 52–78. Retrieved from https://scholarcommons.usf.edu/cgi/viewcontent.cgi?article=1679&context=jss.

Statista (2017a). *Twitter: Number of monthly active users 2010–2017.* Retrieved from www.statista.com/statistics/282087/number-of-monthly-active-twitter-users.

Statista (2017b). *Number of Facebook users worldwide 2008–2017.* Retrieved from www.statista.com/statistics/264810/number-of-monthly-active-facebook-usersworldwide.

Steindl, C., Jonas, E., Sittenthaler, S., Traut-Mattausch, E., & Greenberg, J. (2015). Understanding psychological reactance. *Zeitschrift für Psychologie, 223*(4), 205–214. doi:10.1027/215604/a000222.

Stevens, T. (2010). New media and counter-narrative strategies. In E. J. A. M. Kessels (Ed.), *Countering violent extremist narratives* (pp. 112–123). The Hague: National Coordinator for Counterterrorism. Retrieved from https://assembling security.files.wordpress.com/2015/01/nctb-stevens.pdf.

Stewart, D. W., & Shamdasani, P. N. (2014). *Focus groups: Theory and practice* (3rd edn). Thousand Oaks, CA: SAGE Publications.

Stieglitz, S., & Dang-Xuan, L. (2013). Emotions and information diffusion in social media—Sentiment of microblogs and sharing behavior. *Journal of Management Information Systems, 29*(4), 217–248. doi:10.2753/MIS074222290408.

Stryker, J. E., Wray, R. J., Hornik, R. C., & Yanovitzky, I. (2006). Validation of database search terms for content analysis: The case of cancer news coverage. *Journalism & Mass Communication Quarterly, 83*(2), 413–430. doi:10.1177/107769900608300212.

Sue, V. M., & Ritter, L. A. (2012). *Conducting online surveys* (2nd edn). Thousand Oaks, CA: SAGE Publications.

Sundar, S. S. (2008). The MAIN model: A heuristic approach to understanding technology effects on credibility. In M. J. Metzger & A. J. Flanagin (Eds), *Digital media, youth, and credibility* (pp. 73–100). Cambridge, MA: The MIT Press.

Sundar, S. S., & Nass, C. (2001). Conceptualizing sources in online news. *Journal of Communication*, 51(1), 52–72. doi:10.1111/j.146466.2001.tb02872.x.

Szmania, S., & Fincher, P. (2017). Countering violent extremism online and offline. *Criminology & Public Policy*, 16(1), 119–125. doi:10.1111/174133.12267.

Tajfel, H., & Turner, J. C. (1979). An integrative theory of intergroup conflict. In W. G. Austin & S. Worchel (Eds), *The social psychology of intergroup relations* (pp. 33–47). Monterey, CA: Brooks/Cole.

Tajfel, H., & Turner, J. C. (1986). The social identity theory of inter group behavior. In S. Worchel & L. W. Austin (Eds), *Psychology of intergroup relations* (2nd edn, pp. 7–24). Chicago, IL: Nelson-Hall.

Tanis, M., & Postmes, T. (2003). Social cues and impression formation in CMC. *Journal of Communication*, 53(4), 676–693. doi:10.1111/j.146466.2003.tb02917.x.

Taylor, H. (2012). *Social media for social change. Using the internet to tackle intolerance*. London: Institute for Strategic Dialogue. Retrieved from www.theewc.org/content/download/1892/14891/file/Social_Media_Social_Change%20(2).pdf.

Thackeray, R., Neiger, B. L., Hanson, C. L., & McKenzie, J. F. (2008). Enhancing promotional strategies within social marketing programs: Use of Web 2.0 social media. *Health Promotion Practice*, 9(4), 338–343. doi:10.4018/97-52215.ch003.

Thackeray, R., Neiger, B. L., & Keller, H. (2012). Integrating social media and social marketing. *Health Promotion Practice*, 13(2), 165–168. doi:10.1177/1524839911432009.

The Council of the European Union. (2014). *Revised EU strategy for combating radicalisation and recruitment to terrorism*. (9956/14). Retrieved from http://data.consilium.europa.eu/doc/document/ST-995014-INIT/en/pdf.

The Redirect Method (n.d.-a). *About the method*. Retrieved from The Redirect Method website https://redirectmethod.org/.

The Redirect Method (n.d.-b). *The Redirect Method: A blueprint for bypassing extremism* [Project Information Document]. Retrieved from The Redirect Method website https://redirectmethod.org/downloads/RedirectMethod-FullMethod-PDF.pdf.

Tormala, Z. L. (2008). A new framework for resistance to persuasion: The resistance appraisals hypothesis. In R. Prislin & W. D. Crano (Eds), *Attitudes and attitude change* (pp. 213–234). New York: Psychology Press.

Torok, R. (2016). Social media and the use of discursive markers of online extremism and recruitment. In M. Khader, L. S. Neo, G. Ong, E. Tan, & J. Chin (Eds), *Countering violent extremism and radicalisation in the digital era* (pp. 39–69). Hershey, PA: IGI Global. doi:10.4018/97-52215.ch003.

Tuck, H. (2017). Measuring the impact of your online counter or alternative narrative campaign message [Blog Post]. Retrieved from the VOX-POL website www.voxpol.eu/measuring-impact-online-counter-alternative-narrative-campaign-message/.

Tuck, H., & Silverman, T. (2016, June). *The counter-narrative handbook*. London: Institute for Strategic Dialogue Retrieved from www.strategicdialogue.org/wpcontent/uploads/2016/12/CN-Monitoring-and-Evaluation-Handbook.pdf.

Turner, J. C., Hogg, M. A., Oakes, P. J., Reicher, S. D., & Wetherell, M. S. (1987). *Rediscovering the social group: A self-categorization theory*. Oxford, UK: Blackwell.

USAID (2009). *Development assistance and counter-extremism: A guide to programming*. Retrieved from the USAID website https://pdf.usaid.gov/pdf_docs/PNADT977.pdf.

USAID (2011). *The development response to violent extremism and insurgency: Putting principles into practice*. Retrieved from the USAID website https://pdf.usaid.gov/pdf_docs/Pdacs400.pdf.

Valente, T. W. (2002). *Evaluating health promotion programs*. New York: Oxford University Press.

Valente, T. W., & Kwan, P. P. (2012). Evaluating communication campaigns. In R. E. Rice & C. K. Atkin (Eds), *Public communication campaigns* (4th edn, pp. 83–98). Thousand Oaks, CA: Sage.

Valente, T. W., Palinkas, L. A., Czaja, S., Chu, K.-H., & Brown, C. H. (2015). Social network analysis for program implementation. *PloS one, 10*(6), 1–18. doi:10.1371/journal.pone.0131712.

Valente, T. W., & Pitts, S. R. (2017). An appraisal of social network theory and analysis as applied to public health: Challenges and opportunities. *Annual Review of Public Health, 38*(1), 103–118. doi:10.1146/annurev-publhealth-0318 144528.

Van Atteveldt, W. H. (2008). *Semantic network analysis: Techniques for extracting, representing, and querying media content*. Charleston, SC: BookSurge Publishers. Retrieved from http://vanatteveldt.com/p/vanatteveldt_semanticnetworkanalysis.pdf.

Valkenburg, P. M., Peter, J., & Walther, J. B. (2016). Media effects: Theory and research. *Annual Review of Psychology, 67*, 315–338. doi:10.1146/annurev-psych-1224133608.

Van der Hulst, R. C. (2008). *Sociale netwerkanalyse en de bestrijding van criminaliteit en terrorisme* [Social network analysis for the combat of crime and terrorism]. Justitiële verkenningen, *38*(8), 10–32. Retrieved from www.wodc.nl/binaries/jv0805-volledige-tekst_tcm27018.pdf.

Van der Pligt, J., & Vliek, M. (2016). *The psychology of influence: Theory, research and practice*. London, New York: Taylor & Francis.

Van Ginkel, B. T. (2015, March). *Responding to cyber jihad: Towards an effective counter narrative* [Research Paper]. The Hague: The International Centre for Counter-Terrorism. doi:10.19165/2015.1.02.

Veale, H. J., Sacks-Davis, R., Weaver, E. R. N., Pedrana, A. E., Stoové, M. A., & Hellard, M. E. (2015). The use of social networking platforms for sexual health promotion: Identifying key strategies for successful user engagement. *BMC Public Health, 15*, 85. doi:10.1186/s12881396-z.

Veilleux-Lepage, Y. (2014, December). *Retweeting the caliphate: The role of soft-sympathizers in the Islamic State's social media strategy*. Paper presented at the 6th International Symposium on Terrorism and Transnational Crime, Antalya, TUR. Retrieved from www.researchgate.net/publication/273896091_Retweeting_the_Caliphate_The_Role_of_Soft-Sympathizers_in_the_Islamic_State's_Social_Media_Strategy.

Veldhuis, J., Konijn, E. A., & Seidell, J. C. (2014). Counteracting media's thin-body ideal for adolescent girls: Informing is more effective than warning. *Media Psychology, 17*(2), 154–184. doi:10.1080/15213269.2013.788327.

Veldhuis, T. (2012, March). *Designing rehabilitation and reintegration pro-grammes for violent extremist offenders: A realist approach* [Research Paper]. Retrieved from the International Centre for Counter-Terrorism website www.icct.nl/download/file/ICCT-Veldhuis-DesigningRehabilitation-Reintegration-Programmes-March-2012.pdf

Veldhuis, T., & Staun, J. (2009*). Islamist radicalisation: a root cause model.* The Hague: Netherlands Institute of International Relations Clingendael. Retrieved from www.diis.dk/files/media/publications/import/islamist_radicalisation.veldhuis_and_staun.pdf.

Vergani, M., Iqbal, M., Ilbahar, E., & Barton, G. (2018). The three Ps of radicalization: push, pull and personal. A systematic scoping review of the scientific evidence about radicalization into violent extremism. *Studies in Conflict & Terrorism*, 1–32. doi:10.1080/1057610X.2018.1505686.

Vidino, L. (2010, November). *Countering radicalization in America* (USIP Special Report No. 262). Retrieved from the United States Institute of Peace website www.usip.org/sites/default/files/SR262%20-%20Countering_Radicalization_in_America.pdf Vitale.

Vitale, H. M., & Keagle, J. M. (2014). A time to tweet, as well as a time to kill: ISIS's projection of power in Iraq and Syria. *Defense Horizons*, (77), 1–12. Retrieved from www.files.ethz.ch/isn/185255/DH-77.pdf.

Von Behr, I., Reding, A., Edwards, C., & Gribbon, L. (2013). *Radicalisation in the digital era: The use of the internet in 15 cases of terrorism and extremism* (RAND Publication No. RR-453-RE) [Research Report]. Retrieved from the RAND corporation website www.rand.org/content/dam/rand/pubs/research_reports/RR400/RR453/RAND_RR453.pdf.

von Sikorski, C., & Hänelt, M. (2016). Scandal 2.0: How valenced reader comments affect recipients' perception of scandalized individuals and the journalistic quality of online news. *Journalism & Mass Communication Quarterly (JMCQ)*, 93(3), 551–571. doi:10.1177/1077699016628822.

VOX-Pol. (2019). *About us.* Retrieved from the VOX-pol website www.voxpol.eu/about-us/.

Wagemakers, J. (2009). A purist Jihadi-Salafi: The ideology of Abu Muhammad al-Maqdisi. *British Journal of Middle Eastern Studies*, 36(2), 281–297. doi:10.1080/13530190903007327.

Waldman, S., & Verga, S. (2016, November). *Countering violent extremism on social media: An overview of recent literature and Government of Canada projects with guidance for practitioners, policy-makers, and researchers* (DRDC Scientific Report No. DRDC-RDDC-2016-R229). Retrieved from the website of Defense Research and Development Canada http://cradpdf.drdcrddc.gc.ca/PDFS/unc262/p805091_A1b.pdf.

Wasserman, S., & Faust, K. (1994). *Social network analysis: Methods and applications* (Vol. 8). Cambridge, UK: Cambridge University Press.

Webb, T. L., Joseph, J., Yardley, L., & Michie, S. (2010). Using the Internet to promote health behavior change: A systematic review and meta-analysis of the impact of theoretical basis, use of behavior change techniques, and mode of delivery on efficacy. *Journal of Medical Internet Research*, 12(1), e4. doi:10.2196/jmir.1376.

Weimann, G. (2014). *New terrorism and new media* (Research series vol. 2) [Research Paper]. Retrieved from the Wilson Center's Common Labs website www.wilsoncenter.org/publication/new-terrorism-and-new-media.

Weimann, G. (2015). *Terrorism in cyberspace: The next generation* [E-reader version]. Washington, DC, Woodrow Wilson Center.

Weimann, G. (2016). Terrorist migration to the dark web. *Perspectives on Terrorism, 10*(3), 40–44. Retrieved from www.universiteitleiden.nl/binaries/content/assets/governance-and-global-affairs/isga/perspectives-on-terrorism/201.pdf.

Weinreich, N. K. (2011*). Hands-on social marketing: A step-by-step guide to designing change for good* (2nd edn). Thousand Oaks, CA: Sage.

Wiktorowicz, Q. (2004). *Joining the cause: Al-Muhajiroun and radical Islam.* Memphis, TN: Rhodes College, Department of International Studies. Retrieved from http://insct.syr.edu/wp-content/uploads/2013/03/Wiktorowicz.Joining-the-Cause.pdf.

Wiktorowicz, Q. (2006). Anatomy of the Salafi movement. *Studies in Conflict & Terrorism, 29*(3), 207–239. doi:10.1080/10576100500497004.

Winter, C. (2015). *The virtual 'Caliphate': Understanding Islamic State's propaganda strategy* (Vol. 25). London: Quilliam. Retrieved from www.stratcomcoe.org/download/file/fid/2589.

Winter, C. (2018). Apocalypse, later: A longitudinal study of the Islamic State brand. *Critical Studies in Media Communication, 35*(1), 103–121. doi:10.1080/15295036.2017.1393094.

Wright, K. B. (2005). Researching internet-based populations: Advantages and disadvantages of online survey research, Online Questionnaire Authoring Software Packages, and Web Survey Services. *Journal of Computer-Mediated Communication, 10*(3). doi:10.1111/j.108101.2005.tb00259.x.

Wyer, N. A. (2010). Selective self-categorization: Meaningful categorization and the in-group persuasion effect. *The Journal of Social Psychology, 150*(5), 452–470. doi:10.1080/00224540903365521.

YouTube. (2017). YouTube for press. Retrieved from www.youtube.com/intl/enGB/yt/about/press.

Zeiger, S. (2016). *Undermining violent extremist narratives in South-East Asia: A how-to guide.* Abu Dhabi, UAE: Hedayah Center. Retrieved from www.hedayah-center.org/Admin/Content/File-3182016115528.pdf.

Zelin, A. (2015). Picture or it didn't happen: A snapshot of the Islamic State's official media output. *Perspectives on Terrorism, 9*(4), 85–97. Retrieved from www.terrorismanalysts.com/pt/index.php/pot/article/download/445/876.

Zimmer, M. (2010). "But the data is already public": On the ethics of research in Facebook. Ethics and information technology. *Ethics and Information Technology, 12*(4), 313–325. doi:10.1007/s1067122.

INDEX